REVELATION

ABINGDON NEW TESTAMENT COMMENTARIES

REVELATION

LEONARD L. THOMPSON

Abingdon Press
Nashville

ABINGDON NEW TESTAMENT COMMENTARIES:
REVELATION

Copyright © 1998 by Abingdon Press

This book is printed on recycled, acid-free, elemental-chlorine–free paper.

Library of Congress Cataloging-in-Publication Data

Thompson, Leonard L., 1934–
    Revelation / Leonard L. Thompson.
      p. cm. — (Abingdon New Testament commentaries)
    Includes bibliographical references and index.
    ISBN 0-687-05679-9 (pbk. : alk. paper)
    1. Bible. N.T. Revelation—Commentaries. I. Title.
  II. Series.
  BS2825.3.T465   1998
  228'.07— dc21   98-28389
                                                        CIP

Scripture quotations, unless otherwise indicated, are from the New Revised Standard Version Bible, copyright © 1989, by the Division of Christian Education of the National Council of the Churches of Christ in the United States of America.

Scripture quotations noted RSV are from the Revised Standard Version of the Bible, copyright 1946, 1952, 1971 by the Division of Christian Education of the National Council of Churches of Christ in the USA. Used by permission.

Scripture quotations noted GNB are from the *Good News Bible*—Old Testament: Copyright © American Bible Society 1976; New Testament: Copyright © American Bible Society 1966, 1971, 1976. Used by permission.

Scripture quotations noted AT are the author's translation.

98 99 00 01 02 03 04 05 06 07—10 9 8 7 6 5 4 3 2 1

MANUFACTURED IN THE UNITED STATES OF AMERICA

For my parents
Ruth Alice Dyson Thompson
and
Russell Charles Thompson (in memoriam)

CONTENTS

FOREWORD

The *Abingdon New Testament Commentaries* series provides compact, critical commentaries on the writings of the New Testament. These commentaries are written with special attention to the needs and interests of theological students, but they will also be useful for students in upper-level college or university settings, as well as for pastors and other church leaders. In addition to providing basic information about the New Testament texts and insights into their meanings, these commentaries are intended to exemplify the tasks and procedures of careful, critical biblical exegesis.

The authors who have contributed to this series come from a wide range of ecclesiastical affiliations and confessional stances. All are seasoned, respected scholars and experienced classroom teachers. They take full account of the most important current scholarship and secondary literature, but do not attempt to summarize that literature or to engage in technical academic debate. Their fundamental concern is to analyze the literary, socio-historical, theological, and ethical dimensions of the biblical texts themselves. Although all of the commentaries in this series have been written on the basis of the Greek texts, the authors do not presuppose any knowledge of the biblical languages on the part of the reader. When some awareness of a grammatical, syntactical, or philological issue is necessary for an adequate understanding of a particular text, they explain the matter clearly and concisely.

The introduction of each volume ordinarily includes subdivisions dealing with the *key issues* addressed and/or raised by the New Testament writing under consideration; its *literary genre, structure, and character;* its *occasion and situational context,* including its wider social, historical, and religious contexts; and its *theological and ethical significance* within these several contexts.

In each volume, the *commentary* is organized according to literary units rather than verse by verse. Generally, each of these units is the subject of three types of analysis. First, the *literary analysis* attends to the unit's genre, most important stylistic features, and overall structure. Second, the *exegetical analysis* considers the aim and leading ideas of the unit, deals with any especially important textual variants, and discusses the meanings of important words, phrases, and images. It also takes note of the particular historical and social situations of the writer and original readers, and of the wider cultural and religious contexts of the book as a whole. Finally, the *theological and ethical analysis* discusses the theological and ethical matters with which the unit deals or to which it points, focusing on the theological and ethical significance of the text within its original setting.

Each volume also includes a *select bibliography*, thereby providing guidance to other major commentaries and important scholarly works, and a brief *subject index*. The New Revised Standard Version of the Bible is the principal translation of reference for the series, but the authors draw on all of the major modern English versions, and when necessary provide their own original translations of difficult terms or phrases.

The fundamental aim of this series will have been attained if readers are assisted, not only to understand more about the origins, character, and meaning of the New Testament writings, but also to enter into their own informed and critical engagement with the texts themselves.

Victor Paul Furnish
General Editor

PREFACE

As we approach a new millennium, interest in apocalyptic thought increases, and Revelation—the cornerstone for apocalyptic thinking in the Christian world—becomes the book of the hour. Many who quote the book, however, do not respect the book's coherence or the proportion of its parts. All too often, words or phrases such as "Armageddon," "666," and "whore of Babylon" are wrenched from the book and given an importance not found in Revelation. It is a book of visions and marvels that reveals one way of making sense out of the human story and must be read as a whole in order to learn its message. This commentary is an aid for those who would read the wondrous visions of Revelation and discover a message as timely for the new millennium as for John and his first readers at the beginning of the first millennium of the Christian era.

My debts are several: To Victor Furnish who invited me to write the commentary. To Bernice, Lavena, and Ruth who read Revelation and sent many questions to me. To Virginia Ray and Sue Kane who made useful comments for revising parts of the commentary. To Steve Friesen, a benevolent E-mail correspondent. To Herschel Dyer who organized a group of "beta testers" at the Methodist Retirement Village in Warren, Indiana. My thanks also to Herschel, Violet Bear, Florence Kistler, and especially an anonymous reader who made detailed comments on a draft of the entire commentary. Finally, my deepest appreciation to John H. Elliott, editor extraordinaire, and M. L. Ray, relentless as always, in her insistence on clear writing. Initial research for this commentary was made possible by a sabbatical grant from Lawrence University.

Leonard L. Thompson

LIST OF ABBREVIATIONS

(Reference works for students with knowledge of Greek marked *)
(Essential reference works are marked **)

2 Apoc. Bar.	Syriac *Apocalypse of Baruch* (in OTP)
1 Clem.	*1 Clement* (in *Apostolic Fathers*)
1 Enoch	Ethiopic *Book of Enoch* (in OTP)
2 Enoch	Slavonic *Book of Enoch* (in OTP)
1Q27	*Book of Mysteries* (Qumran Cave 1)
1Q28b	*Rule of the Blessings* (Qumran Cave 1)
1QM	*War Scroll* (Qumran Cave 1)
1QpHab	*Pesher on Habakkuk* (Qumran Cave 1)
1QS	*Rule of the Community* (Qumran Cave 1)
4Q550	*Aramaic Proto Esther* (Qumran Cave 4)
AB	Anchor Bible
**ABD	D. N. Freedman (ed.), *Anchor Bible Dictionary*
Adv. Col.	Plutarch, *Moralia: Reply to Colotes*
Adv. Haer.	Irenaeus, *Against Heresies*
Am. narr.	Plutarch, *Moralia: Love Stories*
ANET	James B. Pritchard (ed.), *Ancient Near Eastern Texts*
ANF	*The Ante-Nicene Fathers*
An recte	Plutarch, *Moralia: Is "Live Unknown" a Wise Precept?*
Ant.	Josephus, *The Antiquities of the Jews*
Anton.	Plutarch, *Lives: Antony*
Apoc. Ab.	*Apocalypse of Abraham* (in OTP)
Apoc. Adam	*Apocalypse of Adam* (in OTP)
Apoc. Elijah	*Apocalypse of Elijah* (in OTP)
Apoc. Peter	*Apocalypse of Peter* (in EANT or HSW)
Apoc. Sedrach	*Apocalypse of Sedrach* (in OTP)
Apoc. Zeph.	*Apocalypse of Zephaniah* (in OTP)

Apol. Chr.	Tertullian, *Defense of Christianity*
Apol. Jud.	Philo, *Apology for the Jews*
***Apostolic Fathers*	Since the seventeenth century, a name given to a collection of Christian writings from the first and second centuries BCE. English translations are available in Kirsopp Lake (trans.), *The Apostolic Fathers (LCL)*
Ap. Rhod.	Apollonius of Rhodes, *The Voyage of Argo*
Arat.	Plutarch, *Lives: Aratus*
Artem.	Artemidorus, *The Interpretation of Dreams*
Ascen. Is.	*Ascension of Isaiah* (in OTP)
Astr.	Lucian, *Astrology*
AT	Author's translation
*BAGD	W. Bauer, W. F. Arndt, F. W. Gingrich, and F. W. Danker, *Greek-English Lexicon of the NT*
Barclay	William Barclay (trans.), *The New Testament: A New Translation.* Vol. 2, *The Letters and the* Revelation. London: Collins, 1969.
Barn.	*Barnabas* (in *Apostolic Fathers*)
BCE	Before the Christian Era (see CE)
Bib. Ant.	Ps.-Philo, *Biblical Antiquities* (in OTP)
Brut.	Plutarch, *Lives: Brutus*
Caes.	Plutarch, *Lives: Caesar*
C. Apion	Josephus, *Against Apion*
Cat.	Lucian, *The Downward Journey*
CE	Christian Era. There is no "common era" for dating events in religious history. 2,000 CE equals 5,760 in a Jewish calendar and 622 CE equals 0–1 AH in an Islamic calendar.
CG	Jean Chevalier and Alain Gheerbrant, *A Dictionary of Symbols* (trans. John Buchanan-Brown; Oxford: Blackwell Publishers, 1994)
Cher.	Philo, *On the Cherubim*
Cic.	Plutarch, *Lives: Cicero*
CIG	*Corpus inscriptionum graecarum*
CII	*Corpus inscriptionum iudaicarum*
ConBNT	Coniectanea biblia, New Testament
Confes.	Augustine, *Confessions*
Conf. Ling.	Philo, *On the Confusion of Tongues*
Crass.	Plutarch, *Lives: Crassus*
De Alex. fort.	Plutarch, *Moralia: On the Fortune of Alexander*

De def. or.	Plutarch, *Moralia: Obsolescence of oracles*
De garr.	Plutarch, *Moralia: Concerning Talkativeness*
De Is. et Os.	Plutarch, *Moralia: Isis and Osiris*
Dem.	Plutarch, *Lives: Demosthenes*
De Pyth. or.	Plurtarch, *Moralia: The Oracles at Delphi*
De superst.	Plutarch, *Moralia: Superstition*
Dial. Trypho	Justin Martyr, *Dialogue with Trypho* (in *ANF*)
Did.	*Didache* (in *Apostolic Fathers*)
Dio Chrys.	Dio Chrysostomus, *Orations (Or.)*
Diod. Sic.	Diodorus Siculus, *The Library of History*
DMeretr.	Lucian, *Dialogues of the Courtesans*
**EANT	J. K. Elliott (ed.), *The Apocryphal New Testament*
Ebr.	Philo, *On Drunkenness*
Ep.	Pliny the Younger, *Letters*
Ep. Arist.	*Epistle of Aristeas* (in *OTP*)
Ep. Diog.	*Epistle of Diognetus* (in *Apostolic Fathers*)
Fab.	Plutarch, *Lives: Fabius Maximus*
Frag.	Plutarch, *Moralia: Other Fragments* in *LCL*
GNB	*The Bible in Today's English Version (Good News Bible)*
Gos. Pet.	*Gospel of Peter* (in *EANT* or *HSW*)
*HCNT	*Hellenistic Commentary to the New Testament*
Hermetica	*Corpus Hermeticum*. I have used the edition by Brian P. Copenhaver (Cambridge: Cambridge University Press, 1992)
Herm. Man.	*Hermas, Mandate(s)* (in *Apostolic Fathers*)
Herm. Sim.	*Hermas, Similitude(s)* (in *Apostolic Fathers*)
Herm. Vis.	*Hermas, Vision(s)* (in *Apostolic Fathers*)
Hist. Eccl.	Eusebius, *The History of the Church*
HNTC	Harper's NT Commentaries
**HSW	*New Testament Apocrypha*
IBC	Interpretation: A Bible Commentary for Teaching and Preaching
IDB	G. A. Buttrick (ed.), *Interpreter's Dictionary of the Bible*
Ign. *Eph.*	Ignatius, *Letter to the Ephesians* (in *Apostolic Fathers*)
Ign. *Mag.*	Ignatius, *Letter to the Magnesians* (in *Apostolic Fathers*)
Ign. *Phld.*	Ignatius, *Letter to the Philadelphians* (in *Apostolic Fathers*)

Ign. *Pol.*	Ignatius, *Letter to Polycarp* (in *Apostolic Fathers*)
Ign. *Smyrn.*	Ignatius, *Letter to the Smyrnaeans* (in *Apostolic Fathers*)
Ign. *Trall.*	Ignatius, *Letter to the Trallians* (in *Apostolic Fathers*)
IGRom.	*Inscriptiones Graecae ad res Romanas pertinentes* (1906–)
JBL	*Journal of Biblical Literature*
Jos. Asen.	*Joseph and Asenath* (in OTP)
JSNTSup	Journal for the Study of the New Testament—Supplement Series
JSOT	Journal for the Study of the Old Testament
Jub.	*Jubilees* (in OTP)
J.W.	Josephus, *The Jewish War*
LCL	Loeb Classical Library
Life	Josephus, *Autobiography* (sometimes appended to *Ant.*)
*LN	Louw, Johannes P. and Eugene A. Nida, *Greek-English Lexicon of the New Testament Based on Semantic Domains* (New York: United Bible Societies, 1988)
LSAM	*Lois Sacrées de L'Asie Mineure*, ed. Franciszek Sokolowski (Paris: E. de Boccard, 1955)
*LSJ	Liddell-Scott-Jones, *A Greek-English Lexicon*
Luc.	Plutarch, *Lives: Lucullus*
*LXX	Septuagint. LXX refers only to the text of Alfred Rahlfs, ed., *Septuaginta*. 5th ed. (Stuttgart: Württembergische Bibelanstalt, 1952)
Lyc.	Plutarch, *Lives: Lycurgus*
Mar.	Plutarch, *Lives: Marius*
Mart. Isa.	*Martyrdom of Isaiah* (in OTP)
Mart. Pol.	*Martyrdom of Polycarp* (in *Apostolic Fathers*)
Math.	Sextus Empiricus, *Against the Professors*
Merc. Cond.	Lucian, *On Salaried Posts*
*MM	J. H. Moulton and G. Milligan, *The Vocabulary of the Greek New Testament*
MT	Massoretic Text
NEB	*New English Bible*
**NHL	*Nag Hammadi Library in English*. James M. Robinson, general ed. 3rd ed. (San Francisco: HarperSan Francisco, 1990)

NJBC	R. E. Brown et al. (eds.), *The New Jerome Biblical Commentary*
Non Pos.	Plutarch, *Moralia: That Epicurus Actually Makes a Pleasant Life Impossible*
**NRSV	New Revised Standard Version
Num.	Plutarch, *Lives: Numa*
**OCD	*Oxford Classical Dictionary*
Odes Sol.	*Odes of Solomon* (in OTP)
Op.	Philo, *On the Creation*
**OTP	J. H. Charlesworth (ed.), *The Old Testament Pseudepigrapha*
Paus.	Pausanius, *Description of Greece*
PDM	Papyri Demoticae Magicae; see Betz 1986.
Pel.	Plutarch, *Lives: Pelopidas*
Per.	Plutarch, *Lives: Pericles*
Peregr.	Lucian, *The Passing of Peregrinus*
**PGM	K. Preisendanz (ed.), *Papyri graecae magicae;* see Betz 1986
*PHI	Packard Humanities Institute. Greek Documentary Texts, CD-ROM #7
Philops.	Lucian, *Lover of Lies*
Plant.	Philo, *On Noah's Work as a Planter*
Pol. *Phil.*	Polycarp, *Letter to the Philippians* (in *Apostolic Fathers*)
Polyb.	Polybius, *Histories*
POxy	B. P. Grenfell and A. S. Hunt (eds.), *Oxyrhynchus Papyri*
Prot. James	*Protevangelium of James* (in EANT or HSW)
Provid.	Philo, *On Providence*
Pss. Sol.	*Psalms of Solomon* (in OTP)
Publ.	Plutarch, *Lives: Publicola*
Pyrr. Hyp.	Sextus Empiricus, *Outlines of Pyrrhonism*
Quaest. conv.	Plutarch, *Moralia: Table Talk*
Quaest. Rom.	Plutarch, *Moralia: Roman Questions*
Sat.	Lucian, *Saturnalia*
Sib. Or.	*Sibylline Oracles* (in OTP)
Somn.	Philo, *On Dreams*
Strabo	Strabo, *Geography*
Str-B	[H. Strack and] P. Billerbeck, *Kommentar zum Neuen Testament*
Sull.	Plutarch, *Lives: Sulla*

Syr. D.	Lucian, The Syrian Goddess
T. 12 Patr.	*Testament of the Twelve Patriarchs* (in OTP)
T. Ab.	*Testament of Abraham* (in OTP)
T. Adam	*Testament of Adam* (in OTP)
T. Asher	*Testament of Asher* (in *T. 12 Patr.*)
T. Benj.	*Testament of Benjamin* (in *T. 12 Patr.*)
T. Dan	*Testament of Dan* (in *T. 12 Patr.*)
*TDNT	G. Kittel and G. Friedrich (eds.), *Theological Dictionary of the New Testament*
Theod.	Theodotion's Greek translation of the Hebrew Bible (see *ABD*, vol. 6, pp. 447-48)
Timon	Lucian, *Timon*
T. Job	*Testament of Job* (in OTP)
T. Jos.	*Testament of Joseph* (in *T. 12 Patr.*)
T. Judah	*Testament of Judah* (in *T. 12 Patr.*)
T. Levi	*Testament of Levi* (in *T. 12 Patr.*)
*TLG	Thesaurus Linguae Graecae, CD ROM #D. Property of the Regents of the University of California, 1992
T. Moses	*Testament of Moses* (in *T. 12 Patr.*)
T. Reuben	*Testament of Reuben* (in *T. 12 Patr.*)
T. Sim.	*Testament of Simeon* (in *T. 12 Patr.*)
Tyr.	Lucian, *The Tyrannicide*
T. Zebulon	*Testament of Zebulon* (in *T. 12 Patr.*)
VH1	Lucian, *A True Story I*
Vita Cont.	Philo, *The Contemplative Life*
Vita Mos.	Philo, *Life of Moses*
WBC	Word Biblical Commentary

INTRODUCTION:
READING REVELATION

Revelation exalts writing. Throughout the book, directives come down from heaven: "Write in a book," commands a suprahuman figure; "Write what you have seen"; "To the angel of the church of Ephesus, write"; "Write this: Blessed are the dead"; "Write this: Blessed are those invited to the marriage supper of the Lamb." In the final directive, God himself commands John, "Write this, for these words are trustworthy and true." In Revelation, the imperative "write" occurs twelve times, but it only occurs three times in the rest of the New Testament. By obeying these commands, John takes us into the wonder of written language: John sends his message across the centuries and the waters—from ancient Patmos in the Aegean to where I sit in landlocked Wisconsin—to get inside my mind (see Pinker 1995). He is able to get his message across to me because he obeyed the command: He wrote rather than spoke his words.

When John spoke to people on the isle of Patmos, where he had his visions, his words communicated only as long as he was there voicing them. After he stopped speaking, the words vanished. The sound waves rippled away and the words disappeared in the air. (So far as we know, John had no device for recording sound.) By writing, however, John could make his words last. They became squiggles on a papyrus, words that could be copied, translated, and displayed in museums. But in this act of writing, John severed his words from the umbilical—rather, vocal—cord that joined them to him. Once they were copied and sent away, they abandoned their creator. The squiggles lay lifeless, like viruses waiting to come alive in another body, waiting to be read by a reader.

Listeners—unlike readers—had the advantage of John's physical presence. When John spoke to people on the isle of Patmos, he was fully present with them: his "here and now" was theirs. Facing his listeners, he could smile, lift an eyebrow, look puzzled, shuffle his feet, point, and do all those things that we do, when communicating through body language. Readers, however, cannot watch John's eyes or the nodding of his head. All the clues for the meaning of his words are in the squiggles on the page. Nineteen centuries later, in a different place and in another situation, we readers are called upon to read the words, find the clues, and close the circuit of communication.

There is a wildness to old words that resists our control. Reading them is like walking at the edges of cultivated land, in hedgerows and commons, slightly off the beaten path. There, the wild and the tame mingle together. The fox, glancing slyly at us through the brush, looks like good dog Fido back home. Similarly, John of Revelation describes an evil empire—just like Bourgeois Capitalism or Big Government or the Soviet Union (before it collapsed)! Land Managers and Master Readers, which we are all capable of being, seek to rid the commons entirely of the wild, so that the fox becomes our dog and the words of Revelation reflect only our values, our feelings, our peculiar vantage point in history. As Master Readers, we read the words to confirm what we already know, to validate what is happening in our time: Floods and earthquakes, social and economic oppression, wars and revolutions, sickness, neuroses, and death. (There is an arrogance—I know of no kinder word—to Master Readers who think that Revelation revolves completely around their life and times.)

If, however, we allow the wild and tame to mingle together, curiosity and the imagination are quickened. The mingling allows us to see new things in the old and old things in the new. We see the world differently. We may even be different. As Paul Ricoeur has written, "It must be said that we understand ourselves only by the long detour of the signs of humanity deposited" in the written word (Ricoeur 1981, 143). Ursula Le Guin puts it this way:

> Word is the whorl that spins me,
> the shuttle thrown through the warp of years

to weave a life, the hand
that shapes to use, to grace. (Le Guin 1991, 214)

John wrote and we read. Both acts are necessary to enter into the wonder of written language. By reading, we breathe life into apparently lifeless words, and they become a part of our "here and now." Yet, to some extent, the words remain alien. They tell us something that we did not know. They crack open our enclosed world and our self-understandings—whether Christian or non-Christian. We give them life, but the words are not our offspring alone. We join with John to produce them, and as with the offspring of all unions, they sometimes shock us, and, if John should hear our talk, they would shock him too.

In what follows, I uncover three paths in the wild of John's words. In the first section, "To the Seven Churches of Asia," I sketch out some local color and regional detail of urban life in Asia (non-Christian and Christian) at the time when John wrote Revelation. What was city life in a Roman province like? How did Christians fit into it? I try to mingle the wild and the tame, so that city life back then is readily recognizable, but not viewed the same as today. Then, in the second section, "In the Spirit," I bring into the foreground visionary elements in Revelation, religious attitudes toward the life sketched out in the first section. In that section, Revelation is a document in religious, visionary history. Finally, in "Dirty Clothes Are Dirty Clothes," I investigate the language of Revelation, its poetic words and how those words are organized.

To the Seven Churches of Asia

A Christian by the name of John sent this remarkable little book—that reaches to the highest heavens, to the depths of hell, and to the end of time—as a letter to "seven churches that are in Asia" (1:4). Who was this letter writer? Where exactly were the seven churches? When did John write it? What was life like in those days of the Roman Empire? For those who lived in the seven cities? For urban Christians? Readers of Revelation often assume that John was writing to isolated backwaters of the empire and that

Christians consisted of the poor and downtrodden. If readers are familiar with the grand Hollywood movies portraying early Christians, they envision Christians being thrown to the lions and cut up by gladiators, while mad emperors (and their women) watch in lustful excitement. It may, therefore, come as a surprise to find that John's "letter" was sent to Christians living in some of the largest, most cultured cities of the empire and that, for the most part, Christians were living quietly, peacefully, and prosperously in those cities.

Being fascinated as we are with personalities, we would like to know all about John's personal life. Who were his parents? Where was he born? Where did he grow up? Was he married? Did he have children? How did he feel about being a prophet? Was it challenging work? But he tells us nothing about those things, at least directly, and probably he would be puzzled by our interest in such personal detail. He tells us all that he considers necessary to know: He is a "servant" of Jesus Christ (1:1) as well as "brother" and "partner" of Christians in the seven churches of Asia (see 1:9). He writes "words of the prophecy" (1:3) so we may conclude that he is a Christian prophet, though he never refers to himself as such. He had a series of visions while living on the island of Patmos, and he was commanded to send a written record of those visions to the churches of Asia. There is no more reliable information in early Christian literature about this John. Perhaps he was a Jewish convert from Palestine, or maybe he grew up in Ephesus. We do not know. Irenaeus, a Christian writing toward the end of the second century CE, assumed that the writer of Revelation was "the Lord's disciple" (*Adv. Haer.* 4.20.11) and Eusebius, the fourth-century historian, referred to him as "apostle and evangelist" (*Hist. Eccl.* 3.18.1). Most scholars today doubt that John of the Revelation was one of the apostles. Probably he was an otherwise unknown Christian in Asia, perhaps in Ephesus.

Just as with personal detail, so John did not consider it important to give a precise date for his writing. (Of course the original recipients of Revelation knew what time it was when they received it. We latter-day readers are the ones in the dark.) He mentions only one person by name—an Antipas, otherwise unknown—who was apparently martyred at Pergamum (2:13). If, in chapter 17, the angel is referring to specific emperors, he does it in such a way that we today are not able to identify them. Nor do references to the temple in Rev 11 require a date prior to the destruction of the temple in 70 CE, for John sees many things in his visions that did not "exist" when he wrote. The lack of evidence about the precise date is, of course, tantalizing to historians who develop various hypotheses to pinpoint Revelation, usually placing it in either the aftermath of Nero's reign (68–69 CE) or in the latter years of Domitian's reign (c. 92–96 CE). We can only be certain, however, that Revelation was written sometime roughly between 68 and 120 CE, for in chapter 17, John adapts stories about Nero's return from the dead or exile, and the book was most likely known in Ephesus by the early years of Hadrian's reign (*Dial. Trypho* 81.4; Justin probably became acquainted with Revelation when he was at Ephesus in 135 CE). Irenaeus wrote that Revelation was written "not long ago," but "close to our generation, towards the end of the reign of Domitian" (*Adv. Haer.* 5.30.3).

John is precise about place (1:4, 9, 11). He is on the island of Patmos (about one hundred kilometers southwest of Ephesus), and he wrote to seven congregations in seven cities of the Roman province of Asia: Ephesus, Smyrna, Pergamum, Thyatira, Sardis, Philadelphia, and Laodicea. The province, Asia, located along the western part of Anatolia (present-day Turkey) looking out on the Aegean Sea, was one of the first provinces of the Roman Empire to be Christianized (before 50 CE). Paul wrote his first letter to the Corinthians from Ephesus (about 54 CE) and was quite excited about the missionary possibilities in and around that city (1 Cor 16:9; cf. Acts 20:31). With respect to the seven churches of Revelation, Paul mentions Laodicea in his letter to the Colossians (Col 2:1; 4:13) and Thyatira is mentioned in connection with Lydia whom Paul met at Philippi (Acts 16:13-14). Ignatius, writing a few years after Revelation, while traveling to Rome in hope of being martyred, demonstrated the continuing importance of Asia for developing Christianity. He sent letters to Ephesus, Philadelphia, and Smyrna (one to the church and one to Polycarp), as well as to Magnesia and Tralles. During the next two centuries, Asia became a center of Christianity unrivaled in the eastern end of the Roman Empire.

Life in the Roman province of Asia during the last quarter of the first century was, on the whole, prosperous and peaceful. The province possessed a wealth of natural resources: river valleys rich in land for agricultural products, forests, pasture for animals, as well as rich veins of copper, iron, salt, and marble (Broughton 1938, 607-26). Many of the cities in Asia were major industrial and trading centers, located strategically on roadways leading from Syria, Palestine, and points further east, to Rome in the west, and on shipping lanes around the Mediterranean Sea. Travelers, the imperial mail service *(cursus publicus),* and small caravans transporting textiles, precious metals, ointments, and other less bulky valuables, used a network of well-kept roads. Craftsmen such as Paul, who worked with bulkier items (cf. Acts 18:3), also traveled those roads, for it was easier to transport workmen than heavy material. They stayed in rooms provided by people in their religious or professional networks, rather than at a "motel."

The province had a triple layer of government control, somewhat comparable to federal, state, and local controls in the United States. The senate and the emperor back at Rome had ultimate authority over Asia. Strictly speaking, Asia was a province of the senate, and so the senate at Rome appointed the proconsul or governor to Asia. In fact, governing Asia (proconsul) was seen as a political plum for one completing his public service. But the emperor could intervene in Asia if he thought it necessary (both Domitian and Trajan did). Either the emperor or the senate could make regulations affecting everyone in the province of Asia, and envoys from Asia to Rome might seek audiences with either the senate or the emperor.

The province was governed locally by an assembly *(koinon)* that had existed in Asia before the province was annexed by Rome. In the time of Revelation, it served as a kind of intermediary between the cities and Rome. For example, at Pergamum the assembly made public the edict of Augustus about the rights of Jews in Asia; it appealed to Domitian to rescind the edict regarding the planting of vines (cf. Rev 6:6?). Sometimes, it even brought charges against a proconsul who abused his office.

Wealthy patrons took responsibility for governing city life. Officials such as city clerk, superintendent of the markets, superintendent of streets and sanitation, city treasurer, chief of police, and city attorney oversaw everyday operations of the city. Only the wealthy could afford to hold any of these offices, for not only were fees paid in order to be "elected," but officers also had to spend their own money to execute their responsibilities. So magistrates, for instance, financed transporting grain, paying the imperial tax, erecting buildings, paving a street, running the gymnasium, funding religious festivals and city banquets, and providing for the food supply. Since the gymnasium was "the chief centre of the social life of the community," its upkeep could be very costly, for it included not only baths and exercise rooms but also lecture halls and sometimes a library (Broughton 1938, 806-7). Cities stayed solvent only by means of the financial support of those patrons, and even then, they sometimes went bankrupt by overspending, as they competed with other cities in having the finest buildings, holding district court, having a temple with the right of asylum for fugitives, or honoring the emperor through temples and festivals.

Civic responsibilities also benefited those with money, for such offices were stepping-stones to imperial service, equestrian status, and eventually, the prestige of being a senator at Rome. Under the Flavian emperors (Vespasian, Titus, and Domitian), opportunities increased for provincials to enter into imperial service. Perhaps the patrons themselves would not become senators, but their children or grandchildren would.

Production of textiles was the most important industry in Asia Minor, though there were also many other crafts and trades. Pergamum produced parchment; Thyatira had tanners, leather workers, and coppersmiths; Smyrna, silversmiths and goldsmiths (Broughton 1938, 817-30). Textiles included Lydian embroideries, red dyes from Sardis, wool traded at Thyatira and worked at Laodicea and Colossae, and hemp from Ephesus. Except for textiles, which were exported, industrial production served local and regional needs. Those industries provided ample opportunities for labor. As indicated by the occurrence of strikes, individual artisans, members of the craft guilds, and their known helpers were almost all free men, not slaves or freedmen. Slaves served primarily as domestics, personal agents, clerks and secretaries, civil servants, and menial laborers, for example in mines and quarries (Broughton 1938, 841).

Professions included architects, physicians, teachers, lawyers, actors, and performers. Public school teaching had little status; fame came from private teaching of wealthy pupils. Sophists of note taught and lectured at Smyrna, Ephesus, and Pergamum. In Pergamum, at the shrine of Asclepius, hero and god of healing, archaeologists discovered a kind of university charter for medicine and rhetoric. At Smyrna there was a school of medicine founded sometime in the first century before Christ. Cities held entertainers and athletes in high honor, with the most popular granted citizenship and honorary council memberships (see Thompson 1990, 154).

Ceremonies involving the emperor became an important feature in city life, for they honored and expressed appreciation for the emperor, the chief benefactor of the province's peace and prosperity. When a city built a statue, temple, or altar to the service of an emperor or Rome, both the local city and the emperor were honored. If a city had a priest responsible for religious ceremony involving the emperor, he not only represented the emperor to the people, but also would sometimes journey to Rome to represent the city to the emperor. A city gained even more status if its imperial honors were sponsored by the provincial assembly rather than just the city. Such cities were given the title, *neōkoros,* custodian of an emperor's temple. In a large city such as Ephesus, there were many reminders of its imperial benefactors: temples to Roma (the city of Rome) and Julius Caesar, to Augustus (Octavian), to Domitian, and to Hadrian, among others; small shrines for Augustus and Hadrian in the temple of Artemis; and statues of emperors and their families in covered walkways (porticoes), on the streets, fountains, city gates, and public buildings.

Cities also held festivals celebrating critical moments in the life of an emperor—his birth (sometimes celebrated at the beginning of each month), a decisive victory in battle, his accession to being emperor, or a significant event in honor of a family member of the emperor. Since there were many events to celebrate, several days in a year were devoted to "imperial days," when festivities, feasts, distributions of food and gifts, and ritual observances were held in a major city. During those festivals, processions would pass through the city consisting of dignitaries from other cities; perhaps the provincial high priest in crown and purple garb surrounded by young, male incense-bearers; garlanded animals being led to slaughter; and bearers of images of the emperor and local deities. As the procession passed by, householders would sacrifice on small altars outside their homes. The festivities brought to a city many visitors—orators, prostitutes, craftsmen, and tinkers. Business among the shops was lively. Athletes and musicians competed in contests. Provincial officeholders, trust funds, and even the emperor himself underwrote the cost of the festivals.

There is considerable evidence that Christians shared in the urban life and economy of Asian cities. Many of them—like Lydia and Paul—were converts from Judaism, and Jews at this time in Asia participated fully in civic life. From inscriptions we know of Jews who served municipal, provincial, and even imperial offices—all the while active in the synagogue; honored members of the synagogue were not troubled by "religious observances connected with citizenship and office-holding" (Kraabel 1968, 221). Jews participated in the gymnasium, held "season tickets" at the theater, and participated in guilds and trade unions. They farmed, grew vines, worked leather and metals, manufactured tents and hob-nailed boots, and sold perfumes. Most common of all, Jews engaged in the manufacture of textiles as dyers, carpet makers, and makers of woolen wares. For Christians converting from Judaism, much of everyday life remained unchanged. Wayne Meeks's description of Christians derived from Paul's letters would fit many Christians in the cities of Asia:

> The "typical" Christian . . . the one who most often signals his presence in the letters by one or another small clue, is a free artisan or small trader. Some even in those occupational categories had houses, slaves, the ability to travel, and other signs of wealth. Some of the wealthy provided housing, meeting places, and other services

for individual Christians and for whole groups. In effect, they filled the roles of patrons. (Meeks 1983, 73)

Christians did not, however, take part in civic and provincial celebrations of the emperor. Followers of Christ did not offer sacrifices as imperial processions went by their homes. They did not even offer sacrifices to local, established deities—Artemis, Zeus, Cybele, Asclepius—that supported public, imperial life. Christian households contained no statues or images of any of the Caesars or of any other god. In short, Christians gave the appearance of not supporting the public order.

Nevertheless, Roman officials at the time of Revelation did not initiate action against Christians, even though they found them—along with Druids and the Bacchae—a troublesome lot. They would, however, respond—albeit reluctantly—to anonymous pamphlets sent to them by locals who accused neighbors of being Christians. So Pliny, in 112, while traveling on behalf of the emperor Trajan through Bithynia and Pontus—provinces north and east of Asia—brought those accused to trial, but simultaneously admonished against anonymous pamphlets (*Ep.* 10.96).

It was in the testing of Christians, not the bringing of charges, that caused religious ceremony involving the emperor to become a central issue. Beginning with Pliny (112 CE, possibly before), when neighbors were accused anonymously of being Christians, the official in charge would require them to make an offering to the statues of Caesar and the gods or say that Caesar is Lord and renounce Christ (cf. *Ep.* 10.96). If they persisted in affirming their Christianity, they were either executed or sent to Rome for trial. Pliny found Christianity distasteful, "a degenerate sort of cult carried to extravagant lengths," but it did not concern him greatly. He interviewed several people who had abandoned Christianity and returned to their traditional religions, so he hoped that this "wretched cult" would soon die out. Pliny's comments also make it clear that he differentiated Christians from Jews. That made Christians more vulnerable to arrest, for Jews were normally not required to make sacrifice before a statue of Caesar.

It is not clear exactly why non-Christians found their Christian neighbors offensive. Christians were probably suspect simply because they were a New Religious Movement that did not honor and respect traditional forms of public, religious life (cf. suspicions about New Religious Movements such as the Unification Church or Church Universal Triumphant in the United States). They met in secret, and it was rumored that in their meetings they had cannibalistic feasts, carried on illicit sexual relations, and blasphemed the gods—at least so the Christian Athenagoras said, several years after Revelation (Athenagoras, *In Defense of the Faith* 3). There may also have been an economic factor in opposition to Christians: If several people converted to Christianity in one area, it could hurt businesses associated with traditional religion, for example, butchers who prepared sacrifices or silversmiths who made images of deities (*Ep.* 10.96; Acts 19:23-27; see Wilken 1984).

For the most part, Christians at the end of the first century did not irritate their neighbors sufficiently for them to make very many anonymous complaints to the authorities. "Maintain good conduct among the Gentiles," wrote the author of 1 Peter to Christians in the area of Pontus, "so that in case they speak against you as evildoers, they may see your good deeds and glorify God on the day of visitation . . . honor everyone . . . honor the emperor" (2:12-17 AT). The writer of 1 Timothy urges Christians to pray "for kings and all who are in high positions, so that we may lead a quiet and peaceable life in all godliness and dignity" (2:1-2, cf. *Mart. Pol.* 10.2). Approximately a century later than Revelation, Tertullian made clear that Christians were not odd and different from others in the empire. He wrote that Christians had the same manner of life, the same dress, and the same requirements for living as non-Christians. They depended upon the marketplace, the butchers, the baths, shops, factories, taverns, fairs, and other businesses. Christians sailed ships, served in the army, tilled the ground, and engaged in trade alongside non-Christians; and Christians provided skills and services for the benefit of the whole society (*Apol. Chr.* 42; cf. *Ep. Diog.* 5). Persecutions were sporadic and minimal. Martyrs were few in number (cf. *Mart. Pol.* 19.1). As Robert Wilken writes, "In most areas of the Roman Empire Christians lived quietly and peaceably among their neighbors, conducting their affairs without disturbance" (Wilken 1984, 16 [For more detail about the Asian cities and Christian activities in them, see Thompson 1990, 116-67.]).

In the Spirit

To the urban Christians of Asia, John, a religious visionary on the periphery of society, sent a message as explosive as a letter bomb. He challenged their quiet life and their willingness to have dealings with non-Christian, Roman society: It was a corrupt and evil society. He heard a voice from heaven calling to them: "Come out of her, my people, so that you do not take part in her [Roman society's] sins, and so that you do not share in her plagues" (18:4). He also challenged local leaders who allowed such trafficking with the devil. For he saw in the near future persecution requiring a martyr's witness, and, beyond that—for those who listened to his message and faithfully kept the witness of Jesus—a time of blessed existence before God's throne in the new Jerusalem.

Let there be no mistake: John evaluates Roman society and the congregations in Asia from a religious perspective. To be sure, he touches on political, economic, and social life in the empire, but he always does so from a religious point of view. Virtually every sentence in Revelation opens the discourse to "something more"— something more fundamental, more comprehensive. The writer comments on local conditions in the cities of Asia in such a way that they disclose cosmic powers at work in the congregations. The moral, social fabric of society—both the good and the bad—is grounded in larger, transcendent powers such as God or Satan. John offers a vision of a total world. That way of thinking is religious, because it works toward what is most fundamental, most compre-hensive, toward that which is at the hub of the web of all that exists, even as it acknowledges a surplus, a "more," a weight of mystery that cannot be altogether scaled. John names that "hub" God.

We can place John more precisely within religious history: He is a visionary. That is, he makes contact with God through ecstatic experience rather than through such institutional forms as sacra-ments, fixed scripture, or prescribed prayers (even though institutional forms sometimes influence his ecstatic experience). When filled with the spirit, he serves as a bridge between the ordinary world of everyday life and the "more" that opens it up. He talks with angels and other divine beings. He ascends to heaven and enters the realm of God and the blessed dead (4:1).

The visionary is a type recognizable in religions throughout the world and in every era. In John's own era, other Christians had visions—Paul, Agabus, Hermas, and Gnostic Christians (Acts 11:28; 21:10-11; 2 Cor 12:2-4; *Herm. Vis.; NHL; Apoc. Peter*). In Judaism, visionaries wrote under the names of Daniel, Enoch, Ezra, and Baruch. Pagan visionaries included the Sibyls and the Egyptian Hermes. I. P. Couliano (1991) catalogs records of such experiences in locations such as ancient Mesopotamia, Egypt, Taoist China, ancient Iran, and Greece, in religions such as Buddhism and Judaism, and in Dante. Robert M. Torrance (1994) gives detailed descriptions of the spirit-possessed, mediums, and shamans among tribal religions throughout Malaysia, Indonesia, Eurasia, and the Americas. Visionaries continue to exist today: in the corners of mainline religious groups and in New Religious Movements such as Church Universal and Triumphant or Divine Light Mission (see Melton 1992). Mokichi Okada, founder of Johrei, describes an experience in which he, like John, was ordered to write:

At about midnight one night in 1926, the most peculiar sensation came over me, a feeling I had never experienced before. It was an overwhelming urge that I simply cannot describe; I had an irresistible compulsion to talk. There was no way to suppress the power that was using my voice. So I gave in. The first words were, "Get something to write with." Just as soon as my wife brought paper and pen, a torrent was let loose. (Schmidt 1988, 355, quoting Okada 1984, 161-62)

Various explanations have been given for visionary experience, some more skeptical than others. (Skepticism of the visionary can be found wherever visionaries exist; it did not arise with modernization and "scientific thinking.") At the time when John wrote, some ridiculed any notion of a divine providence (see Artem. 1.1). Plutarch, a contemporary of John, rejected any simple notion that

God takes control of the visionary: "Certainly it is foolish and childish in the extreme to imagine that the god himself after the manner of ventriloquists . . . enters into the bodies of his prophets and prompts their utterances, employing their mouths and voices as instruments" *De def. or.* 9, 414E). Today, some view the visionary experience as an abnormal psychological sickness; others find analogues in near-death or out-of-body experiences, movement into the fourth dimension, and altered states of consciousness triggered by singing, dancing, or hallucinatory drugs (see *De def. or.* 40, 432F; Thompson 1990, 71-72; Couliano 1991; Pilch 1993, especially 241; Goodman 1990).

Most visionaries live on the periphery of society, where they challenge the central values transmitted by institutions at the center. So, John (literally at the periphery, on an island) sees a new Christian golden age that will eventually replace an evil Roman Empire (for other examples, see MacMullen 1966, 146-51). He turns the existing social order upside down. The Roman peace is really a time of war and conflict. Prosperity and well-being deceive, for they depend upon cooperating with evil forces. The poor are rich; the rich are poor (2:9; 3:17). Wealthy patrons gain their wealth by "fornicating" with Rome. The glorious buildings in the cities of Asia are a sham, compared to the new Jerusalem. Quietly working a trade and participating in the guilds and all that goes with it involve idolatry. Living peaceful lives in a neighborly relationship with non-Christians constitutes blasphemy. True blessing comes with martyrdom. I recall a delicious exchange in Shakespeare's *Coriolanus.* The tribunal has just voted to exile Coriolanus from his country. He, however, stands alone in the face of those who have just condemned him, and responds: "I exile you . . . for there is another country"! In Revelation, followers of the Lamb are killed by the Dragon or the beast and as they die, they cry "Victory, we have conquered!" Such reversals do more than puzzle others; they threaten existing values and the present social order.

Not surprisingly, then, those committed to a stable social order view the ideas and stories of visionaries as dangerous: they can destabilize a "sane, steady world" (MacMullen 1966, 162). Visionaries can be the catalyst for civic unrest and even open rebellion. In the later part of the second century CE, Roman rulers would seize and execute visionaries—perhaps Druids, sometimes Christians—for spreading unrest and perplexity in the towns. Rome established a bureaucracy to control visionaries, prophets, diviners, and astrologers. Augustus began that control, by not allowing "divinatory consultations without the presence of a third person" (11 CE). He forbade any speculation and prediction of his or anyone else's death. Augustus also burned "more than two thousand books" of prophecy and did not allow private ownership of such books. Tiberius checked the circulation of the Sibylline Oracles. In the Justinian code there is a law—MacMullen dates it before the middle of the second century (150)—which prohibits, by threat of death, the reading of "the books of Hystaspes or the Sibyl or the [Jewish] prophets" (MacMullen 1966, 128-31). Any prophet, including John, could be banished for spreading unrest among the people through his visions.

Thus the visionary and those who "keep the world steady" oppose each other, for when they walk the streets of Ephesus, they see different things. Those trying to keep society steady view visionaries as ill-informed, ignorant, and slightly mad. On occasion, if the visionaries become too irritating, the State may even initiate temporary hostilities by imprisoning and killing a few of them. Visionaries, on the other hand, see the "steady-staters" as manifestations of the devil, opposing and warring against those who speak for God.

Contrast, for example, Pliny's and John's views of the empire. As mentioned above, the emperor Trajan sent Pliny to Pontus and Bithynia to straighten out some problems in those two provinces— inadequate sewage disposal, overpaid athletes, corruption in the post office, and potentially seditious organizations such as the Nicomedian volunteer fire department, a benefit society at Amisus, and—so some locals claim—secret meetings of Christians. Pliny, representing the ruling powers, didn't really care to bother with Christians, except that he found them to be degenerate, distasteful, and possibly subversive. "I am convinced," he wrote to the emperor, "that their stubbornness and unshakeable obstinacy ought not to go unpunished" (*Letters* 10.96). John, on the other hand, would lump Pliny in with a corrupt bureaucracy characterized in chapter 13 as an earth beast who tells people to "make an image for the [sea] beast" and then to "worship the image" or "be killed" (13:14-15). In response to these evil forces, he urges Christians to be steadfast and to endure. One man's stubborn obstinacy is the other man's steadfast faithfulness and enduring hope.

John even had a peripheral relationship with the "centers" of Christianity in Asia, the local congregations and their leaders. For example, in chapters 2 and 3, John mentions, only to condemn, Christian leaders in the churches—for example, so-called apostles, Nicolaitans, Balaamites, and "Jezebel." (It is not clear how familiar he was with the seven churches of Asia; he certainly does not communicate the kind of familiarity and intimacy found in Paul's letters.) His visions do not occur while worshiping with one of the congregations (1 Cor 14:26), but on the island of Patmos, at a distance from the seven churches. Whether or not he was banished there because he was seen by Roman "authorities" as a marginal person disrupting the central institutions in the cities of Asia, John has his visions in a place away from Christian centers in Asia. John was probably a wandering prophet, an ascetic without home or possessions—similar to those prophets regarded ambivalently in the *Didache,* a church manual written a few years later than Revelation, or to Peregrinus, whom Lucian found so disgusting (*Did.* 11.7–13.4; *Peregr.*; cf. Yarbro Collins 1992 and "liminal poverty" in Turner 1974, 265).

From the periphery, the location of novelty and innovation, John saw an alternative to the social accommodation of those Christians at the "center." He wrote to persuade them that social intercourse with non-Christians in the context of city life was wrong (chapters 2–3). He called upon them to come out of the "evil empire," the craftwork, the trades, and he disdained the economic benefits of the whore. He wrote to attack their complacency and compromise, that is, the fact that they were living quietly and at ease with their neighbors. Those who follow the Lamb should be living a life apart and at odds with those around them. They should expect persecution, not friendly relations with their neighbors. To underscore that point, visions throughout the book portray Christians as martyrs suffering at the hands of evil powers, and godly forces from heaven avenge—sometimes spitefully—the treatment of Christians (see especially chapters 11 and 19). John assures Christians, however, that they will ultimately be victors in their battle with society, if they are willing to live as he directs.

Those responsible for keeping order at the center do not view John with favor, for he sees things differently and offers alternatives to the status quo, such as a new day coming when all will be transformed and destinies will be reversed. As Fintan O'Toole once wrote in *The Irish Times,* "The apocalypst [*sic*], the magician, and the mystic are the ultimate critics of the world as it is." And one can add, they—or at least the apocalyptist—are the ones who offer new ways of seeing and being in the world, ways that encompass, but transcend the planning and projecting of human endeavor.

DIRTY CLOTHES ARE DIRTY CLOTHES

If it would be a mistake to picture John as a unique visionary, isolated on a barren isle, untouched by any cultural or religious tradition, so also it would be a mistake to assume that Revelation is a writing peculiar in its time. If a seer wants to communicate a vision, he writes in the style and form that his readers will recognize as visionary literature, just as a person writes in the style and form of a letter, if she wants to communicate by letter. Revelation belongs to a circle of revelatory, visionary texts that include some Hebrew prophets in the Old Testament, Jewish visionaries outside the Bible (see *OTP,* especially vol. 1), and to a lesser extent, prophecies and oracles elsewhere in the Greco-Roman world. To read Revelation with understanding, one eye must be on the large circle of revelatory texts, the other on the specific language and themes in John's book; with that dual vision, readers can better understand how John uses a common stock of motifs and images to communicate his distinctive message.

In light of the close connection between having a vision and communicating it in words, we could ask: Did John have visions or did he simply write in the form of visionary writings? Did his visions create the words or did the words create the visions? There is a more basic question, which I will ask but will not attempt to answer: In the poetic language of Revelation, can the seer have images without words or words without images? Like the language of all poets, his is sensual and literal. Even when John "names marvelous and impossible things"—a pale green horse, a bottomless pit, a red dragon, a sea beast, a whore on a scarlet beast—he, like all poets, depends "on a literal mind" (Hall 1995, 84). His poetic language also creates an intensity, an excitement, an enhancement of consciousness, which comes to expression as vision (Wilder 1971, 92). John writes words for the ear! To appreciate them fully, readers must listen to their form and shape, just as lovers of architecture savor the details of proportions in columns, arches, and porticoes of Greco-Roman temples.

"Image" is, I think, the best term to use in describing John's visionary words. A word-image is material and concrete, but at the same time it creates a surplus of meaning, a "more" that transcends its concreteness. For example, Christ praises a few among Christians at Sardis "who have not dirtied their clothes" (3:4 AT). He urges those at Laodicea to put on "white" clothes to keep the "shame of [their] nakedness from being seen" (3:18). The images should be taken literally. However, they also point to something more (in reverse order): "White": pure, godly, victorious, heavenly, immortal, transfigured, enlightened. "To change clothes": transform, transfigure, conquer. Cordelia says to Lear: "Be better suited: These weeds [clothing] are memories of those worser hours: I prithee, put them off" (*King Lear* 4.7.7-9). "Dirt": stain, stench, defilement, desecration. Northrop Frye takes "dirt" even further: "Dirt" is an image of excretion, and, he writes, "I suspect that it is the metaphorical kernel of the ultimate separation of heaven and hell" (Frye 1990, 262). By being both concrete and metaphorical (pointing to something more), John's images should be understood both literally (descriptively) and figuratively (metaphorically). That is, an image refers to the material object that the word names, and it also opens an empty space to be filled by the disciplined imagination (see Mitchell 1993).

John's material images and sensual language contrast with the abstract language of argument, the presentation of ideas as allegory, and the linear progression of logic. When read as moral allegory, for example, various godly characters in Revelation represent virtues, evil characters represent vices, and the book becomes a kind of Bunyan's *Pilgrim's Progress*. Other "spiritual" interpretations make Revelation into a theological system or events in our individual psyches. When we hear that Christians at Ephesus will be given "permission to eat from the tree of life that is in the paradise of God" (2:7), it's better to imagine a coconut tree on a South Sea island than to paraphrase into abstract religious, moral, or psychological concepts. John's sense-lines form the cadence of a dance, as one line proceeds after another in circular, kaleidoscopic fashion. Words, phrases, and motifs are repeated; one line echoes a preceding one; cadence may be broken for emphasis; and a stanza ends where it begins:

After this
I looked and, behold, an open door in heaven.
And the first voice that I had heard sounding like a trumpet, spoke to me:
"Come up here and I will show you
What must take place
after this." (Rev 4:1 AT)

In short, John does not offer a set of teachings or doctrines about God, Jesus, or humans. He presents us with sense perceptions, visionary experiences, personal encounters—a style of seeing. He refines our perceptions, "so that for a moment our eyes can see and our ears can hear what is there about us always," as Father Vaillant says about miracles, in Willa Cather's, *Death Comes for the Archbishop*.

Using images as raw materials, John creates scenes that he saw while "in the spirit." In some scenes, John joins images to narrate action: the earth beast exercises authority, makes the earth worship the sea beast, makes fire come down from heaven, deceives the inhabitants of the earth, gives breath to an image of the sea beast and kills those who do not worship it (chapter 13). Other scenes describe the actors: the locusts that came up from the abyss are like horses, with crowns on their heads, with faces like humans, hair like women's hair, teeth like lions, scales like iron breastplates, and wings that make a roaring noise (9:7-10). Still other scenes describe the setting in which the actors act: The new Jerusalem, radiant like a rare jewel, is marked off by a great, high wall with twelve gates and twelve foundations. It forms a cube of fifteen hundred miles in all directions. It houses no temple; but a river, with trees on each side, flows through it (21:9–22:5).

John arranges scenes in a loose and fluid manner, for he uses a limited number of images over and over. As one listens to scene after scene, images combine and recombine: some fall away, new ones are added, old ones return in different combination. They form one scene after another—each similar to, yet different from the other. They are like petroglyphs found on stones in the southwestern United States where a small number of straight lines of different lengths combine with one another and with a few curved lines to form a wide variety of figures and shapes on the rocks. John Brandi describes those rock drawings as maps "that rotate and unfold into myriad dimensions; exploding ideograms—tenseless, dream connected, associated with . . . ritual magic . . . rain, lightning, eclipses, earthquakes, procreation" (1991, 77). So John's audiograms explode and unfold, as we listen to one scene following another.

Images in one scene form ratios and harmonies with those in another (Thompson 1990, 89; Berry 1990, 89). God is to Satan as the Lamb is to the beast, as the faithful are to the inhabitants of the world, as heaven is to earth, as the future is to the present, as the temple is to space outside it, as activity of worship is to everyday activity. Babylon, the Great whore, fornicator with kings of the earth (17:2), is "clothed in fine linen, in purple and scarlet" and "adorned with gold" (18:16). Her "scarlet" matches the color of the beast upon which she sits (17:3). Her fornication echoes the prophetess, Jezebel, at Thyatira, who beguiles Christians "to practice fornication" (2:20). The whore's linen is matched by that of the Bride of the Lamb, though the bride's is " 'bright and pure'—for the fine linen is the righteous deeds of the saints" (19:8), who are ransomed by the Lamb (5:9) and whose blood makes the great whore drunk (17:6). The "gold" with which the great whore is adorned is also what Christ makes available to the Laodiceans (3:18) and that out of which the new Jerusalem is made (21:18).

A single image can accumulate multiple meanings as it joins various others throughout the book. "Sea" occurs twenty-six times in Revelation. It first appears before the " heavenly throne," along with "thunder," and "lightning," images of the divine presence (chapter 4). At 5:13 it joins with "earth," "heaven," and "under the earth" to describe various areas within the created universe. At 13:1, it is an image of the primordial abyss that holds the waters of chaos: A beast arises out of it as a Dragon stands on the shore. Finally, at 21:1 it disappears; "the sea was no more," in the "new heaven" and "new earth."

In a kind of reverse development, one scene can draw together images from many different scenes. For example, 19:11-13 describes in detail the principal actor in the drama. That description accumulates images from earlier scenes:

Then I saw heaven opened [4:1], and there was a white horse [6:2]! Its rider is called Faithful and True [1:5; 3:7], and in righteousness he judges and makes war [6:10; 2:16]. His eyes are like a flame of fire [1:14], and on his head are many diadems [12:3]; and he has a name inscribed that no one knows but himself [2:17]. He is clothed in a robe dipped in blood [1:5; 7:14], and his name is called the Word of God [1:9].

As one reads, dominant images rotate like a turning kaleidoscope. The first sequence of visions (1:9–3:22) anchors the book in the life of the seven Christian congregations of Asia. In this sequence, the Likeness of a Human (1:13) appraises, exhorts, encourages, threatens, complains, promises, and advises each of the seven churches. Most important, he who has the "keys of Death and of Hades" (1:18) ends each of the prophetic pronouncements with various images of immortality—tree of life, crown of life, new name, white robes, a place on the throne—for the one who conquers. Many of the images that recur throughout the book thus have Christian life in Asia as their reference point even as they "rotate" to the heavenly realm.

The next two series of visions (4:1–8:1; 8:2–11:19) establish the divine powers that judge the world and destroy evil. The twin visions in chapters 4 and 5—the vision of the throne and the enthronement of the Lamb—become the touchstones for describing divine forces of good in the rest of the book. The text of 12:1–14:20 and 15:1–16:20 introduces various evil beings that oppose and war with divine beings and the faithful on earth. Chapter 13, in presenting a concentrated series of evil images, stands as polar opposite to chapters 4 and 5. Forces of evil mentioned elsewhere in the book point ahead or back to those images of chapter 13—beast, blasphemy, idolatrous worship of an image, deceptive signs, and tattoos on hand or forehead. Even the visions of Babylon the whore (17:1–19:21) build on chapter 13, though the kaleidoscope of evil images has turned slightly in those chapters. The final rotation of images brings into focus the grand finale (20:1–22:5) of Satan's defeat, the final judgment, and the renewal—the transformation—of earth, heaven, and Jerusalem. Images in that series are not new: they draw upon previous ones, especially in chapters 2–5.

Some readers find John's visionary style of writing bizarre. George Bernard Shaw concluded that Revelation was "a curious record of the visions of a drug addict" (quoted in McGinn 1984, 35). John describes objects like a human holding seven stars in his hand and seven-headed beasts. Likewise, Ezekiel sees an elaborate structure of wheels within wheels, with rims "tall and awesome" and "full of eyes." In Ezra's vision, a weeping woman is suddenly transformed into a city "being built." Bizarre! Those same readers, however, may read visual representations in their newspapers of a dog sitting on top of his doghouse with a typewriter, beginning a novel, "It was a dark and stormy night." Or they may read a book in which a person climbs into a small booth, shuts the door, and opens it in a different century or on a different planet. Indeed, readers may find personal, moral, and religious insights in the dog and in space and time travel. Why don't regular readers of *Peanuts* and *Dr. Who* find them bizarre? The answer, put succinctly, is because those readers are familiar with the genre of cartoon and science fiction and with what is possible within those genres. Readers recognize and implicitly accept the "contract" that writers have made with them.

So the relevant question is not, Why do visionaries like John write in such a bizarre manner? but What do we need to know about the genre of visionary writing (apocalypse)? What are characteristics of the genre, apocalypse, in which Revelation is written? In what form does John shape his visions, and what kind of "contract" does he make with his readers?

First of all, John says the words are not his; they were given to him (for the following see Collins 1979; Thompson 1996). That is not bizarre. In fact, artists and theorists often have had the same experience. Homer and Virgil named a Muse as the source of their words. Einstein dreamed parts of his theories and felt that his ideas came from outside him. The pianist, Keith Jarrett, explains that he does not make music; he only allows the music to be played. Dizzy Gillespie said, "All the music is out there in the first place, all of it. From the beginning of time, the music was there. All you have to do is try to get a little piece of it. I don't care how great you are, you only get a little piece of it" (quoted in Hillman and Ventura 1992, 59).

John, of course, receives his inspiration in a very different setting from Dizzy Gillespie or Keith Jarrett. As we have seen, John exemplifies a type of religious visionary. Among visionaries, John is more the shaman than medium, for in his extra-corporeal flights and clairvoyant experiences, he "remains wholly himself while becoming other" (Torrance 1994, 137-38). Further, what he sees is determined by his particular religious tradition and social experience. When John is taken up in the spirit, he sees the Lord God sitting on a heavenly throne, not the Master in a Caribou House. He sees Jesus Christ, the Slain Lamb, not an enlightened Buddha sitting under a tree. He encounters personal beings, not impersonal forces; angels, not ancestors; eagles, not cranes.

His visions take shape from a stock of words, phrases, and motifs drawn from reading—or listening to lectors reading—books now a part of the Christian Bible, from visionary literature outside the Bible, from street vendors hawking various religions and philosophies, from public, religious festivals, from conversations, or from simply walking the city streets and roads of the province of Asia. For example, John drew images primarily from the Old Testament and Jewish visionary literature to describe "one like the Son of Man" (1:12-16), but he may have read "the keys of Death and of Hades" (1:18) on a roadside epitaph or heard of a divine being holding "seven stars" from someone at Miletus (1:16). He adapted those various sources freely, for he was composing from them, not commenting upon them. Further, it is unlikely that he had a library of scrolls at Patmos, and even if he did, it is even less likely that the page of the source was open as he wrote (see Achtemeier 1990). Whether he alluded to a text or used stock conventions, John composed from a variety of sources a symphony of images distinctive to Revelation in order to proclaim the Christian message revealed to him.

Second, John recorded his visions in the form of a story about what he saw and heard. The skeleton of the book thus reads as a narrative:

I, John, your brother . . . Then I turned to see . . . After this I looked, and there in heaven a door stood open . . . After this I saw four angels . . . And I saw another mighty angel . . . And I saw a beast rising from the sea . . . After this I heard what seemed to be the loud voice of a great multitude in heaven . . . Then I saw a new heaven and a new earth . . . I, John, am the one who heard and saw these things.

Within that first-person narrative, one scene after another balloons out, each with its own cast of characters. Within the scenes are also dialogues, monologues, and heavenly scenes of worship, but all are presented within the simple story line of what John saw and heard.

Third, John's narrative reveals hidden, religious dimensions in ordinary life, dimensions that he describes in two ways: that which is "yet-to-come" and that which is "above." Contemporary culture critics (Christian and non-Christian) associate Revelation most often with the yet-to-come (see Kumar 1995). They borrow its imagery of doom and disaster and expect an Armageddon to end the world as we know it (Rev 16:16). In contrast to modern apocalypses that bring the world to an end in the heat of atomic wars or the iciness of entropy, John describes those coming disasters as birth pangs or a refining fire that leads to a new, transformed world portrayed by powerful, elemental images such as "the water of life," "the tree of life," "no more night," "crying and pain will be no more" (chaps. 21–22). Further, that "yet-to-come" is God's business and will arrive when he brings it. Humans are to prepare for and not speculate on the time of God's coming. The "yet-to-come" gives weight to the present: What we do matters. Human behavior is not rendered meaningless by life's impermanencies (or its constant changelessness). Waylon Jennings is not talking about John when he sings, "He was talking about tomorrow while I was struggling with today."

The "above"—the other way John describes hidden, religious dimensions in ordinary life—exists in the present. When John goes through the open door to heaven (4:1), he describes a throne scene to which he returns at several points throughout the book. There, he sees angels and other heavenly creatures worship and sing praises to God and the Lamb. Heavenly songs celebrate the present rule of God and his Christ and the justice of their judgments. That is, the rule of God and his just judgment of earthlings do not await a future eschaton; they are present, hidden realities. Those scenes of the heavenly throne, which punctuate regularly the story that John tells, keep the religious dimension from being simply a distant hope of a coming end. The good God has not lost control of the world, and the faithful followers of the Lamb are given assurance regularly throughout Revelation that they will ultimately take their place before the throne of God and rejoice in the radiance of his presence, no matter what horrors they may face on earth. The eschaton— when the heavenly throne comes down as the new Jerusalem—simply brings universal recognition of what presently exists.

In sum, John creates his visionary scenes from images that both refer to concrete things and open to something "more." From the clay of images, John forms one scene after another—each similar to, yet different from the other. Reading the scenes in sequence is like turning a kaleidoscope, in which a limited number of tiny, glass particles reflect ever-changing sights. Moreover, John constructs his visionary scenes in such a way as to communicate to his readers that they are reading visions that John has received. Finally, those images that form scenes and sequences of scenes as part of the visionary genre do not simply create an imaginary world, unrelated to the life and times of John and his readers. The analogies and harmonies in the work both reflect and shape those by which John and his responsive readers live. They form the "whorls that spin him," and thoughtful readers (Christian or non-Christian) will weigh their possibilities for "spinning a life."

WELCOME TO THE COMMENTARY

Victor Furnish points out in the foreword that each unit of Revelation is analyzed in three different ways: literary analysis, exegetical analysis, and theological and ethical analysis. The analyses will be most helpful if you read the literary analysis, then the unit in Revelation, and, finally, the exegetical and theological analyses of the unit.

Literary analysis focuses upon the unit itself, its overall structure, its constituent forms, its stylistic features, and its coherence (e.g., one issue, one actor, or one sustained narrative point of view). There also I weigh the relative importance given to action, actor, scene, supporting actors, purpose of action, and dramatic development.

The exegetical section forms the bulk of the commentary. In that section you will find references to other writings that share with Revelation words, phrases, images, and motifs. Those references taken together form a circle of texts. By studying each text individually and then in relation to the others in the circle, you can learn a lot about the religious and social setting in which John lived, as well as the particular point that he gives to the common language. It would be the worst kind of anachronism to limit John's circle of texts to writings in the Christian Bible, for in his day there was no Christian Bible. John formed and proclaimed his message in the multicultural world of the Roman Empire, and in order to understand fully what he wrote, we need to consider the whole range of religion and society that he knew. To enter his world, *The Oxford Classical Dictionary (OCD)*, with its many references to the culture, society, and history of the Roman Empire, is as important as a dictionary of the Bible, and writings found in *The Old Testament Pseudepigrapha (OTP)*, *The Apostolic Fathers*, the *Apocryphal New Testament*, *Papyri graecae magicae (PGM)*, and many authors in the Loeb Classical Library (LCL) are nearly as important as those found in the Christian Bible.

Comments in the third section of analysis draw upon a study of the references in the exegetical section. John and his first readers shared a common stock of knowledge about their culture and society, and so his first readers easily recognized allusions and meanings in Revelation that we discover by searching laboriously through many obscure references. (Consider how difficult it would be for an alien of our cultural and social institutions to place the following fragment in its proper cultural setting: "Welcome to the Ascended Masters Network. This page is dedicated to helping you enter the world of enlightened spiritual beings called Ascended Masters. Scroll down. . . .")

The following comments about the opening of the seventh seal (8:1) exemplify those three types of analyses: "When the Lamb opened the seventh seal, there was silence in heaven for about half an hour." *Literary:* In Revelation, the seventh in a sequence serves as a marker to the reader and to those listening that a major segment has come to a close. Dramatic tension builds from the previous six seals. All attention is given to the "act" of silence. The scene is "in heaven." No actor, supporting actors, or purpose is given. *Exegetical:* There is a wide circle of texts that refer to silence and its importance. Zephaniah commands: "Be silent before the Lord GOD! For the day of the LORD is at hand" (1:7; see also Hab 2:20). Baruch wonders if at the end, "will the universe return . . . to its original silence?" (2 *Apoc. Bar.* 3, cf. 2 Esdr 6:39; 7:30). Adam, explaining the hours of the night, says to his son Seth that "the twelfth hour is the waiting for incense, and silence is imposed on all the ranks of fire and wind until all the priests burn incense to his divinity" (*T. Adam* 1.12). In the Mithras Liturgy, Silence is called a symbol of the living God: "So at once put your right finger on your mouth and say: 'Silence! Silence! Silence! Symbol of the living, incorruptible God! Guard me, Silence, Nechtheir Thanmelou' " (*PGM* 4.558-60). *Theological and Ethical:* So, on the basis of the circle of texts involving "silence," we may conclude first that at Rev 8:1 "silence" is not just an absence; it is an activity marking the presence of God, often preceding the day of the Lord, and, second, it is a sign of revelations to come (cf. 1 Kgs 19:12, theophany to Elijah; Job 4:16, to Eliphaz).

Unless otherwise indicated, English translations are from the NRSV and Greek transliterations are from the Greek text of Nestle-Aland, *Novum Testamentum Graece* (27th revised edition; Stuttgart: Deutsche Bibelgesellschaft, 1993). Usually I use the form of the Greek word in the text. In addition to the references marked in the "List of Abbreviations" and "Select Bibliography," I find two other references invaluable: *The American Heritage Dictionary of the English Language,* 3rd ed. and M. H. Abrams, *A Glossary of Literary Terms,* 4th ed. (New York: Holt, Rinehart and Winston, 1981). The index includes a reference to key images, as well as other topics.

COMMENTARY

INTRODUCTION TO THE VISIONS (1:1-8)

John begins with a genealogy of Revelation: God gave it to Jesus Christ who gave it to an angel who gave it to John who testified to it by writing it down. The genealogy (1:1-2) is written in lean prose, no details are given as to where this transmission occurs, the actors are named without further attributes, and no motivation is given for the divine revelation beyond God's desire to let people know "what must soon take place." After the genealogy and a blessing for reader and hearers (1:3), John makes a unique shift for a visionary: He greets his readers in the form of a pastoral letter (1:4-6). Two prophetic sayings (1:7-8) then make a transition from pastoral letter to the first vision (1:9–3:22). The sayings' oracular, cryptic style contrasts with the matter-of-fact style in 1:1-6 and prepares the reader for the vision to come.

The aim of the introduction is clear. The visions are true because they come from God. Those who listen carefully will be blessed. The greeting in second-person "you" (1:4) draws the audience into John's orbit, and the "us" in the doxology (1:5-6) at the conclusion of the greeting unites John and his readers as one Christian community. Through matter-of-fact assertions, promises, greetings, and joint praise to Jesus Christ, John's Christian audience is led to accept what he writes as God's word—at least if they want to share in communion with John, Jesus, and God.

◊ ◊ ◊ ◊

1:1-2: John uses several quasi-technical terms to describe this chain of transmission: The term "revelation"—only here in Revelation—refers to a process of disclosure (*apokalypsis*, the "-sis" suffix marks it as a process); for example, land is revealed as a river

47

recedes from it (MM under *apokalyptō*), or a person's hidden evil nature becomes evident when he or she gains power (*Sull.* 30.5.8). Here it refers to the disclosure of things hidden with God. Amos writes, "Surely the Lord GOD does nothing, without revealing his secret to his servants the prophets" (3:7; cf. Dan 2:22, 28). In the Jewish community at Qumran, the Teacher of Righteousness discloses "all the mysteries of the words of his servants, the prophets" (1QpHab VII.5). At Rev 1:1, "servants" probably refers to Christian prophets, but the term could refer to all Christians. "Show" *(deixai)* also has a technical meaning of "disclose." In a prayer of thanksgiving occurring several times in visionary literature, a seer rejoices "because you have shown us yourself" (*PGM* III.597, note 114). "Made it known" *(esēmanen)* refers to an event or situation not fully disclosed (John 12:33; Acts 11:23; Dan 2:45; *Ant.* 7.214; 10.241). So, Heraclitus said that the oracle at Delphi always indicates or points to something more *(sēmainei)*, rather than revealing it fully *(legei)* or concealing it completely (*kruptei; De Pyth. or.* 21, 404E). "Testified" *(martyrein)* refers to a highly personal act of disclosure, such as witnessing in a court of law or as a martyr. In this chain of transmission, both Jesus Christ and John "testify" to the word of God: Jesus Christ through an angel (22:16, 20); John by writing.

1:3: The scene of the beatitude in verse 3 is an assembly of Christians at worship where a reader (lector) reads aloud to the others. Such an arrangement was necessary since only a small number of Christians in the churches of Asia could read, probably about one out of ten (see Gamble 1995, 5). Moreover, in the first centuries after Christ most reading was done aloud, whether public or private. Recall Augustine's surprise that Ambrose *always* read silently, "his heart perceived the sense, but his voice and tongue were silent" (*Confes.* 6.3.3. For examples of reading silently, cf. *De Alex. fort.* 7, 340A; *Brut.* 5.2, and Gilliard 1993, 694, as well as his letter to the editor in *Times Literary Supplement* [Aug. 8, 1997], 19). We know little about church readers (lectors) in this early period of Christianity, but they probably had some control over what exactly was read before the congregation. By offering a blessing, John encourages them to read his book. Only six other beatitudes occur in Revelation (14:13; 16:15; 19:9; 20:6; 22:7; 22:14). Prophecies and revelations were regularly spoken or read in services of worship (Acts 11:28; 13:27; 1 Cor 14:26-33; 1 Tim 4:14).

To "hear" is to be involved in an aural, sensory event involving communication and learning. If members of the congregation hear the word properly, they will "keep" it (cf. 2:26; 3:3, 8, 10; 12:17; 14:12; 16:15; 22:7, 9). "Prophecy" *(propheteias)*, an expression of Christian visionary experience, connects closely with "testified," for as an angel says later in Revelation, "the testimony of Jesus is the spirit of prophecy" (19:10; cf. 22:7, 10, 18, 19). The nearness of the time when God will judge all humans (11:18) motivates the hearers to obey (cf. 22:10).

1:4: John, the last recipient in the chain of revelation (1:1), is now the main actor who sends greetings to "the seven churches that are in Asia" (1:4). "Grace" and "peace" are typical elements in Christian greetings, usually from a double source, God and Jesus Christ (Rom 1:7; 1 Cor 1:3; Titus 1:4; *1 Clem.*). The greeting expresses a wish, "May you have grace and peace." As noted earlier, Revelation is unique in combining the letter with vision-reports.

Here "grace" and "peace" derive from a triple source: God (note 1:8), "the seven spirits," and "Jesus Christ." "The seven spirits" are identified with "seven flaming torches" at 4:5 and with "seven eyes" of the Lamb at 5:6 (cf. Zech 4:10). John is probably alluding to the seven watchful archangels who stand before the divine throne ready to do God's will (8:2; *1 Enoch* 20; Tob 12:15). He may, however, be referring to some other cluster of heavenly, perhaps astral, powers.

1:5-6: Of the three sources of grace and peace, John emphasizes Jesus Christ. John gives him three attributes, followed by a doxology. First, he is "the faithful witness" *(martys;* cf. "testimony *[martyrian]* of Jesus Christ," 1:5). This phrase associates Jesus with the royal line of David (Ps 89:37; Isa 55:4) and with death (2:13; John 3:11-15). If John's readers were familiar with the story of the crucifixion as told in the Gospels, they might recall Jesus' faithful witness in contrast to the false witnesses who testified against him at his execution (cf. 1 Tim 6:13). Second, he is "firstborn." The Davidic king is also called "firstborn" (Ps 89:27), but here John gives the term a twist: Jesus is "firstborn *of the dead*" *(prōtotokos tōn nekrōn)*, that is, he is "preeminent among the dead" (cf. Pol. *Phil.* 7.1 where heretics are called *prōtotokos tou satana,* "preeminent of Satan"). The grammatical construction, genitive without preposition, does not move Jesus out of the sphere of the dead. (For the construction, cf. 20:5; Heb 12:23; Col 1:15; *Sib. Or.* 8.314 in contrast to Col 1:18, which has the preposition *ek: prōtotokos ek tōn nekrōn.*) Third, "ruler of the kings of the earth" (cf. Isa 55:4; Ps 89:28) parallels "firstborn of the dead": Jesus Christ is preeminent over both the dead and the living kings of the earth (cf. Rom 14:9, "For to this end Christ died and lived again, so that he might be Lord of both the dead and the living."). Later in the book, "kings of the earth" are associated with evil forces such as the "beast" and the "whore," but here at the beginning John makes clear that Jesus Christ has ultimate power over them (cf. 21:24. For "kings of the earth," cf. 6:15; 17:2, 18; 18:3, 9; 19:19).

A doxology brings the letter greeting to a close (cf. Rom 16:27; Gal 1:5). Doxologies occur primarily in the domain of worship, but then letters are also read in worship (Col 4:16). Three elements make up the skeleton of a doxology: first, the one given praise is addressed, for example, "to him"; then words of praise such as "glory" *(doxa,* note 4:9-11) and "dominion" follow *(kratos,* note 5:13-14; cf. 1 Pet 4:11); finally, the doxology ends with an "amen," often preceded by a temporal phrase, "forever and ever" (5:13; 7:12). The efficacy of Jesus' blood for deliverance from sin is a common theme in early Christian literature (note 5:9-10; Luke 22:20; Acts 20:28; Rom 3:25; 5:9; 1 Cor 11:25; Eph 1:7; 2:13; Heb 10:19; 1 Pet 1:2, 18; 1 John 1:7). Into this doxology, John has inserted a statement about what Christ has done for Christians (for "kingdom and priests"; see 5:10).

1:7: This enigmatic oracle is charged with dramatic tension. The rider of the clouds, though not specified, would be associated by listeners with Jesus Christ in the doxology. The verb translated "is coming" in the NRSV would better be rendered "is moving" *(erchetai)*, for in contrast to passages such as 10:1; 11:12; or 1 Thess 4:16, movement here is not specified as toward or away from the audience. (*Atēh* in Dan 7:13 is also movement without a direction specified.) We should here see Jesus' movement as crossing the sky like lightning (Matt 24:27), similar to the end time "figure of a man" in 2 Esdras who "flew with the clouds of heaven" (13:3 and Dan 7:13). "Riding the clouds" is a divine attribute (see Isa 19:1). As the eschatological (end-time) Jesus is moving across the sky, his appearance has global dimensions: "every eye" and "all the tribes of the earth" see him.

In the Christian story as the Fourth Evangelist tells it, the "pierced one" is the crucified Jesus (John 19:34-37). "Those who pierced him" also associates the figure with the Lord God and with the mourning of Hadad-rimmon (a Canaanite deity) in Zech 12:

And I [the Lord God] will pour out a spirit of compassion and supplication on the house of David and the inhabitants of Jerusalem, so that, when they look on me [MT] whom they have pierced, they shall mourn for him, as one mourns for an only child, and weep bitterly over him, as one weeps over a firstborn *[prōtotokoi]*. On that day the mourning in Jerusalem will be as great as the mourning for Hadad-rimmon in the plain of Megiddo. The land *[gē]* shall mourn, each family *[kata phulas]* by itself. (Zech 12:10-12)

In this oracle as a whole, the heavenly figure referred to in Dan 7:13 and 2 Esdr 13:3 is brought into connection with "wailing" *(kopsontai)*, which occurs most often in a funerary context (18:9; 1 Kgs 13:29; Luke 23:27; *Gos. Pet.* 7.25; 12.52; *Ant.* 8.273). "The tribes of the earth" *(phylai tēs gēs)* wail "on his account" *(ep' auton;* cf. 18:9; 2 Sam 1:12; contrast *Apoc. Peter* 6 and the long recension of Ign. *Trall.* 10 where the text is changed to read "and they shall wail 'for themselves *[eph' heautois]'* "). Here, as in Zech 12, we enter the domain of ritual lamentation of a hero or deity (see Hvidberg 1962, 119). The lament over "the pierced one" is comparable to the ritual lamentation over Achilles (*Paus.* 6.23.3), Adonis (*Syr. D.* 6, "and then, they say he lives and they send him into the air [sky]"), or Attis (Diod. Sic. 3.59.7). Note also that the "man" flying with the clouds in 2 Esdras comes from "the heart of the sea," that is, Sheol, the place of the dead.

1:8: This final oracle brings the introduction to a close. The repetition of "who is and who was and who is to come" at 1:4 and 1:8 exemplifies ring composition (or an envelope pattern), in which a word or phrase is repeated at the beginning and at the end of a unit and thus forms a ring around the block of text. The "I" of God here also provides a transition to the "I" of John in 1:9. A declaration of God speaking in first person *(ego eimi),* one of the most audacious forms found in religious literature, functions as a form of divine self-revelation (Exod 3:14; Isa 41:4; John 8:28; Isis sayings from Cyme in Grant 1953, 131-33). By revealing himself as "the Alpha and the Omega," God declares that he takes in all that is, from A to Z (cf. 21:6; 22:13 referring to Christ; Isa 41:4; 44:6). More common in religious literature is the phrase, "who is and who was and who will be" (see Charles, 1:10-11). By changing the last part, John emphasizes that God is the one who comes (cf. 11:17; 16:5; Isa 40:10; John 14:23). The expression, "the Almighty" *(pantokrator),* appears only in Revelation among New Testament books (at 2 Cor 6:18 as part of an Old Testament quotation). In the Septuagint, the term translates *Sabaoth,* a Hebrew word associated with the warrior-God of the ark of the covenant (cf. Josh 5:14; 10:12-14; Judg 5:11-21; 2 Sam 5:22-25; Pss 103:19-21; 148:1-5; Dan 8:10; James 5:4). Elsewhere in Revelation, these epithets of God occur primarily in heavenly liturgies (4:8, 11; 11:17; 15:3; 16:5, 7; 19:6).

◊ ◊ ◊ ◊

The verbs used to narrate the genealogy of Revelation—"revelation," "show," "made it known," and "testify"—place this writing in the cultural domain of prophecy, oracles, and visions. In that domain, revelation opens the ordinary world of everyday life to more than it appears to be: to a "heavenly" dimension above (cf. 4:1-2), as well as to a future hidden in the present (4:1; 22:6; Matt 24:6), for the God who discloses "what must soon take place" *(ha dei genesthai en tachei)* also brings it to pass (4:1; 22:6; Matt 24:6;

Dan 2:29, 45 Theod.). Revelation is, however, always filtered through the person who presents the revelation. John, like all writers, is present in what he writes in this sense: It is his values and beliefs that shape the visions that God gives him.

John begins Revelation matter-of-factly with an omniscient third-person point of view. He even knows what God, Jesus, and the angel did in transmitting the revelation. As readers, we hardly think about the fact that someone is making these assertions. At verse 4, John removes the veil of narrator and speaks plainly and openly, "John." His intended hearers also become explicit: "To the seven churches that are in Asia." They are addressed directly in the second person, "Grace to you. . . ." Then, as we have seen, the first-person plural, "us, our," in the doxology establishes and assumes a community to which John, the reader, and the hearers all belong.

In the rest of the book, beginning with 1:9, John reports, in first person, visions that he experienced. In those vision-reports, John has a dual role. On the one hand, his ego ("I") frames the visions by phrases such as "I heard," "I saw," "After this I looked." On the other hand, he is a character within the visions interacting with other characters, for example, "So I went to the angel and told him to give me the little scroll; and he said to me, 'Take it, and eat . . .' " (10:9). As both framer and character in the frame, John's role in writing becomes much like that of an actress presenting a one-woman show of the life of someone such as Emily Dickinson.

That shift to first person affects the kind of moral and religious authority expressed in the rest of the book. From 1:9 to the end, John reports personal experience. We are told only that which flows through his center of consciousness. He knows only that which he experiences, deduces from his experiences, or learns from others. Moreover, he has privileged access to these experiences. Hearers cannot see exactly what he sees. They have no access to what lies behind the report (cf. 1 Cor 13:2; 1 Thess 5:19-22). For that reason, a seer's words (including John's) are always liable to be suspect. That suspicion is, however, abated by the way John uses first person to reflect his psychological and religious state in which his ego blurs with either God's or Christ's, or both. Note, for example, the sequence of "I" in 1:8-18: "I am the Alpha and the Omega . . . I, John, your brother . . . I was in the spirit . . . I turned . . . I fell . . . I am the first and the last . . . I was dead, and see, I am alive." By that blurring, John exemplifies what Christ says in the *Odes of Solomon*, "Then I arose and am with them, and will speak by their mouths" (42.6).

JOHN'S FIRST VISION (1:9–3:22)

John identifies himself as a "brother," sketches out the circumstances in which he wrote his book, and then tells about his initial vision (1:9-11). Prominent in the vision is a Likeness of a Human, whom John describes in detail (1:12-17) and who directs John not to be afraid (1:17-18), to write down what he sees (1:19), and to take dictation in the form of a prophetic pronouncement to each of the seven churches (2:1, 8, 12, 18; 3:1, 7, 14). The pronouncement to the church at Laodicea brings John's first vision to an end (3:14-22) and provides a transition to his second vision, which begins at chapter 4.

Brother John (1:9-11)

Neither here nor earlier in the greeting does John claim any special role such as apostle, elder, or prophet. He is simply a "brother" and a "partner" of those to whom he writes. After stating the basis of their common communion (1:9a), John tells where he is, when he has his visions, and what religious-psychological state he is in (1:9b-10a). His initial vision begins when he hears a voice behind him telling him to write in a book all that he sees and to send it to "the seven churches" (1:10b-11). When he turns "to see whose voice it was that spoke," the vision begins (1:12).

◊ ◊ ◊ ◊

1:9a: In the first part of verse 9, John establishes a relation with his hearers by stating the basis of Christian community: "I, John, your brother and partner in affliction, royal power, and patient endurance, which we share with Jesus . . ." (AT). "Brother" *(adel-*

phos) is a way of referring to a member of a religious association such as a burial society, a sacred athletic association, or a congregation of Theos Hypsistos ("The Most High God," see BAGD under *adelphos).* It is used over three hundred times in the New Testament to refer to followers of Christ (6:11; 12:10; 19:10; 22:9; Acts 1:15; 15:23; Rom 11:25; 1 Cor 5:11; 10:1; Phil 1:12). "Partner" *(sygkoinōnos)* underscores what John shares in common with his hearers and with Jesus, namely, "affliction" *(thlipsis;* the NRSV incorrectly translates this as "persecution"), "royal power" *(basileia;* NRSV: "the kingdom"), and "patient endurance" *(hypomonē).*

In Revelation, "affliction" *(thlipsis)* is associated with "poverty" (2:9-10), the suffering of Jezebel (2:22), and the ordeal out of which those before the throne came (note 7:13-14). Elsewhere in the New Testament it occurs in a variety of situations, such as childbirth (John 16:21), persecution (Acts 11:19), marriage (1 Cor 7:28), and being an orphan or a widow (James 1:27). At Matt 24:9 it is a sign of the end of the age. Paul is grateful that the Philippians share in *(sugkoinōnēsantes),* his afflictions (Phil 4:14).

Christians share "royal power" with Jesus, because he gave it to them by means of his death (see 1:6; 5:10). John would probably agree with Barnabas that "the royal power of Jesus is on the wood," that is, the cross *(Barn. 5).*

"Patient endurance" is associated with "toil" and "bearing up" (2:2-3; cf. 3:10), as well as "love, faith," and "service" (2:19). Paul makes a connection between "affliction" and "patient endurance": "affliction produces patient endurance, and patient endurance produces character, and character produces hope" (Rom 5:3-4 AT; cf. Ps 62:5). "Patient endurance" moves in the orbit of "manly prowess," the quality of a good soldier *(Anton.* 43.3) who is "steadfast" when tortured and not afraid to die (4 Macc 1:11; 17:17; Pol. *Phil.* 9.1). In that orbit of good soldiers and martyrs, Cato the elder gives sage advice: There is "a difference between valuing courage highly and life cheaply." Plutarch develops the point: "There is no disgrace in avoiding death, so long as a man does not cling to life dishonourably; but neither is there any patient endurance in meeting it if this is done out of contempt for life" *(Pel.* 1).

1:9b-11: In contrast to the lean third-person prose of 1:1-3, John details in first person the circumstances of his revelation. "I . . . was on *(egenomēn en)* the island called Patmos," which is one of the Sporades Islands in the Aegean Sea, about one hundred kilometers southwest of Ephesus. "I" was there "because of *[dia]* the word of God and the testimony of Jesus." The syntax allows for two possible meanings: retrospectively, John was there as a result of (my preaching) the word of God and the testimony of Jesus, or prospectively, to receive the word of God and the testimony of Jesus. The latter meaning echoes 1:2, where the phrase refers to the revelation that John received. Later Christian interpretation, however, favors the first meaning (*Hist. Eccl.* 3.18).

Second, John says, "I was in the spirit" *(egenomēn en,* parallels "I was on" above), that is, "I was under the power of God's spirit" *(en pneumati).* In that state, John is not "possessed," that is, he does not lose his own center of consciousness (note 4:2-3). His traveling to Patmos may be related to his being in the spirit (compare the relation between traveling and spirit at 4:2; 17:3; 21:10; cf. Ezek 11:24; 37:1; Luke 2:27; 4:1; Acts 19:21). "The Lord's day" most likely refers to the day when Christians gathered for worship (Ign. *Mag.* 9; *Did.* 14; *Gos. Pet.* 12.50). Thus, John receives his visions in the same ritual time that the reader reads them (1:3). The phrase, "Lord's day," may have developed in early Christianity as a reference to the Christian Lord, analogous to "Augustus Day," in reference to the emperor (cf. Deissmann 1980, 359). It is not uncommon in religious history for visionary prophecy to have a ritual setting (*De Pyth. or.* 21; *NHL* VI.7; Plut., *Num.* 9.8).

From the start of the vision, John's language creates a situation larger than life. First, he hears a mysterious voice from behind him, the location from which Lycurgus, an early lawgiver of Sparta, also heard a heavenly voice (*Lyc.* 23.2). For the significance of "trumpet," note 8:2.

John is directed to write in a scroll all the visions that he will see, which is the book that we are reading. It was, however, first intended for "the seven churches": Ephesus, Smyrna, Pergamum, Thyatira, Sardis, Philadelphia, and Laodicea.

◊ ◊ ◊ ◊

At 1:9 John states succinctly his understanding of Christian community. It is an egalitarian community in which all are "brothers and sisters." They share with Jesus in the present the three attributes of "affliction," "royal power," and "patient endurance" (so also do some Cynics and Stoics, see Seeley 1992, 135-36). That presentness differs from statements in, for example, 2 Thessalonians or 2 Timothy where Christians endure affliction patiently in the present, but will share "royal power" in the future (2 Thess 1:4-5; 2 Tim 2:12). By sharing presently in all three of those characteristics, Christians mirror John's earlier description of Jesus Christ (1:5-7; cf. Heb 12:2). It is impossible to tell from 1:9 whether John is introducing himself to the seven congregations or whether they have a previous relationship. It is also impossible to know whether those in the congregations shared John's understanding of the brotherhood.

Those verses cannot be used as evidence for widespread political persecution of Christians in John's time. *Thlipsis* should not be translated as "persecution," since it has a much broader meaning (note 1:9*a*). John even states ambiguously his reason for being on Patmos (note 1:9*b*-10). As a visionary, John views as hostile the social world in which the brotherhood lives, and he has some basis for this view in the occasional prosecution of Christians, although other factors shape his understanding of Christian community. For example, Rev 1:9 emphasizes the theme of imitating Jesus, who reigns from the cross. He also wishes to sharpen the boundaries between the brotherhood and the social world around it. John may have expected—even hoped for—political persecution in the near future, but there was no widespread persecution during his lifetime, nor for several decades after (see pp. 27-30).

A Likeness of a Human (1:12-20)

These verses revolve around an apparition that is compared to a human figure—the sacred setting in which he appears (1:12), a detailed description of his clothes as well as visible parts of his body (1:13-16), and an encounter that he has with John (1:17-20). John begins describing the vision in first person, "I turned to see. . . ." The scene builds to a climax when the apparition speaks in first person. Then John's "I" recedes in the presence of the "I" of the other. The scene concludes with the Likeness of a Human explaining the identity of two objects in the vision, "the seven stars" and "the seven lampstands" (1:20). That explanation functions as a transition to the prophetic pronouncements that follow (chapters 2–3).

◊ ◊ ◊ ◊

1:12: John first sees in his vision "seven golden lampstands." Zechariah had a similar vision in which he saw one golden lampstand with seven lamps, with each lamp having seven lips (Zech 4:2-3). At the time of Judas Maccabee, when the Jerusalem temple was rededicated, new holy vessels were brought into the temple, including a lampstand with lamps (1 Macc 4:48- 50; cf. 1 Kgs 7:49). By first seeing lampstands, John associates his vision with that sacred, visionary tradition in Judaism.

1:13-16: "In the midst of the lampstands," John sees a "Likeness of a Human" (AT: literally "likeness of a son of man," *homoion huion anthrōpou;* NRSV: "one like the Son of Man"). John identifies this figure only by what he is "like." In Revelation, "likeness" *(homoios)* occurs when John presents something or someone as suprahuman, such as those in the throne scene at chapter 4 (vv. 3, 6, 7), locusts from the bottomless pit (9:10), beasts from the sea or land (13:2, 4, 11), or the two awesome cities (18:18; 21:11, 18). Readers familiar with the concept of the Son of Man coming on the clouds (Matt 24:30) might associate this being in 1:13 with 1:7 (cf. Dan 7:13; 2 Esdr 13:3). If that were the point of this phrase, however, one would expect "*the* son of man," rather than "son of man," that is, "a human," a fairly common way of identifying visionary apparitions (14:14; Ezek 1:26; 8:2; 9:2, 11; Dan 10; *Apoc. Ab.* 10.1–11.6; *1 Enoch* 46.1; 62.14).

The detailed description of this Likeness of a Human (1:13-16) is similar to that of suprahuman beings, especially angels and archangels, seen in other visions and, in a few instances, to the appearance of those having a sacred office, such as priests:

"long robe [podērē]" Ezekiel's vision of the man with a writing case (Ezek 9:2); Zechariah's vision of Joshua (Zech 3:4); garb of priests (Sir 45:6-13; *Ep. Arist.* 96); garb of Dionysus (Paus. 5.19.6).

"golden sash [zōnēn chrysan] across his chest [mastois]" angels at 15:6; the archangel Eremiel (*Apoc. Zeph.* 6.12); the high priest (*Ant.* 3.154-55, 184-85); Aseneth (*Jos. Asen.* 14.14); Job's daughters (*T. Job* 46.9).

"white hair" Iaoel (*Apoc. Ab.* 11.2); the "Ancient of Days" (Dan 7:9; cf. the One before time at *1 Enoch* 46.1); Noah (*1 Enoch* 106.10).

"fiery eyes" rider of the white horse (19:11); Gabriel (Dan 10:6); Michael (*Jos. Asen.* 14.9); Mithras (*PGM* IV.700); Noah (*1 Enoch* 106.10); Samoila and Raguila (*2 Enoch* 1.5).

"feet like burnished [polished] bronze" Gabriel (Dan 10:6); Michael (*Jos. Asen.* 14.9); Eremiel (*Apoc. Zeph.* 6.11); Prince of the congregation (1Q28b V.26).

"Voice . . . like the sound of many waters" the 144,000 (14:2); great multitude (19:6); wings of creatures (Ezek 1:24); glory of the Lord (Ezek 43:2); voice in the fire (*Apoc. Ab.* 17.1; 18.2).

"in his right hand . . . seven stars" either the seven planets (e.g., *Cher.* 22; *Astr.* 10) or, more likely, the Bear constellation (e.g., *Ep.* 114; Strabo, *Geography* 1.1.21), which Mithras also holds in his right hand (*PGM* IV.700; cf. Iaoel *Apoc. Ab.* 11.3: a "golden staff").

The "sharp, two-edged sword" the word of God (19:15; Isa 49:2; Eph 6:17; Heb 4:12; Wis 18:15-16).

"face . . . like the sun" a mighty angel (10:1); transfiguration of Jesus (Matt 17:2); Gabriel (Dan 10:6); Michael (*Jos. Asen.* 14.8-9); Eremiel (*Apoc. Zeph.* 6.11); Iaoel (*Apoc. Ab.* 11.2); Noah (*1 Enoch* 106.5); Samoila and Raguila (*2 Enoch* 1.5).

1:17-18: John's response to the Likeness of a Human and then the Likeness's response to John are typical elements in reports of visions (19:10, an angel; cf. 22:8; Matt 17:6, transfiguration of

Jesus; cf. Matt 14:27; Acts 26:14, Paul on the road to Damascus; Dan 8:18; 10:5, Gabriel; Ezek 1:28, the glory of the Lord; *1 Enoch* 14.24-25, the Great Glory; *Apoc. Ab.* 10.1-4, Iaoel; *Apoc. Zeph.* 6.4-8, Eremiel; *Jos. Asen.* 14.1-9, Michael).

The Likeness of a Human moves on the boundary between life and death and the human and the divine. By speaking in first person *(ego eimi)* and calling himself "the first and the last," he identifies himself as divine (cf. 1:8). "The living one" *(ho zōn)* may suggest divinity, but usually that phrase without further qualification refers to an ordinary human (see Eccl 7:2; John 11:26; 2 Cor 4:11; 1 Thess 4:15). Thus, the Likeness of a Human lived as a human, "was dead" *(egenomēn nekros),* and is "alive forever and ever" *(zōn eimi eis tous aiōnas tōn aiōnōn),* a mark of divinity. Now he has "the keys of Death and of Hades" *(kleis tou thanatou kai tou haidou;* cf. Aeacus in Apollodorus, *The Library* 3.12.6; Rice and Stambaugh 1979, 244-45; Pluto in *Paus.* 5.20.3; key-holders of the gates of hell in *2 Enoch* 42; Uriel, *Sib. Or.* 2.227-230, *Apoc. Pet.* 4; Eremiel, *Apoc. Zeph.* 6.15 = Jeremiel, 2 Esdr 4:36; Remiel, *1 Enoch* 20.8; Iaoel, *Apoc. Ab.* 10. Also, Persephone in an Orphic hymn; Grant 1953, 110; Osiris in *De Is. et Os.* 35, 364F; further removed, Odysseus in Dio Chrys. 4.37; Dionysus in Paus. 2.31; Euridice in Apollodorus 1.14.5; Heracles in *Pyrr. Hyp.* 1.228; Orpheus in Fronto 10.3.5). There is no hard line between life and death or the human and the divine (see Nock 1944, 144 for other examples).

1:19: The Likeness of a Human then commands John to write. I think that this verse should be translated as follows: "Write down what you see, both what you see presently and what you will see after this" (AT). What is and what will take place explain further what John sees. The second phrase, "what you will see after this" *(ha mellei genesthai meta tauta,* contrast *ha dei genesthai,* note 1:1-2; 4:1; 22:6), may refer to what will take place at or near the end (Matt 24:6; Dan 2:29 Theod.), but it need not refer to the end (Isa 48:6 LXX; Acts 27:33). So far as I can tell, John does not begin describing "last things" until chapter 20, possibly earlier in chapter 18.

1:20: Verse 20 reads as a kind of addendum. Two features of the previous vision are called a mystery (note 10:3-7), which the Likeness of a Human explains: The stars are angels (cf. *PGM* I.74-75 and more remote, *Plant.* 12) and the lampstands are churches (cf. Matt 5:15). That way of explaining objects in a vision, "this means that," occurs only here and in chapter 17. This addendum provides a transition to the pronouncements to the seven churches in chapters 2 and 3.

◊ ◊ ◊ ◊

The apparition whom John sees shares characteristics with archangels, divinized heroes, and eschatological emissaries of God. That Likeness of a Human, who will later be identified unambiguously as Jesus Christ (2:3), has especially close connections with some heroes who die and become minor supernatural beings. He died, "turned into a corpse," entered the grave and Hades, as do all who die, and dwelt in the shadowy existence of the grave. But he has the keys to Death and Hades, as does that "most pious of men," Aeacus who, after his death, is also given the keys. Christ is now in a position to help his community of followers in life and death.

Finally—and this is significant for those "who read aloud and hear" the words—the Likeness of a Human can lead others out of the dark regions of the grave. He (like the Persian god, Mithras), with the Bear constellation firmly in his right hand, gives revelation and leads his initiates upward in ritual ascent so that they may gain immortality, that is, live closely to the One God. In this emerging picture of individual eschatology (continued existence after death), two features should be noted: First, neither the seer nor the apparition avoids or fears death, dying, and being among the dead in the grave and Hades. Artemidorus comments that living members of an association would customarily "go to the house of the deceased members" to be received there by the deceased (Artem. 5.82). Second, a richer, fuller existence near God does not come automatically at death, but occurs when a supernatural being who has power ("the keys") over Hades takes the shadowy wraith up to the heavenly spheres.

This last point recurs at the end of each of the seven following pronouncements: Christ assures those who conquer that he will give them a blessed existence after death.

Pronouncements to the Seven Churches
(2:1–3:22)

Chapters 2 and 3, the Likeness of a Human's dictation to John, concludes John's first vision. Each of the seven messages that he dictates takes the form of a prophetic pronouncement, "These are the words of him who holds . . ." (NRSV), or "Thus says the one holding . . ." (AT; *tade legei;* cf. Amos 1:6, "Thus says the LORD . . ."; cf. Acts 21:11; Diod. Sic. 40.3.6; *Sat.* 10; *Life of Adam and Eve* 22.3). Each of the pronouncements begins with a command to write, then an identification of the one dictating ("these are the words of . . ." followed, for the most part, by phrases found earlier in 1:12-19), and concludes with a sentence appraising the congregation ("I know . . ."). Each pronouncement ends with a command to "listen to what the Spirit is saying" and a promise to the one "who conquers." The middle of the pronouncements consists of complaints, exhortations, threats, acknowledgments, encouragements, or advice.

In each pronouncement, John is directed by the Likeness of a Human to write to the "angel of the church." About that phrase, the following can be said: First, everything has an angel over it (e.g., 7:1-2, winds; 9:11, the abyss; 14:18, fire; 16:5 and *1 Enoch* 66.2, waters; Dan 10:13, 20-21, nations; cf. *Jub.* 2.2). Second, "angel" relates to "church" as "head" relates to "state" in the phrase, "head of state," or "tip" to "finger" in the phrase, "tip of the finger." That is, "angel," here, is a part of "church" and can even represent the church (cf. "head of state"). That point is confirmed by the use of singular and plural "you" in the pronouncements. For the most part, "you" singular is used, as one would expect, since "angel" is singular. But a few times, the speaker shifts back and forth. For example:

Do not fear what you [sing.] are about to suffer. Beware, the devil is about to throw some of you [pl.] into prison so that you [pl.] may be tested, and for ten days you [pl.] will have affliction. Be faithful [sing.] until death, and I will give you [sing.] the crown of life. (2:10; cf. 2:23-24)

Third, on the basis of the mystery that the Likeness of a Human solves (1:20), the seven angels have their place in John's vision as the seven stars that the Likeness of a Human holds in his right hand. The prophetic pronouncements in chapters 2 and 3, however, clearly address situations in the seven congregations of Asia Minor. So, an element in John's vision is also an element in Asian church life. Blurring of vision and church life also occurs at 2:3: There the Likeness of a Human (part of the vision) says, referring to himself in first person, "I also know that you are . . . bearing up for the sake of my name" (congregational life in Asia). In those instances, there is either a confusion of the visionary world with that of Asian church life (like my saying, "Today, I am having lunch with Sherlock Holmes") or, more likely, John's vision opens Asian church life to something more, to dimensions otherwise hidden.

Since the pronouncements to the seven churches in Asia are placed early on in the book, church life in Asia becomes the initial context—the base line—for images and symbols that recur later in the book. In later visions, the dominant imagery rotates to heavenly scenes, demonic powers, cosmic conflicts, and a final transformation and renewal of the earth and heavens, but Christian life in Asia is the touchstone for those later scenes. For example, those who keep the faith at Ephesus are promised permission to eat from the tree of life (2:7). "Tree of life" recurs later in the vision of the new Jerusalem, growing beside "the river of the water of life" (note 22:1-5). In chapters 17–18, John sees the great whore Babylon, who is condemned for her fornication with the kings of the earth, but for those who first read the pronouncements, Babylon the whore mirrors Jezebel, the prophetess at Thyatira, who "refuses to repent of her fornication" (2:21). The early placement of those pronouncements keeps John's visionary world grounded in Asian church life, and the rest of the visions help Christians in Asia to see their situation correctly.

To the Church at Ephesus (2:1-7)

This first pronouncement is linked closely to what precedes by a repetition of "seven stars" and "seven golden lampstands" (1:20; 2:1). After a command to write and an identification of the speaker (2:1), the Likeness of a Human appraises the church positively (2:2-3). Then he "drops the other shoe" with a complaint (2:4), an exhortation, and a threat (2:5), only to end his evaluation with a positive acknowledgment (2:6). The pronouncement concludes, as do the other six, with an exhortation to listen to the Spirit and a promise to everyone who conquers (2:7).

◊ ◊ ◊ ◊

2:1-3: "Ephesus" was a city of more than two hundred thousand people. Its geographical location was ideal for the growth of business, for its harbor looked out on the Aegean (and Mediterranean) Sea, and a major highway from the eastern province of Syria ran through the town and then northwest to Cyzicus, on the Sea of Marmara. Ephesus housed a civic center with city, provincial, and imperial buildings; a commercial district near the harbor; baths, gymnasia, a jogging track, a theater with a seating capacity of twenty-five thousand; and all the other amenities of a cosmopolitan city. District court was also held there.

The Likeness of a Human identifies himself by referring to the "seven stars in his right hand" (see 1:16) and the "seven golden lampstands" (1:12; at 2:1 he "walks among" them). In appraising the church, he underscores their "works," which involve a moral, religious quality that requires "toil" (see 14:13; 1 Cor 15:58; 1 Thess 1:3; Wis 3:11) and a capacity to endure (note 1:9a). As an alternative to "I know your works," Barclay translates, "I know the life that you have lived." Also, they cannot "tolerate evildoers," perhaps identified with the false apostles. Those calling themselves apostles make a sincere claim, but the speaker and at least some of the Ephesians challenge their claim (*Did.* 11; Paul also opposed apostles in 2 Cor 11:5, 13). A similar statement is made about Jesus in Luke 23:2 (cf. *Herm. Man.* 11.16, also "those who say that they are Jews," Rev 2:9 and 3:9; and "Jezebel, who calls herself a prophet," 2:20). Finally, the speaker commends the church for "bearing up because of *my* name," that is, "my name" is the cause for and means of the action of "bearing up" (AT; note the play on "bear evildoers" above, cf. Matt 10:22; 24:9; John 15:21; 1 John 2:12). The Likeness of a Human's reference in first person, "for the sake of my name," identifies him for the first time as Jesus Christ. (In the following, I often refer to John's Christ as the Likeness of a Human as a reminder that "Christ" refers to the apparition that John sees.)

2:4-6: "But I have this against you" (2:4) is a complaint that echoes a judicial charge in a court of law (cf. 2:6, "But you have this" [AT]; "Yet this is to your credit" [NRSV]). "The works you did at first" (when first becoming Christians) contrast with "the works of the Nicolaitans," as "love" contrasts with "hate" (note the imitation of Christ by hating). "Love" *(agapēn)* is an action-oriented attitude of loyalty and attachment to Christ and the brothers and sisters, as well as a detachment and aversion to those outside "our group" (cf. 1:5; 2:19; 3:9; 12:11 "Our comrades did not love their earthly lives" [AT]; 20:9 contrast "hate" at 17:16; 18:2). So the community at Qumran loved and hated in terms of their "group" (1QS 1.4, "to love everything which [God] selects and to hate everything that he rejects; in order to keep . . . from all evil"). On "remember," see note on 18:4-5. On "repent," see 2:16; also 2:21; 3:3, 19; 9:20-21; 16:9, 11. Irenaeus says that the "Nicolaitans" are followers of Nicolaus who went astray (*Adv. Haer.* 1.26.3; cf. Acts 6:5; note 2:14-15). The Likeness of a Human exhorts those at Ephesus to express that exclusivism that they had at first; otherwise, he will remove their lampstand, that is, he will not walk with them (2:1). Repentance keeps Christ from coming to the church, so this "coming" is not a reference to Christ's appearance at the end.

2:7: In each of the seven pronouncements, the Likeness of a Human repeats the command to listen to the Spirit. Three noticeable shifts occur: the Spirit, not Jesus Christ, speaks; there is a shift from second to third person, for example, from "Yet this is to *your* credit" to "*everyone* who conquers"; and more than one church is addressed—"churches" (the seven or more), not the church at Ephesus. The phrase could also be translated: "Let anyone who has an ear listen. What does the Spirit say to the churches? Whoever conquers I will give permission to eat from the tree of life." "Conquer" *(nikaō)* occurs frequently in Revelation, not only at the end of each of the pronouncements, but also at 5:5 (Lion of Judah), 6:2 (rider of a white horse), 11:7 (beast over prophets), 12:11 (comrades over dragon; note 12:10-12), 13:7 (beast over saints), 15:2 (saints over beast), 17:14 (Lamb over beasts), 21:7 (contrast with sinners in 21:5-8).

Eating has some unusual associations in Revelation (2:14; 10:10; 17:16; 19:18). The Ephesians who conquer will be granted "to eat from the tree of life," of which Adam and Eve were not allowed to eat (22:2, 14, 19; Gen 3:22; cf. *T. Levi* 18; *1 Enoch* 25; *2 Enoch* 8; *2 Esdr* 8:52). Paradise is either an earthly garden of delight (Isa 51:3; Ezek 28:13; *Life of Adam and Eve [Apocalypse]* 22) or a heavenly place (2 Cor 12:4; *2 Enoch* 8.1-3). Whichever, it is the place where the righteous dead dwell (Luke 23:43; 2 Esdr 7:36; *Pss. Sol.* 14.3; *1 Enoch* 60.8).

◊ ◊ ◊ ◊

A variety of religions and temple organizations abounded in Ephesus. The temple of Artemis ranked as one of the seven wonders of the ancient world, and it had right of asylum for fugitives. There were imperial precincts dedicated to Rome and various emperors, a temple of Serapis (a god combining Greek and Egyptian features), and temples dedicated to the worship of many other Greco-Roman deities such as Athena, Dionysus, Demeter, Cybele (a goddess of Phrygian origin, also called Magna Mater, the Great Mother), and various heroes (see *ABD* under "Ephesus"). There was also a Jewish community at Ephesus that had the legal right to observe its religious traditions. Two gravestones have been found at Ephesus that charge the Jewish community to care for the graves of those buried (see Thompson 1990, 143).

The Christian congregation, which had been in existence for several decades, consisted of converts from both Jewish and non-Jewish communities. In the early 50s, during the reign of Claudius,

Paul wrote his letters to the Corinthians from Ephesus (1 Cor 16:19). According to Acts, he made Ephesus the center of a ministry that extended into other regions of Asia Minor (Acts 18–19). Later, in the second century, Ignatius of Antioch wrote to the church, and around the middle of the second century, Justin Martyr debated with Jews in Ephesus.

In this pronouncement, as in the following six, John's Christ has a clear notion as to how Christians should live in the world, and he evaluates each congregation accordingly. He commends the Ephesians for their "toil" or "labors," for, as is said later, when Christians die, "they will rest from their labors, for their deeds follow them" (14:13). The Ephesians show "patient endurance" in the way they live, an attribute central to John's understanding of being a follower of Christ (note 1:9a). The Likeness of a Human also evaluates the congregations on how sharply they distinguish themselves from others. The Christ of these pronouncements values exclusion rather than inclusion. The Ephesians are praised for not tolerating "apostles" and for "hating the works of the Nicolaitans," for they are not true brothers and sisters. In the following pronouncements, the Likeness of a Human will direct the congregations to separate from other groups.

To the Church at Smyrna (2:8-11)

The church at Smyrna is only one of two churches—the other is at Philadelphia—against which the speaker makes no criticism or complaint. After the command to write and a statement identifying the speaker, The Likeness of a Human appraises the congregation positively (2:9). Then he encourages them as he apprises them of imminent persecution, promising the faithful "the crown of life" (2:10). The pronouncement ends with an admonition to listen to the Spirit and a promise to those who conquer (2:11). The Likeness of a Human's description of their situation involves several ironic reversals: they appear poor, but they are rich; Jews at Smyrna are not Jews; death is the means to life.

◊ ◊ ◊ ◊

2:8-9: "Smyrna" (modern Izmir), located about sixty-five kilometers north of Ephesus on the coastal road leading to Cyzicus, on the Sea of Marmara, had a population of over one hundred thousand during the first century CE. There was also a road west to Sardis that passed north of Mount Olympus—at least in the Flavian dynasty. According to Philostratus, people there took great pride in the beauty of the city, so much so that Apollonius urged them to be crowned with good men rather than "porticos and pictures, or even with gold in excess of what they needed" (*Life of Apollonius* 4.7). Smyrna, along with Ephesus, Sardis, and Pergamum, was a center for the provincial assembly and also maintained a district court. It had both a civic agora (for political gatherings) and a commercial agora (marketplace) near the harbor, as well as a stadium, a gymnasium, a theater that seated twenty thousand people, and a large grain market.

The Likeness of a Human identifies himself as "the first and the last, who was dead and came to life" (cf. 1:17-18), the first phrase indicating his divinity (note 1:8). The "affliction" (note 1:9*a*) and "poverty" (only here in Revelation, cf. 2 Cor 6:10; 8:2, 9) of those at Smyrna—and the fact that there are no factions in the church—make them an ideal congregation. The phrase, "those who say that they are Jews," is in form like the comment about apostles at 2:2. For "synagogue of Satan," see comments on 3:8-9. The "slander" *(blasphēmian)* of the Jews could refer to false accusations that Jews make against Christians (cf. Rom 3:8, Paul; 1 Pet 4:4, Christians; Jos. *Life* 260, false accusations madee against Josephus), but, more likely, the Jews slander Christ by rejecting his divine claims, for in Revelation "slander" refers to either contemptuous names for God or false claims to divinity (cf. 13:1, 5, 6; 16:9, 11, 21; 17:3; Dan 3:29 Theod. For similar slander, see John 10:33; Acts 18:6, though Josephus says that Jews aren't inclined to "blaspheme," C. *Apion* 236-37. One person's *blasphēmia* is, of course, another person's confession of faith; cf. Artemis at Acts 19:37; Jesus on the cross at Matt 27:39; Gentiles at 1 Pet 4:4; Epicurus at *Non Pos.* 19, 1100D). Too little is known about the Smyrnean situation at this time to document conflict between Jews and Christians. It is possible, though I think not likely, that "Jews" here is a reference to a

Christian group (cf. Gal 2–3; *The Book of Elchasai* in HSW 2:685). *Synagôgê* does not necessarily refer to a Jewish community (cf. Jas 2:2 NRSV: "assembly"; *Herm. Man.* 11.9).

2:10-11: "Suffer" (*paschein,* "endure, undergo") occurs only here in Revelation. The devil, who will throw some of those at Smyrna into prison, will later be imprisoned (20:7). "Prison" *(phylakēn)* can be understood in its ordinary sense (cf. Luke 12:58; Acts 16:23) but, also, in the sense of Hades or the abyss (1 Pet 3:19; Rev 20:7; note 18:1-2). Imprisonment itself is the "test" (*peirasthēte,* to test or to tempt; cf. 2:2; 3:10; 1 Thess 3:5). Daniel, Hananiah, Mishael, and Azariah are also tested "for ten days," when they eat food that did not defile them (Dan 1:12).

"Crowns" are associated with royalty, the priesthood, benefactors, and victorious warriors, but they have special significance in connection with rites of transformation, such as initiation and funerary rites (note 4:4; also *Odes Sol.* 1, 17, 20; Apuleius, *The Golden Ass* 11.24). In rituals associated with the dead, a crown is laid upon a corpse, indicating its transformed state of being (see *Per.* 36.9; *Arat.* 53; *Merc. Cond.* 28; *Mart. Pol.* 17.1). According to the *Ascension of Isaiah,* the Christian dead are crowned only after Christ has "plundered the angel of death" and ascends into the seventh heaven (*Ascen. Is.* 9.6-18, 7.22). In the *Odes of Solomon* 20, the righteous person who comes into paradise is urged: "make for yourself a crown from his tree . . . put it on your head and be refreshed, and recline upon his serenity" (cf. Wis 5:16). And in an Orphic plate from Thurii, Italy, a soul addresses Persephone, "I have reached the crown I longed for, I bury myself in the lap of the Lady who rules Hades" (Grant 1953, 109). Of course, in Christian literature, Christ rules Hades (1:17-18; 2:8). He promises that those who receive the "crown of life" will not "be harmed by the second death" (see see 20:6, 14).

◊ ◊ ◊ ◊

At Smyrna there was a great temple of Zeus, a temple for Aphrodite giving right of asylum, a temple honoring Rome and the emperor Tiberius, and a temple for worship of the Great Mother,

Cybele. Although there is no inscriptional evidence of Jews at Smyrna before the second century CE, there was undoubtedly a community of Jews at Smyrna when John wrote Revelation. Ignatius does not mention any conflict between Jews and Christians in his letter to either Smyrna or Polycarp, though in the *Martyrdom of Polycarp*, Jews cry out for Polycarp's death; but that account has been patterned after the arrest of Jesus as told in the Gospels (see Thompson 1990, 126, 143). According to Ignatius, Christians in Smyrna were of both Jewish and non-Jewish backgrounds (Ign. *Smyrn.* 1), and they represented different social classes (Ign. *Pol.* 4). Also, according to Ignatius, the church at Smyrna had a "godly bishop," a "revered presbytery," and deacons, but of those offices we hear nothing in Revelation (Ign. *Smyrn.* 12).

The caption for this pronouncement could be the phrase "Be faithful until death, and I will give you the crown of life" (cf. Jas 1:12). The Likeness of a Human identifies himself as the one "who was dead and came to life," and so he assures his afflicted and impoverished followers, about to be imprisoned and killed in the luxurious city of Smyrna, to be "faithful until death." He underscores the promise of life after death through two images: they will receive the "crown of life," and they "will not be harmed by the second death," that is, eternal punishment in the lake of fire (see 20:14).

To the Church at Pergamum (2:12-17)

After appraising the congregation at Pergamum (2:13), the Likeness of a Human draws up a complaint (2:14-15), followed by an exhortation to repent. If they do not repent, he threatens war against them (2:16). The pronouncement ends with the customary closing of a directive to listen to the Spirit and a promise to the one who conquers (2:17). In this pronouncement, the appraisal, complaint, and exhortation/threat are emphasized equally.

◊ ◊ ◊ ◊

2:12-13: "Pergamum" (modern Bergama) was about ninety kilometers north of Smyrna and approximately twenty-five kilometers inland from the Aegean coast, slightly north of the Caicus River.

It was located on the north/south road from Ephesus to Cyzicus on the Sea of Marmara. Another road went east out of Pergamum and then south to Thyatira and Sardis. It probably had a population of at least one hundred thousand. In it was located a district court, a theater of about ten thousand seats, a civic center, several gymnasia for different age groups, a smaller auditorium, baths, and an arena for wrestling. At one time, it also housed a library of some two hundred thousand volumes that competed with the great library of Alexandria.

By ringing the appraisal—"where Satan's throne is . . . where Satan lives"—"Satan" (note 12:7-9) is given prominence in the description of Pergamum. Three possibilities have been suggested for "Satan's throne": the hospital of Asclepius (see Grant 1953, 53-55), ceremonies honoring the emperor (e.g., *IGRom.*, no. 353; Lewis 1974, 125), or the religious community around the large altar of Zeus. "Satan's throne" (or "ruling power") is probably con-nected somehow with the martyrdom of Antipas (Antipater?, *Ant.* 14.10), a Christian otherwise not mentioned in early Christian literature. Martyrs were few and known by name. By calling Antipas "my witness, my faithful one," the Likeness of a Human repeats descriptions of Jesus Christ at 1:5.

2:14-15: The Likeness of a Human complains to the angel of the church that the congregation allows Balaamites and Nicolaitans in its midst. Concerning the Balaamites, Num 25:1-2 is the relevant passage: "While Israel was staying at Shittim, the people began to have sexual relations *[ekporneusai]* with the women of Moab. These invited the people to the sacrifices of their gods *[eidōlon]*, and the people ate and bowed down to their gods." Later it is said that Balaam caused the Israelites to go astray (Num 31:16 ; cf. *Ant.* 4.137). Although Balaam is assessed negatively elsewhere in the New Testament and in some Jewish literature (2 Pet 2:15-16; Jude 11; Philo, *Cher.* 32; *Conf. Ling.* 65, 159), he is also spoken of favorably (Mic 6:5; *Ant.* 4.104-5; *1 Enoch* 1.2). Balaam's fourth oracle (Num 24:17) is even used to describe the Messiah in *T. Levi* 17.3; *T. Judah* 24; and 1QM 11.6. It is possible that at Pergamum there was a prophetic school associated with the name, Balaam, similar to the followers of Jezebel at Thyatira. The Likeness of a Human approves of neither (see comments on 2:20-23). The Nicolaitans are here also associated with the Balaamites.

2:16: The complaint is followed by an exhortation and a threat (cf. 2:5). In Revelation, "to repent" is "to turn away from," for example, "her fornication" (2:21), "works of their hands," (9:20), "murders, sorceries, fornication, thefts" (see 9:21), or "deeds" (16:11); and it is a turning to something more desirable, such as "the works you did at first" (2:5) or "giving glory to God" (see 16:9). By the use of "make war," the Likeness of a Human sets himself, the angel, and the angel's church in oppostion to "them," that is, the Balaamites and the Nicolaitans (cf. 12:7; 13:4; 17:14; 19:11; Jer 21:5). For "the sword of my mouth" (AT), see 1:16.

2:17: To everyone who conquers at Pergamum, the Likeness of a Human promises "hidden manna" and a "white stone" with a "new name" written on it. Although "manna" is often referred to in medical literature (recall the Asclepieum [hospital] at Pergamum) as a pinch of frankincense with medicinal properties (for eyesores, Dioscorides Pedanius, *Materials of Medicine* 1.68.6; or a nosebleed, MM under *manna*), it refers here to the bread from heaven given to the Israelites in the desert (e.g., Exod 16:4; Num 11:7; Deut 8:3; *Ant.* 3.31). That heavenly food of the angels (Ps 78:25) is hidden in heaven—it is this *hidden* manna that the Likeness of a Human promises to those at Pergamum—where the righteous in Paradise will eat it once again, in contrast to the unrighteous who will burn "with torches all day, throughout eternity" (*Sib. Or.* Frag. 3.46-49; cf. *Sib. Or.* 7.148-49; 2 *Apoc. Bar.* 29.8). There may also be here an allusion to the Eucharist, as in John 6 and 1 Cor 10:3.

A "white stone" with secret writing on it (cf. 19:12) is an amulet that both protects one from evil and can aid in divination (cf. *PGM* IV.930–114; for the social and religious significance of amulets, see the examples given in Gager 1992, 218-24). The "new name" is probably one that refers to Christ (cf. 3:12).

◊ ◊ ◊ ◊

Pergamum's greatest "temple" was probably the Asclepieum, a shrine dedicated to Asclepius. It had rights of asylum for fugitives, and it served as a hospital for the healing arts practiced in connection with Asclepius, the God of healing. In 74 CE, the emperor Vespasian declared that "physicians, teachers, and medical practitioners" could practice tax-free without malpractice suits (Sherk 1988, no. 84), but about twenty years later, Emperor Domitian threatened to take away those privileges that were being abused (Sherk 1988, no. 108). The great second-century physician, Galen, practiced at Pergamum for many years. Pergamum's great altar to Zeus was dismantled, reconstructed, and is now at the Pergamum Museum in Berlin. In 29 BCE, Augustus granted the request that a provincially sponsored temple be built in Pergamum for him and Rome. Temples also existed to Athena, Dionysus, Demeter, Persephone, Hera, Serapis, and Isis (the latter two, built in the early second century CE, were Egyptian in origin), as well as Mithras or Attis. There was a Jewish synagogue at Pergamum from at least the first century BCE (Thompson 1990, 143). Within Christian circles, Pergamum was apparently not significant. It is not mentioned elsewhere in early Christian literature.

This prophetic pronouncement illustrates nicely how Israel's sacred traditions are alluded to, but never quoted in Revelation (cf. the allusion at 2:7 to the story of Adam and Eve). The Likeness of a Human summarizes succinctly at 2:14 the plot of the Balaam story (Num 22–24; 31:16), but elements of it also appear throughout the pronouncement. The Likeness of a Human identifies himself by "the sharp two-edged sword" (2:12; cf. 1:16), which he threatens to use against the Balaamites and Nicolaitans (2:16), just as the "angel of the LORD" threatened Balaam (Num 22:23, 31). Both Christ and the angel are "adversaries," which in Num 22:32 translates the Hebrew *satan*. "Satan," however, occurs in Revelation as an opponent of Christ and his faithful. Finally, The Likeness of a Human promises "manna" to those who conquer, just as the Israelites received manna in the desert of Moab where Balaam appeared as "a stumbling block before the people" (22:14 AT). For the offense of the Balaamites at Pergamum, see the following pronouncement involving "Jezebel." Both followers of Jezebel and the Balaamites ate "food sacrificed to idols" and practiced "fornication."

To the Church at Thyatira (2:18-28)

The purpose of this prophetic pronouncement is to call Jezebel and her followers to repentance and to encourage the faithful at Thyatira. Here, as in previous pronouncements, the church is too inclusive for the Likeness of a Human. The pronouncement consists of an appraisal (2:19), a complaint (2:20-23), and exhortation (2:24-25), a promise (2:26-28), and an exhortation to hear the Spirit (2:29). According to the Likeness of a Human, there are two factions within the church: those who follow the prophetess, Jezebel, and the rest.

◊ ◊ ◊ ◊

2:18-19: Thyatira (modern Akhisar) was about seventy kilometers south of Pergamum and further inland, on the Pergamum-Sardis road. It was under the district court of Pergamum until the third century, when Caracalla granted Thyatira a court of its own. In the first century CE, it was not an important city in provincial or imperial affairs. It did, however, have a significant number of guilds—potters, tailors, leather workers, shoemakers, linen weavers, bakers, smiths, slave merchants, and especially, dyers and wool workers—that were important economically for the city and the region (Jones 1983, 83; see, e.g., *IGRom.*, 1252, 1265; Acts 16:14).

The shift in terminology from "likeness of a human" (1:13 NRSV: "Son of Man") to "Son of God" is not as significant as might appear at first. Both refer to heavenly figures closely associated with God. So, in Matthew, the high priest asks Jesus whether he is "the Christ, the Son of God," and Jesus responds "From now on you will see the Son of Man seated at the right hand of Power and coming on the clouds of heaven" (Matt 26:63-64; cf. 2 Esdr 13:32; *Odes Sol.* 36.3).

The ethical and religious behavior of those at Thyatira ("your works") is depicted here as "love" (note 2:4-6), "faith" (2:13; 13:10; 14:12), "service *[diakonia]*"—what the writer of Ephesians calls any kind of "ministry *[diakonia]*, for building up the body of

Christ" (Eph 4:12; cf. Acts 11:29; 1 Cor 16:15)—and "patient endurance *[hypomonē]*," closely associated with "faith" (2:13; 13:10; 14:12; note 1:9*a*). In contrast to Christians at Ephesus (2:4), those at Thyatira have increased rather than decreased in their religious commitment.

2:20-23: The Likeness of a Human complains that this congregation tolerates one who calls herself a prophetess *[prophētin]*—in the Greek, he emphasizes her female character—whom he calls "Jezebel" as a way of condemning her (note 2:1-3). She "teaches," an activity limited in Revelation to Jezebel and the Balaamites, and "beguiles" or "deceives," an activity Jezebel shares with Satan and his cohorts (note 13:13-15). By her teaching, she encourages those at Thyatira "to practice fornication and to eat food sacrificed to idols," as Balaam taught the Israelites (2:14). Jezebel was the foreign wife of King Ahab (1 Kgs 16:31). Prophets of her god Baal came into conflict with Elijah, Elisha, and other Israelite prophets (cf. 2 Kgs 9:22; *Ant.* 8.347). Her fornications involved not her sex life but her idolatry (2 Kgs 9:22; see also Lev 17:7; Deut 31:16; Jer 2). The upshot is that the Likeness of a Human condemns a prophetess and her followers at Thyatira for the idolatrous activity of eating food offered to idols. If she and her followers do not repent, he will come to destroy them, throw them "into great distress" (note 1:9*a*) and destroy them. Then, the Likeness of a Human says, "all the churches will know that I am the one who searches minds and hearts, and I will give to each of you as your works deserve."

2:24-25: The speaker then exhorts the "rest of you [plural]" at Thyatira, who "do not hold this teaching" of the prophetess. "This teaching" is further described by "whoever does not know the deep things of Satan, as they [the prophetess and her following] say" (AT; cf. 1 Cor 2:10). The speaker is probably being sarcastic, but it is not clear whether the prophetess does claim to know "the deep things of Satan" (either the deep things about Satan or the deep things that Satan reveals). Is this some esoteric revelation or is it the knowledge that Satan has no power, that "no idol in the world really exists . . . there is no God but one" (1 Cor 8:4)? On "the rest" the speaker places no further burden (cf. Acts 15:28): only "hold fast to what you have until I come," that is, to bring judgment upon the prophetess.

2:26-29: A double promise is given to everyone who conquers. First, just as Jesus Christ has been given authority from his father, so he gives to his followers "authority over the nations," that is, they will function in a manner similar to the royal messiah (Pss 2:8-9; 12:5; 19:15; *Pss. Sol.* 17.23-24; *Sib. Or.* 8.245). The "morning star" is also an image of the Messiah. At the end of Revelation, Jesus identifies himself as "the root and descendant of David, the bright morning star" (22:16). In *Joseph and Aseneth,* the "morning star" is "a messenger and herald" of the great day of the Lord (14.1). Kingly attributes are also given to the high priest, Simon: "How glorious he was. . . . Like the morning star among the clouds" (Sir 50:5-6). The association of star, king, and messiah derives ultimately from Balaam's fourth oracle, "a star shall come out of Jacob, and a scepter shall rise out of Israel" (Num 24:17), but a star becomes associated with both the priestly and royal messiah (cf. *T. Levi* 18.3; *T. Judah* 24; cf. also *Bib. Ant.* 33.5; *1 Enoch* 104.2; *T. Moses* 10.9; 4 Macc 17:5).

◊ ◊ ◊ ◊

Religious devotion in Thyatira was directed to Apollo Tyrimnaios (a syncretic union of Apollo and Tyrimnos, a deity of Asia Minor; *IGRom.* 1215), and Artemis (*IGRom.* 1225), among others. Jews were also present there (*IGRom.* 1281; Schürer 1986, 19). We do not know when or how Christianity developed at Thyatira. In the third and fourth centuries, Thyatira sent a bishop to church councils (Hammond 1981, map 28).

The issue of eating food offered to idols is discussed elsewhere in early Christian literature. According to Acts, the apostles and elders from the church at Jerusalem sent an edict to believers at Antioch, Syria, and Cilicia concerning persons who converted from a Gentile (non-Jewish) religion: "For it has seemed good to the Holy Spirit and to us to impose on you no further burden than these essentials: that you abstain from what has been sacrificed to idols and from blood and from what is strangled and from fornication. If you keep yourselves from these, you will do well" (Acts 15:28-29; cf. *Did.* 6.3). The issue also arose in the Corinthian church. Paul, however, was not as strict as the Jerusalem apostles. He forbade the Corinthians from eating food offered to idols as part of a meeting in a pagan temple (1 Cor 10:14-22), but they could eat whatever was sold in the meat market, even if it came from a pagan temple service (1 Cor 10:25). Moreover, they could eat whatever was set before them when dining at the house of an unbeliever (1 Cor 10:27).

Thus, the prophetess at Thyatira takes a position more in line with Paul, whereas the Likeness of a Human (the Christ of John's visions) takes the position of the Jerusalem apostles. The prophetess may have been even more liberal than Paul and more like the Corinthians of whom Paul was critical. Whether her position was similar to Paul's or the liberal Corinthians', the Likeness of a Human threatens her and her followers with sickness and death if she does not repent. Then, he says, "all the churches" (the seven or more; cf. 1 Cor 4:17; 14:33; 2 Cor 8:18; 11:28) will know that the Christ of John's vision is the true judge.

The issue of "eating food sacrificed to idols" may tell us something about social classes in the churches of Pergamum and Thyatira. Both cities, especially Thyatira, were known for their many crafts and guilds. According to Acts, Paul, at Philippi in Macedonia, met a "dealer in purple cloth" from Thyatira (Acts 16:14). Paul also had a craft, as did many apostles and prophets who traveled among the congregations (*Did.* 11.3–12.3). In the guilds, Christians and non-Christians came together and participated in meals that included meat dedicated to different deities. It is probably not coincidental that Paul defends his working at a trade in the context of discussing the eating of meat offered to idols (1 Cor 8:13–9:7). The prophetess at Thyatira was probably involved in crafts (like Lydia at Philippi) and was a person around whom other people engaged in crafts and guilds gathered. The Likeness of a Human does not approve of those "successful" Christians who "eat food sacrificed to idols" when they enter into the social and professional life of the cities, for he believes that they compromise their allegiance to him (see Thompson 1990, 122-24).

To the Church at Sardis (3:1-6)

The Likeness of a Human has almost nothing positive to say about this church. Through exhortation and threat, he hopes to awaken them. The pronouncement moves from a negative appraisal (3:1) to exhortation and threat (3:2-3), acknowledgment of a few faithful followers (3:4), promise (3:5), and the command to listen to the Spirit (3:6).

◊ ◊ ◊ ◊

3:1: "Sardis," a thriving commercial center of about one hundred twenty thousand, was approximately fifty kilometers south and a little east of Thyatira. The north road coming down from Pergamum and Thyatira extended on southeast to Philadelphia, then to Hierapolis, Laodicea, and Colossae. An east-west road extended west to Smyrna on the coast. The city had a distinguished history as capital of the kingdom of Lydia, where, among others, the wealthy Lydian king Croesus had his palace, before his kingdom fell to the Persians. Like the other major cities, it had gymnasia, baths, a civic center, business district, stadium, and a theater that could seat up to fifteen thousand people. It also housed a district court.

The "seven stars" are the seven angels of the churches (1:20) that the Likeness of a Human holds in his right hand (1:16). The "seven spirits of God" are mentioned at 1:4, but not in connection with Christ. The phrase "has the seven spirits of God" foreshadows 5:6. The Likeness of a Human appraises those at Sardis, as later those at Laodicea (3:15), negatively: "You have a name of being alive, but you are dead." (He qualifies his total condemnation somewhat at 3:4.) "Alive" and "dead" are images for describing the behavior or manner of life of the congregation at Sardis. They have a reputation (among the other congregations in Asia?) for living the way of life that Christ reveals (toiling, enduring patiently, holding fast, loving), but to the one "who searches minds and hearts" (2:23), they do so only in appearance.

3:2-4: The Likeness of a Human gives them a series of directives that will correct their imperiled spiritual state: "Wake up" *(ginou grēgorōn)*, a term associated with being prepared for the coming of Christ (3:3; 16:15; Matt 24:42); "strengthen what remains" *(stērison)*, mentioned only here in Revelation, but elsewhere it occurs in critical contexts such as Jesus' appearance after the crucifixion or Christ's imminent coming (e.g., Luke 22:32; 2 Thess 3:3; Jas 5:8; 1 Pet 5:10); "remember" (note 18:4-5); "obey" (cf. 1:3, "keep"); and "repent" (note 2:4-6). He must exhort them, because they have not finished or brought to completion (NRSV: "perfect") the manner of life that they began (contrast those at Thyatira). The Likeness of a Human also threatens that if they do not heed his exhortations, he "will come like a thief" (cf. 2:5, 16; 3:11; 16:15; Matt 24:42; 1 Thess 5:2-7; 2 Pet 3:10). At 3:4 the Likeness of a Human does acknowledge that there are a few faithful followers at Sardis, which he characterizes through the image of "soiled" and "white" garments (soiled: note 14:2-5; cf. 16:15; 22:14; 1 Cor 8:7; cf. Exod 19:10, 14; *Ascen. Is. 3.25*).

3:5-6: Three promises are given to those who conquer, each of which involves the transformation of the righteous from death to life: "white robes" (note 4:4; 6:10-11; cf. 3:18; 7:9, 13-14; 19:14; Mark 16:5; *Herm. Sim.* 8.2.3; *1 Enoch* 62.16; *2 Enoch* 22.8-10; *Ascen. Is.* 1.9; 9.2, 9, 17; 11.40; 2 Esdr 2:39; Artem. 2.3); "the book of life" (3:5; 13:8; 17:8; 20:12, 15; 21:27; Exod 32:32; Ps 69:28; Dan 12:1; Mal 3:16; Luke 10:20; Phil 4:3; *Jos. Asen.* 15.3; *Herm. Vis.* 1.3.2); and "confession of the name" before God and angels (cf. 14:10; Matt 10:32; Luke 12:9; 15:10).

◊ ◊ ◊ ◊

With respect to religion at Sardis, the temple of Artemis, offering right of asylum, was most striking. The Greek goddess Artemis (adapted to local religion) and the Phrygian Cybele were the patron deities of Sardis. Coins from Sardis in the second century CE show sanctuaries of Aphrodite, a great altar of Zeus, and an altar with statues of Heracles and Zeus (Yamauchi 1980, 68-69). Devotion to the emperor was present on both the urban and provincial level.

Jews lived in Sardis for at least a century BCE (see, possibly, Obad 20). In the early third century CE, Jews had a synagogue—the largest yet discovered from the time of the empire—right in the civic center. From early on, Jews assimilated to the life of the city (see Thompson 1990, 141-42). This is the first reference to a Christian community at Sardis, but sometime later than 160 CE, Melito, bishop of Sardis, wrote a commentary on the Revelation (*Hist. Eccl.* 4.26.2). Probably Christians at Sardis "soiled their clothes" by participating in the commercial life of the city, of which the Likeness of a Human does not approve.

Here at Sardis (3:3), as throughout the seven pronouncements, the primary danger to the congregations is Christ's coming. With the exception of the martyr Antipas at Pergamum (2:13), imminent (not present) persecution at Smyrna (2:10), and possible oppression by Jews at Smyrna and Philadelphia (2:9; 3:9), Christ is the greatest threat to the congregations. He warns those at Ephesus to repent, or "I will come to you and remove your lampstand" (2:5); to those at Pergamum: Remove the followers of Balaam and the Nicolaitans, or "I will come to you soon and make war against them with the sword of my mouth" (2:16). Christ acts to destroy Jezebel and her followers (2:21-23). He reassures the Philadelphians that he will protect them from "the hour of trial," which will accompany his coming (3:10-11). Finally, he is about to "spit" the Laodiceans "out of [his] mouth" (3:16).

To the Church at Philadelphia (3:7-13)

Like the pronouncement to Smyrna (2:8-11), this pronouncement praises the church without qualification. The completely positive appraisal (3:8) is followed by the Likeness of a Human's oath to vindicate his followers before those "who say that they are Jews" (3:9), his pledge to keep them "from the hour of trial" (3:10), and his promise to come soon (3:11). The pronouncement then concludes with the customary promise and command to listen to the Spirit. Images of place and location dominate this pronouncement.

◊ ◊ ◊ ◊

3:7: "Philadelphia" (modern day Alasehir), about forty-five kilometers southeast of Sardis, was situated on the main road from Sardis to Hierapolis and Laodicea. Another road went northeast out of Philadelphia and joined the road to Sardis. It is the smallest and least important of the seven cities in Revelation. Sometime in the second century CE, Philadelphia was granted a district court, but in the first century, it was within the legal orbit of Sardis. It had a theater and a stadium, but no shrine with the right of asylum. Guilds played an important part in the political life of this town, especially guilds of wool workers, leather producers, and textile workers (Jones 1983, 92).

In contrast to the previous five pronouncements, the speaker does not identify himself with language reminiscent of 1:12-18. The phrase "holy and true" occurs here and at 6:10, but in no other writings independent of Revelation (see TLG, PHI). "Holy" *(hagios)* is attributed only to a deity or that which has been consecrated to a deity (God: 4:8; 6:10; Jerusalem: 11:2; 21:2, 10; 22:19; those reigning with Christ: 20:6; cf. also 5:8). "True" refers to the dependability and trustworthiness of God and those associated with him (cf. 3:14; 15:3; 16:7; 19:2, 9, 11; 21:5; cf. 1 John 5:20). The rest of the speaker's identification draws on the language of Isa 22:20-25, where Eliakim is promised "the key of the house of David; he shall open, and no one shall shut; he shall shut, and no one shall open" (Isa 22:22). Having the "key" indicates the power and authority of its holder, in this case, over the royal house. The reference to "David" and "opening" also foreshadows 5:5 where "the Root of David, has conquered, so that he can open the scroll and its seven seals" (cf. also 3 *Enoch* 18.18; Matt 16:19).

3:8-9: The Likeness of a Human promises the church "an open door" of salvation (cf. 3:7; 21:25; Isa 60:11-12, "Your gates shall always be open; day and night they shall not be shut, so that nations shall bring you their wealth . . . the nation and kingdom that will not serve you shall perish"; see also Matt 25:10; John 10:7). For "keep my word," see 1:3; "deny my name" and "deny my faith," cf. 2:13. As an alternative, the phrases can be translated, "You have followed my commands and have not denied me [your faith in

me]." "Satan" (note 12:7-9) occurs four times in the pronouncements of chapters 2 and 3: "Satan's throne" (2:13), "the deep things
of Satan" (2:24), and "synagogue of Satan" (2:9; 3:9). The point
here is that those who claim to be Jews really belong to Satan (see
comments on 3:12-13). The image of worshiping or "bowing down
before your feet" is drawn from Isa 60:14, "The descendants of
those who oppressed you [Jerusalem] shall come bending low to
you, and all who despised you shall bow down at your feet; they
shall call you the City of the LORD." That is a very bold, if not
blasphemous statement, for "worship" *(proskynēsousin)* in Revelation is reserved for God, except for false worship of the beast (cf.
chapter 13; even angels reject worship, 19:10; 22:8).

3:10-11: The reciprocity in verse 10 takes the form of a word
play: "Because you have kept . . . I will keep. . . ." "The hour of
trial" *(ek tēs hōras tou peirasmou)* is a time of universal, divine
judgment (14:7, 15; 18:10; Dan 12:1; Luke 8:13) that is coming to
test (note 2:10-11) the "inhabitants of the earth," a phrase that
refers to non-Christians (note 6:10-11). The Likeness of a Human
also urges those at Thyatira to "hold fast," that is, "remain
committed to Christ" (2:25; cf. 2:13, "holding fast to my name";
2:14, holding "to the teaching of Balaam"; 2:15, holding "to the
teaching of the Nicolaitans"; cf. Mark 7:3; 2 Thess 2:15). If the
Philadelphians "hold fast," no one can seize their crown (note
2:10-11; cf. Isa 62:3).

3:12-13: "Temple *[naos]*" refers to the innermost sanctuary that
houses an image of the god, while *hieros* includes the surrounding
sacred area (see MM under *naos*). The Philadelphians are to be in
the *naos*, the shrine proper. A "pillar" can be either a part of the
supporting structure of a temple or freestanding. The Likeness of a
Human refers here to the heavenly temple, where the dead praise
God (cf. 7:15; 11:19; 14:15, 17; 15:5, 6, 8; 16:1, 17; 21:22). By
writing a name on the pillar (or person), the Likeness of a Human
claims it as belonging to "my God," "the city of my God," and
"me" (cf. 21:14; Isa 62:2). John's Christ uses the first-person
possessive "my" also at 2:13, "my name"; 2:28, "my Father"; 3:2,

"my God"; 3:10, "my word of patient endurance"; 3:16, "my mouth"; and 3:21, "my throne."

◊ ◊ ◊ ◊

On coins from Philadelphia, there are temples of Artemis Anaitis (a syncretic combination of the Greek goddess Artemis and a Persian goddess), Artemis of Ephesus, Helios (a sun god), Dionysus, Zeus, and Aphrodite (Yamauchi 1980, 78). This pronouncement is our only evidence for a Jewish community at Philadelphia in the first century CE. In the early second century, Ignatius passed through Philadelphia on his way to Rome, and later, from Troas, wrote a letter back to Philadelphia in which he suggests some kind of conflict between Jews and Christians (Ign. *Phld.* 6). According to still-later church tradition, some Christians from Philadelphia were martyred along with Polycarp, "the twelfth martyr at Smyrna," in 156 CE (*Mart. Pol.* 19.1).

This pronouncement to Philadelphia and the one to Smyrna indicate conflict between Jews and Christians in some of the Asian cities. That conflict is primarily theological. Christians claimed to be the heirs of Jewish sacred history and to have replaced the Jews as the people of God, for theirs are the kingship of David and the Jerusalem temple (3:7, 8, 11-12), and Jews are to submit to Christians (3:9). Yet, in the cities of Asia, Jews continued to exist and to meet together in prayer and study at their synagogues. How were Christians (and others) to understand that situation (cf. Thompson 1990, 130)? The Christ of John's vision explains it by stating that "those who say that they are Jews" are lying; they come together in synagogues that are of Satan, not of God (3:9; cf. 2:13, 24; note 12:7-9; 1 Tim 1:20). There may also be a social dimension to this conflict, for Jews living according to their traditions were also active participants in municipal life (see Thompson 1990, 133-45). For their accommodation to Roman life, the Likeness of a Human would not approve of them.

To the Church at Laodicea (3:14-22)

This pronouncement to Laodicea, like that to Sardis, condemns the practices and inadequate faith of the church. The negative appraisal of the Likeness of a Human ends with a warning (3:15-16). He then advises them to turn to him (3:17-18), warns and exhorts them (3:19), and ends with a conditional promise to them (3:20). The pronouncement concludes with a promise and the command to listen to the Spirit. Throughout this pronouncement, appearances contrast with reality, and intimate metaphors and images express unremitting condemnation. This pronouncement brings the first vision to a close (1:9–3:22).

◊ ◊ ◊ ◊

3:14: "Laodicea" was located about eighty kilometers southeast of Philadelphia and about one hundred fifty kilometers inland from Ephesus, in the Lycus Valley, just a few kilometers from Colossae and Hierapolis (Pamukkale). The road that came down from Philadelphia went on southeast to the port of Attaleia on the southern coast of Asia Minor. That road intersected with the east-west road that extended from the Syrian province to Ephesus. Laodicea had a gymnasium and baths, two theaters, a stadium for athletic events and gladiator fights, and, at least in the third century, a fountain house with a large statue of Isis, taken over later by a Christian church (see *ABD* under "Laodicea"). It was a town devoted to textile manufacturing, commerce, and banking. In the latter part of the first century CE, it was apparently a wealthy town (Strabo 12.8.16). Its supposed manufacture of eye salve and its springs of tepid water are two features often related to the prophetic pronouncement in Revelation.

The speaker identifies himself by alluding back to language at 1:5, but with some signficant changes: "Amen," a Hebrew word meaning "trustworthy," is added as a title of Jesus (cf. 2 Cor 1:20; Isa 65:16 MT: *āmēn*; LXX: *althinon*; Symmachus, *amēn*; Aquila, *pepistōmenos*; see Charles 1920, I:94). Also "true *[alēthenos]*" has been added (note 3:7). In contrast to "ruler *[archōn]* of the kings of the earth" (1:5), the Likeness of a Human is here "ruler *(archē)* of the creation of God" (NRSV: "origin of God's creation"), a cosmic ruler, first in rank and time of all God's creation (cf. 1:7, 16; Col 1:15-20; Prov 8:30, where Wisdom is an artisan [Heb. *āmōn*], and 8:22). This epithet foreshadows 3:21 and the enthronement of the Lamb/Christ in chapter 5.

3:15-16: The Likeness of a Human appraises negatively their "works," that is, their moral and religious qualities. "Lukewarm" *(chliaros)* water is used as an emetic to cause vomiting (cf. BAGD under *chliaros*). "Cold" *(psychros)* can, by itself, indicate a state of halfheartedness (Epictetus, *Discourses* 3.15.7; *Timon* 2) and "hot" *(zestos),* a fickle state (BAGD under *zestos*). Here, however, "hot" and "cold" are contrasting states, either one of which is desirable when compared to being "lukewarm," that is, halfhearted in enacting behavior appropriate to followers of Christ.

3:17-20: Their self-understanding contrasts with the Likeness of a Human's understanding of them: "rich," "have prospered," "need nothing" contrasts with "wretched, pitiable, poor, blind, and naked" (3:17). Elsewhere in Revelation, "prospered" *(peploutēka)* refers to the merchants and shipmasters who have gained wealth from Rome's economy (18:3, 15, 19; cf. Zech 11:5; 1 Cor 4:8). "Wretched" *(talaipōros)* occurs only here and Rom 7:24 in the New Testament (cf. Jas 5:1, "Come now, you rich people, weep and wail for the miseries *[talaipōriais]* that are coming to you"). "Pitiable" *(eleeinos)* occurs only here and in 1 Cor 15:19. "Poor" contrasts, of course, with "rich" (cf. 13:16 and the Smyrneans who appear poor but are rich, 2:9). For "blind," cf. 2 Pet 1:9. On "naked," see 16:15-16. Their condition can be remedied only by "buying" from Christ—"buy" *(agorasai)* translates the same Greek word as "ransomed" (note 13:16-17)—true "gold" (21:18, 21 contrast 17:4; 18:16), "white robes" (note 3:5-6), and "salve to anoint your eyes" ("salve" *[kollourion],* may be an image drawn from the Laodicean locale where eye salve was manufactured (see MM under *kollourion),* or it may be an allusion to salve that makes for a clear vision of Christ; cf. *PGM* VII, 335-47).

The Likeness of a Human condemns the Laodiceans with language of intimacy: They are as tepid water in Christ's mouth that he will spew out; he implores them to be hot or cold; he knocks and urges them to "open the door," an allusion to the lover seeking entrance to the beloved in Cant 5:2. Even the reproof in 3:19 is softened by "those whom I love" *(philō)*.

3:21-22: Christ will give to the one who conquers what his "father" has given him, namely, a place on his—and his father's—throne. So in *1 Enoch,* those who love God will be brought "out into the bright light . . . and seat[ed] . . . one by one on the throne of his honor" (108.12; cf. Matt 19:28).

◊ ◊ ◊ ◊

Zeus was an important deity in the worship life of Laodicea, as were Apollo and Asclepius, the god of healing. Coins from Laodicea portray Dionysus Helios, Hades/Serapis, Mithras, Hera, Athena, Tyche (goddess representing fate or chance), and Aphrodite (Yamauchi 1980, 143-45). Inscriptions from the second and third centuries CE indicate a Jewish presence assimilated into the culture and society of Hierapolis, a town only a few miles from Laodicea. There was undoubtedly a synagogue in Laodicea as well (Thompson 1990, 139-40; Cicero, *Flaccus* 68; *Ant.* 14.241-3). According to Col 4:16, Paul wrote a letter to the Laodiceans, but this letter is not extant. In the latter half of the second century CE, Melito mentions that there was a debate at Laodicea about when to observe Easter (Hall 1979, frag. 4).

Laodicea is the last of the congregations to whom the Likeness of a Human sends prophetic pronouncements. It forms a pair with the congregation at Sardis, for John's Christ appraises them both negatively, probably for the same reason: They have "soiled their clothes" and gotten wealthy by participating in urban commercial life. In those two congregations, there are no factions—such as Balaamites, followers of Jezebel—and no conflict with Jews. Those two congregations contrast most clearly with those at Smyrna and Philadelphia—two congregations that the Likeness of a Human praises without qualification, for they are poor, have little power, and in some way come into conflict with the Jewish synagogue. Thus low social and economic status, hostilities with Jews, and unqualified praise from John's Christ contrast with higher social and economic status, no conflict with Jews, and virtually unqualified condemnation by John's Christ.

Of the remaining three congregations, those at Pergamum and Thyatira can be positioned somewhere between those two contrasting pairs, for those two include factions that participate in urban commercial life—Balaamites and Jezebel who "eat food sacrificed to idols"—but they also comprise other groups whom John's Christ praises as worthy Christians. When the seven congregations are grouped in that way, the church at Ephesus stands by itself, for it has no factions—Christians there test those who claim to be apostles and hate the Nicolaitans—and receives almost unqualified praise. The Likeness of a Human only complains that they "have abandoned the love" they had at first.

In these seven pronouncements, the Likeness of a Human is concerned to lay out the hallmarks of Christian identity by prescribing how true Christians should live in the world. The model Christians at Smyrna and Philadelphia suffer "affliction" and "poverty," but keep Christ's word and do not deny his name. Other congregations are praised for "toil," "patient endurance," "bearing up," "not growing weary" (Ephesus), "holding fast to my name," not denying "your faith" (Pergamum), having "love, faith, service, and patient endurance" (Thyatira), and no "soiled clothes" (Sardis).

In relation to others, the Likeness of a Human stresses exclusion rather than inclusion, differentiation rather than integration. Those at Ephesus do well to hate the Nicolaitans (who also claim to be Christians) and to test those who call themselves apostles (also Christians). Those at Pergamum are to exclude the Balaamites (Christians), and those at Thyatira should bar Jezebel and her followers (Christians) from the congregation. There should be no dealings with Jews, for they are of the "synagogue of Satan," and the behavior of "Jezebel," "the Balaamites," and probably the "Nicolaitans" was wrong precisely because they engaged socially and economically with non-Christians—in their neighborhood and in guilds and other organizations related to their crafts and trades.

Conversely, the relationship of those true followers of John's Christ is close and egalitarian. They are brothers and sisters in

Christ, and all stand equally under his guidance. There is no mention of bishops, elders, or other hierarchs. Personal identity is achieved by becoming a "partner," sharing with others "affliction, royal power, and patient endurance in Jesus" (see 1:9). Members are to be loyal to one another and attached to each other; in short, they are to love one another (2:4; cf. 1 John 4:20). Like another tight community, the Jews at Qumran, they are "to love everything which [God] selects and to hate everything that he rejects; in order to keep . . . from all evil" (1QS I.4). In this close fellowship, Christians experience interpersonal communion with Jesus Christ who promises that if they "keep the faith" and "bear up for the sake of my name," they will have a continued personal identity after death, in the company of those who rejoice in the presence of God. Eternal life is communal life.

In young, grassroots organizations—religious or political—it is not easy to find the balance between maintaining solidarity and faithfulness (identity), on the one hand, and living in a larger, diverse community, on the other. John's Christ calls for Christians to separate from non-Christians by making high boundaries between themselves as "true" Christians and the rest of society. At least some of the local leaders in the seven congregations assumed lower, more porous boundaries between various Christian groups as well as between Christians and non-Christians. Ernest Colwell makes a valid point when he writes that ordinary Christians did not "live as separately and aloof as [some of] their leaders desired," and for that reason they eventually overcame the "opposition of the heathen masses" (Colwell 1939, 70). On the other hand, John's visionary separatism established a strong Christian identity that flourished and was nourished by uncovering opposition and conflict with the larger non-Christian society.

VISIONS OF THE HEAVENLY THRONE AND THE SEVEN-SEALED SCROLL (4:1–8:1)

John's ascent into heaven introduces a second series of seven visions that center upon the opening of seven seals of a scroll. He frames in this new series with "I looked *[kai eidon]*" (4:1)—John's

"I" repeating the "I" of the Likeness of a Human in 3:21. The initial vision in the series introduces the first of several throne scenes in Revelation. After John surveys the whole scene (4:1-11), he focuses upon a scroll that the one seated upon the throne holds in his right hand. A Lamb takes the scroll, for he is worthy "to open its seals," and is enthroned alongside the "Lord God the Almighty." Upon being enthroned (5:1-14), the Lamb opens six of the seven seals (6:1-17). John then sees the sealing process reversed, as 144,000 from "the people of Israel" are sealed "on their foreheads" with the seal of God (7:1-8). A throne scene follows, in which "a great multitude" "who have come out of the great ordeal" wave palm branches and acclaim God for their salvation (7:9-17). The opening of the seventh seal brings this series of visions to a close (8:1).

Revelation 4:1 unambiguously begins a new series of visions, but images of "door," "voice," "open," and "throne" carry over from the pronouncement to the Laodiceans (3:14-22). In fact, the final promise in chapter 3 serves as a caption for the heavenly scenes in chapters 4 and 5: "To the one who conquers I will give a place with me on my throne, just as I myself conquered and sat down with my Father on his throne" (3:21).

Enthronement (4:1–5:14)

This unit consists of two scenes involving kingship and enthronement. After John is taken up to heaven "in the spirit," he first sees a throne, and on the throne a figure seated. Then John describes many sights and sounds located on, around, and in front of the throne (4:1-7). The scene rises to a climax with heavenly worship of the one seated on the throne: "Four living creatures" around and on each side of the throne sing a version of the Sanctus ("Holy, holy, holy," 4:8), and twenty-four elders, seated on twenty-four thrones around the central throne, respond with a hymn acclaiming God as "worthy . . . to receive glory and honor and power" because he created all things (4:11).

John's attention is then drawn to a scroll in "the right hand of the one seated on the throne" (5:1). A "mighty angel" heralds throughout the universe a challenge to a contest: "Who is worthy to open the scroll and break its seals?" One of the elders reports to John that the contest—which occurs offstage, out of John's vision—has been won by "the Lion of the tribe of Judah," a descendant of the royal household of David: He is worthy. Onstage, in John's vision, this figure takes the form of "a Lamb" with "seven horns and seven eyes," "standing as if it had been slaughtered" (5:6). The Lamb takes the scroll from the one on the throne, an act that initiates an enthronement ceremony (5:8). Incense and music fill the air. All creatures in heaven bow down before the Lamb and acclaim him in a hymn similar in form to the one sung to the creator-God: "You are worthy . . . for you were slaughtered and . . . ransomed for God saints from every tribe" (5:9). Myriads of angels respond in acclamation: "Worthy is the Lamb that was slaughtered" (5:12). Then all creatures in the cosmos respond with a doxology to the one seated on the throne and to the newly enthroned Lamb (5:13). The four living creatures bring the enthronement ceremony to an end with their "Amen" (5:14).

◊ ◊ ◊ ◊

4:1: By means of an emphatic particle ("and there"), great emphasis is placed on the opening in heaven, a "door standing open" (cf. 3:8, 20; note 9:1). This concrete image connotes a passageway connecting one dimension to another—the apparent to the hidden, the human to the divine, the "below" to the "above," the present to the future (Luke 3:21, Jesus' baptism; Acts 10:11, Peter's vision; Acts 7:56, Stephen's vision; Ps 78:23, manna; Ezek 1:1, Ezekiel's vision; *1 Enoch* 14.15, Enoch's vision; *T. Levi* 5, Levi's vision; *2 Apoc. Bar.* 22.1, Baruch's vision; 3 Macc 6:18, an angelic epiphany; *Herm. Vis.* 1.1.4, a vision of Hermas). On passing through the open door, John sees not only a heavenly realm that transcends the earthly, but also a future that transcends the present.

4:2-3: As John ascends, he undergoes a psychological transformation associated with that of other prophets and visionaries (note 1:9*b*-11; cf. Zech 7:12; Acts 11:28; Eph 3:5; 5:18; 2 Pet 1:21; *Did.*

11.7; Strabo 9.3). Compare the following description of an initiat being drawn to heaven:

> When you have said these things, you will hear thundering and shaking in the surrounding realm; and you will likewise feel yourself being agitated. Then say again: "Silence!" [the prayer]. Then open your eyes, and you will see the doors open and the world of the gods which is within the doors, so that from the pleasure and joy of the sight your spirit runs ahead and ascends. (*PGM* IV.625-629, the Mithras Liturgy)

John sees "a throne," a commonplace object in heavenly visions within Jewish and Christian traditions (1 Kgs 22:19; Ps 11:4; Ezek 1:1, 26; Matt 23:22; Acts 7:49; Heb 8:1; *1 Enoch* 14.15-25; *2 Enoch* 22; *T. Levi* 5.1; *2 Apoc. Bar.* 22.1; *Apoc. Ab.* 18). All else orients in reference to the throne. The one on the throne is a colorful figure, who can be described only by what he is like (cf. "a Likeness of a Human," 1:13): green "jasper" (21:11, 18, 19, 20) and red "carnelian" (21:10), with a "rainbow" that surrounds him like a brilliant green emerald (cf. the chariot vision at Ezek 1:26; the new Jerusalem in chap 21; the Garden of Eden in Ezek 28; and the priest's breastplate at Exod 28:17-20).

4:4: Surrounding the central throne are twenty-four thrones upon which sit "twenty-four elders." These elders serve two func tions in Revelation: they render homage to the one sitting upon th throne (4:10; 11:16; 19:4) and to the Lamb (5:8, 11), and the explain things to John (5:5; 7:13). As heavenly servants, the number may have been influenced by the number of attendan *(lictores)* that marched before a dictator (see *OCD* under *fasce* also *Fab.* 4.3), by the twenty-four courses of priests at the Jerusale temple (1 Chron 24:7-19; *Ant.* 7.14.7), by the twenty-four deca in astrology, or perhaps by something else. According to Nu 11:16, Moses appointed seventy "elders" *(presbyteroi)* as an of cial council (cf. 1 Kgs 8:1; 2 Kgs 23:1; Ezek 14:1; 20:1), and, a later time in Asia Minor, in Jewish, Christian, and civil commu ties, "elders" had specific duties (e.g., Matt 15:2; Acts 4:8; 15 Titus 1:5; see also Schürer 1986, 102; Deissmann 1988, 154, 23

Perhaps one or another of those references to elders influenced John's naming of the heavenly servants. They wear "white robes" and "golden crowns," concrete images of that which belongs to the heavenly and divine ("white robes": note 3:5-6 and 6:10-11; cf. *Philops.* 25; *CIG* 2.2715 quoted in *HCNT* 564-65. "Golden crowns": note 2:10-11 and 6:1-2; cf. 14:14; 2 Sam 12:30; Ps 20:4; Zech 6:11; 1 Macc 10:20).

4:5-8: From the colorful throne come forth (present tense) sounds that signal the divine presence—"flashes of lightning, and rumblings and peals of thunder" (note 6:1-2; cf. Exod 19:16-19; 20:18; 2 Sam 22:14-15; Pss 29; 77:18; Isa 29:6; Ezek 1:13-14; Rev 11:19; Wis 16:22; *Vita. Mos.* 1.118; *Provid.* 2.45; Herodotus 3.86). The "seven spirits" in John's salutation (note 1:4) are here identified with "seven flaming torches" in front of the throne (cf. Exod 25:37; Zech 4:2, 10; see also 5:6). The likeness to a "sea of glass" *(hōs thalassa hyalinē)* may be patterned after the "sea" *(thalassa)* before the Holy of Holies in the Jerusalem temple (1 Kgs 7:23-26; 2 Chron 4:2-5; Ps 29:10; Jer 52:17), which probably represented the cosmic sea, divided at creation with earth sandwiched in between. Other visionaries also saw a vast sea or ocean in their heavenly visions (*2 Enoch* 3.3; *T. Levi* 2.7; *T. Ab.* 8.3). The comparison, "like crystal," may indicate that the sea is solid like ice (cf. 22:1; Exod 24:10; Ezek 1:22; *Somn.* 1.21; *Ant.* 1.30; *1 Enoch* 14.10-14).

The "four living creatures" seem to be slightly more authoritative than the twenty-four elders. They render homage to the one on the throne (4:8; 5:14; 7:11) as well as—later in Revelation—command the four horsemen (6:1-7) and parcel out the seven bowls (15:7). Since they are full of eyes, they see in all directions, watchful of what goes on elsewhere and of any creature who comes near the throne. Ezekiel also saw "four living creatures," though in his vision, each living creature has the same four faces mentioned by John (Ezek 1:5-22; 10:12). These four creatures compare to "seraphim, cherubim, and ophanim," seen by other visionaries (Isa 6:2; *1 Enoch* 71.7; cf. *Apoc. Ab.* 18; *2 Enoch* 22). The four living creatures with six wings sing the Kadosh or Sanctus ("Holy, holy,

holy") without ceasing, as do the seraphim in Isaiah's call-vision (Isa 6:1-3; cf. *1 Enoch* 39; *2 Enoch* 21; *3 Enoch* 20; 40). John fills out the Sanctus with his own language (note 1:8). By being located "in the midst of *[en mesōi]*" and "around *[kyklōi]*" the throne (AT), the four living creatures may actually be a part of, or a support for, the throne, as were the cherubim (winged oxen; cf. Ezek 1:10; 10:14) in the inner sanctuary of the Jerusalem temple (1 Kgs 6:23-29; 2 Chr 3:10-14), and in the ark of the covenant (Exod 25:18-21; Ps 18:10; Isa 37:16).

4:9-11: Throughout Revelation, various terms are used to indicate praise. "Glory *[doxan]*": "weight," "luminescence," "majesty," and "royalty" (1:6; 5:12, 13; 7:12; 11:13; 14:7; 16:9; 19:1, 7; 21:26; *PGM* XIII.185-90; Matt 4:8; 6:29; Luke 9:32; Acts 22:11), as well as "praise," "esteem," "fame," and "dignity." "Honor *[timēn]*": "value and worth" along with "respect and status" (5:12, 13; 7:12; 21:26). "Thanks *[eucharistian]*": gratitude for benefits and blessings (7:12). "Power *[dynamis]*": "ability, capacity, and competence" to do mighty deeds, often associated with ruling (5:12; 7:12; 11:17; 12:10; 17:13; 19:1). Only the one seated on the throne and the Lamb are worthy *(axios)* of these attributes; that is, only those two beings are sufficiently high on the scale of being to receive such praise (here and 5:9, 12; note 5:2-4).

The twenty-four elders respond by singing a hymn, praising God for his wondrous deeds (5:9, 12; cf. Sir 36:19; *PGM* V.400-421; *Hermetica* 1.26): "You are worthy [you deserve] . . . for *[hoti]* . . . ." The divine is addressed as "our Lord and God *[ho kyrios kai ho theos hēmōn]*." Those two terms are connected by "and" only twice in the New Testament, here and in John 20:28, a few times in the Septuagint (Ps 35:23; Jdt 5:21; Tob 13:4), and in reference to the Roman emperor (Thompson 1990, 104-7; *HCNT* 565). God created marvelous things, and throughout Revelation he is praised for what he has done (cf. *1 Enoch* 81.3).

5:1: Scrolls were sealed in order to authenticate the one who sent them and to reserve their contents only for those who were authorized and worthy to read them. They were sealed with either wax or clay imprinted by a precious stone or ring that only the sender possessed. So, when Jezebel had Nathan the prophet killed, she wrote letters in the name of King Ahab, her husband, and sealed them with his seal (1 Kgs 21:8; cf. Jeremiah's sealed deed of purchase of land, Jer 32:11; a king's decree against the Jews, Esth 3:10; a marriage contract, Tob 7:14; sealing a door with the king's signet, Bel 14; Polybius's note to Demetrius, Polyb. 31.13; also sealed letters as evidence, Dionysius of Halicarnassis, *Roman Antiquities* 4.57). Especially apt is a fragment from Qumran about another scroll sealed with seven seals. "The books of his father were to be read in front of him [a Persian king]; and among the books was found a scroll sealed with seven seals of the ring of Darius, his father . . . I read the beginning and found written in it: 'Darius the King [. . .] will rule after me and to the attendants of the Empire, peace' " (4Q550; cf. *Jub.* 32:20-22).

Messages of prophets and visionaries were sometimes sealed. Isaiah sealed up his teaching among his disciples, for the Lord was hiding his face (Isa 8:16; cf. 29:11). God told Ezra to "make public the twenty-four books that you wrote first, and let the worthy and the unworthy read them; but keep the seventy that were written last, in order to give them to the wise among your people. For in them is the spring of understanding, the fountain of wisdom, and the river of knowledge" (2 Esdr 14:45-47; cf. 6:20). Daniel was ordered to keep the "book sealed until the time of the end" (12:4; cf. 8:26). In *1 Enoch*, future mysteries are sealed (106.19), as are the coming judgments (108.6-10; contrast 81.1-2). Later, even John is ordered to seal up some of what he hears (10:4), though he is not to "seal up the words of the prophecy of this book" (22:10).

5:2-4: It is not clear on what scale to measure "worthy," but since "able *[edynato]*" substitutes for "worthy *[axios]*" (5:3), it is probably some combination of physical strength, moral quality, and legal authority (note 4:11). "Weeping" is a motif in various apocalypses (cf. 2 Esdr 5:13; 6:35; *1 Enoch* 90.41; *2 Enoch* 1.2; *3 Baruch* 1.1; *Ascen. Is.* 2.10; Dan 10:2; see Himmelfarb 1993, 107).

5:5: The elder refers to "conquering" ["prevailing, *enikēsen*"], suggesting a conflict or contest in which something must be overcome, perhaps a previous victory by the Lion that makes possible his opening the scroll (cf. note 2:7). Judah is called a lion in his father Jacob's last words and from him the king (anointed) will come: "Judah is a lion's whelp; . . . The scepter shall not depart from Judah, nor the ruler's staff from between his feet" (Gen 49:9-10; cf. Heb 7:14; 1 Macc 3:4). In Revelation, the "root *[riza]* of David" means the same thing as "the offspring of David" (22:16; 3:7; Isa 11:1, 10; Mark 10:47; Rom 15:12). Ezra also associates a lion with David's offspring: "And as for the lion whom you saw rousing up out of the forest and roaring and speaking . . . this is the Anointed One whom the Most High has kept until the end of days, who will arise from the offspring of David" (2 Esdr 12:31-32). It is, then, this Lion—the anointed, the Messiah—who is worthy and able to open the scroll.

5:6-7: John, however, in his vision sees a Lamb *(arnion)*, not a Lion (cf. *T. Jos.* 19.8). He appears "in the midst of" (*en mesōi*; NRSV: "between," imprecise location) the throne and those around it (cf. 7:17), as the Likeness of a Human appears "in the midst of" the lampstands in John's previous vision (1:13). The Lamb appears frequently in John's later visions, sometimes with emphasis on his being slaughtered (7:14; 12:11), and other times on being a wrathful warrior (6:16; 17:14). "Slaughtered" relates him to sacrifice, especially to that of the Passover lamb (cf. 5:9, 12; 13:3, 8; Exod 12:6; Lev 14:13; Ezra 6:20; Isa 53:7; John 1:29; 1 Cor 5:7; 1 Pet 1:19; *Am. narr.* III, 774D, *Lyc.* 22.2). "Seven horns" (peculiar to Revelation) is an image of power and strength, especially that of a king (cf. *1 Enoch* 90; *T. Jos.* 19 Aramaic; Num 23:22; Ps 89:17; Dan 7:20), and "seven eyes" or "seven spirits" is an image of omniscience (Zech 4:10; note 1:4; 4:5). Those images of the Lamb thus combine elements of royalty and sacrifice seen previously in the description of Jesus Christ (1:5-7). This Lamb took the book lying upon the right hand of the one seated on the throne.

5:8: As the Lamb took the scroll, the four living creatures and the twenty-four elders offer homage to him (1:17; 4:10). "Harps" are familiar instruments (cf. MM under *kitharizō*) used in worship (15:2; 1 Chron 16:42; 2 Chron 9:11; 1 Macc 4:54; 13:41). Only here in Revelation do "bowls" hold "incense" (contrast 15:7; 17:4), that is, they hold "the prayers of the saints" (see also 8:3-4; Ps 141:2; Luke 1:10). The "saints" (i.e., "holy ones") are elsewhere associated with prophets, witnesses, servants, and those fearing the name (11:18; 13:7; 16:6; 17:6; 18:20, 24; 19:8). Probably "saints" is a general term for Christians (cf. Acts 26:10).

5:9-10: While bowing before the Lamb, the heavenly servants "sing a new song." In the first vision, those at Pergamum were promised a "new name" (2:17) and those at Philadelphia the name of "the new Jerusalem" and Christ's "new name" (3:12). A "new song" is sung in response to a new deed of salvation and deliverance (Pss 40:3; 144:9; Isa 42:10; Jdt 16), and is often associated with a ritual of divine enthronement (Pss 33; 96; 98; 149; *ABD* IV.43-44). The "new song" takes the form of a hymn (note 4:9-11), though here, the Lamb is worthy to receive "the scroll" rather than general qualities such as "glory and honor" (4:11) or a kingdom (*J.W.* 1.390-393; Dio Chrys., *Or.* 11.141). Praise is motivated (*hoti;* NRSV: "for") "because" the Lamb was "slaughtered" (see 5:6), because he "ransomed" (cf. 3:18; 13:17; 14:3-4; 18:11; 1 Cor 7:23), and because he "made" those ransomed "a kingdom and priests" (Barnabas calls them "a new people," *Barn.* 7.5; cf. 1:5-6; Exod 19:6; 1 Pet 2:9). The ransomed consist of different categories of people—"tribe," "language," "people," "nation" (note 7:9). At the end of the "new song," the subject shifts to "the ransomed," who "will reign on earth" (20:4-6; 22:5). Thus, "the ransomed" are here promised to reign with the Lamb.

5:11-12: The vision expands to include in the liturgy the participation of innumerable angels around the throne, a commonplace in visions (Dan 7:10; Heb 12:22; *1 Enoch* 14.21-22; 40.1). They reaffirm the "worthiness of the Lamb" in their acclamation (note 5:2-4; 7:10; 11:15; 12:10). They attribute to him "power" (*dynamin;* note 4:9-11), "wealth" (*plouton;* abundance, fullness; Rom

11:33; Eph 3:8), "wisdom" (*sophian*, 7:12; *1 Enoch* 48-49; 51; *Ps. Sol.* 17:23, 37), "might" (*ischyn*; strength, 7:12; 2 Thess 1:9), "honor" (*timēn*; note 4:9-11), "glory" (*doxan*; note 4:9-11), and "blessing" (*eulogian*; "praise, speak well of," 5:13; 7:12).

5:13-14: Then the vision expands further to include the whole cosmos: Every creature responds with a doxology to the one seated on the throne and to the Lamb, the two now praised together (cf. 7:10). The totality of creation is emphasized by repetition ("every creature," "all that is in them"), by placement ("every creature" is placed in first position in Greek), and by designating the four cosmic regions ("in heaven," "on earth," "under the earth," and "in the sea"; cf. *De. def. or.* 23, 422F, "the heavens, the water, the air, the earth, and Olympus"). The theme of creation, plus the fact that the doxology addresses both the one seated on the throne and the Lamb, unites chapters 4 and 5 into one throne scene. The whole of creation attributes to the two figures, "blessing, honor, glory" (note 5:12) as well as "might" (*kratos*; cf. *dynamin, ischyn*— "force," or "control," especially political power; see MM under *kratos*). The four living creatures say the "amen" (cf. 1:6), and the twenty-four elders worship the one seated on the throne and the Lamb.

◊ ◊ ◊ ◊

Chapters 4-5 (actually asserted first at 3:21) mark an important transition in how Jesus Christ is presented: In the first vision John sees him as a "Likeness of a Human," who has the characteristics of a hero guiding his followers (seven congregations) in life and death. In chapter 5, Christ is portrayed through the image of a Slain Lamb who is enthroned as *cosmokrator,* ruler over the whole cosmos.

The language of chapters 4 and 5 draws extensively from the political domain of king and emperor. John sees the Creator seated upon a heavenly throne, surrounded by lesser powers who offer obeisance to him by casting their crowns before his throne (4:10; so Herod before Caesar, *J.W.* 1.390-393). They offer, in song, liturgical praise to the Creator, just as a singers' guild at Pergamum offers homage to the emperor on special days (*IGRom.* IV. no. 353; Lewis 1974, 125). The Creator is here called "Lord and God," as were emperors (Suetonius, *Domitian* 13.1; Statius, *Silvae* 1.6.81-84 [Domitian]; *HCNT,* no. 943 [Hadrian]; see Thompson 1990, 104-7). The Creator is offered homage in the form of an acclamation, as are kings (Peterson 1964, 5).

In contrast to the Creator-King in chapter 4, who sits idly, the Lion/Lamb of chapter 5 takes action by conquering, taking the scroll, and receiving sovereign power. The sealed scroll is a critical element in the process of enthronement, for only the victorious Lion/Lamb is worthy to take the scroll. Once the Lamb "takes" it, the enthronement liturgy begins. First, the servants around the throne sing to him a "new song," a kind of psalm that was earlier used to celebrate the Lord God's accession to his royal throne. For example,

> O sing to the LORD a new song;
>> sing to the LORD, all the earth.
>
> . . . .
>
> Declare his glory among the nations,
>> his marvelous works among all the peoples.
>
> . . . .
>
> Say among the nations, "The LORD is king!
>> The world is firmly established; it shall never be moved.
>> He will judge the peoples with equity."
>
> . . . .
>
> He will judge the world with righteousness,
>> and the peoples with his truth. (Ps 96)

In Revelation, however, the "new song" takes the form of a hymnic acclamation (also note 7:10), a form used in establishing a person as king (see Peterson 1926, 141, 176-80, 318, on the acclamation in later times). When Herod came before Caesar Augustus at Rhodes, he laid aside his diadem before Caesar and asked for safety. Caesar replied, "No, you shall not only be safe from danger, you shall be king, . . . for you are worthy to reign over a great many subjects *[axios gar ei pollōn archein]*" (*J. W.* 1.390-393; cf. Aeneas in Dio Chrys., *Or.* 11.141; *Caes.* 6.5.4; *Cic.* 25.4.4, a joke about one of Crassus's sons). The choir of angels acclaims that the Lamb is worthy of receiving divine attributes (5:12), and, as we have noted, the enthronement liturgy ends with a doxology to the Creator and the Lamb (5:13). Both are now established as worthy of receiving royal acclaim by the whole cosmos (cf. 3:21). At the same time, the creator God supports the enthronement of the Lamb, so that there is no confusion about the primacy of the Creator.

As a part of the enthronement ceremony, the Lamb takes the book of destiny (the scroll) in his own hands, just as Marduk, when he was enthroned, took "the Tablets of Fate . . . Sealed them with a seal and fastened them on his breast" (*ANET* 67b; cf. Ps 149). As a book of destiny, the sealed scroll is related to the books of judgment and life described at 20:11-15 (cf. 3:5; 13:8; 17:8; 21:27) as well as the phrase, "what must take place," at Rev 4:1 (also comment on Rev 5:1-4 in *HCNT*).

The sequences of images at various points in the first five chapters of Revelation form a pattern: slaughtered → enthroned (5:12-13); conquered → enthroned (3:21); dead → keys of Death and of Hades (1:18); pierced → riding the clouds (1:7); blood → kingdom (1:5*b*); eminent among the dead → ruler of kings of earth (1:5*a*). John draws freely upon language from a variety of religious traditions in his culture—practices involving the dead, so-called mystery religions, homage to the Roman emperor, creation mythology, and Jewish eschatology—to express the Christian conviction that Christ's suffering and death was his exaltation or the transformational event to his exaltation (cf. Phil 2:7-8; Col 1:18; Heb 1:3; *Barn.* 8.5) and to state that his followers should imitate him by following the same pattern. The upshot is that by the end of chapter 5, Christ is clearly enthroned as a cosmic ruler and his followers are a "kingdom" (5:10; cf. *Apoc. Peter* 6).

In those two chapters, God and his Christ are established as that which is the ground of all being, at the center of the web of all that exists. Images of transformations (open door, enthronement) and figures of speech communicate that religious significance of God and Christ. Chapters 4 and 5 establish the cosmic rulers on their thrones. All other throne scenes in Revelation build upon or elaborate what is presented in those two chapters.

Opening of the Seven Seals (6:1–8:1)

With the opening of the seals, destinies begin to be revealed. The opening of the first six seals presents a relatively uncomplicated sequence of visions and images describing divine judgment measured out by the newly enthroned Lamb (6:1-17). Chapter 7 consists of two scenes. The first one reverses the unsealing process by narrating a sealing of 144,000 from the twelve tribes of Israel (7:1-8). The second is a throne scene in which a great number of peoples praise God and the Lamb in an acclamation of salvation (7:9-17). The opening of the seventh seal brings silence to heaven (8:1).

As each of the seals is broken, a little vision balloons up with its own scene, characters, and actions. Those scenes alternate between describing disasters upon the earth and deliverance of the saints. At first, the weight is on disasters (6:1-8, 12-17), but by the end, it shifts to heavenly celebrations of salvation (6:9-11; 7:9-17).

◊ ◊ ◊ ◊

6:1-2: The first living creature (note 4:5-8) assists the Lamb in carrying out his decrees by issuing a command, "Come!" A "white horse" and its rider come out from somewhere not indicated (cf. Zech 6:1, "coming out from between two mountains . . . of bronze"). "Thunder" identifies their speech as a hierophany or a sacred manifestation (note 4:5-8; 14:2; 19:6; Ps 103:7; Sir 43:17). "I looked, and there" *(kai eidon kai idou)* calls attention to the horse and rider (cf. 4:1). In contrast to Zechariah's emphasis on a "red horse" (Zech 1:8; 6:2), Revelation underscores "white," probably reflecting the significance of white horses in the Greco-Roman world: high ranking officers rode white horses (*DMeretr.* 315 [13.1]); a white horse was a valuable gift (Athenaeus, *The Learned Banquet* 151C; *Jos. Asen.* 5.5); sometimes a white horse is offered as a sacrifice, especially to the sun (*Am. narr.* III, 774D; Philostratus, *Life of Apollonius* 31; Heliodorus, *An Ethiopian Story,* 10.28; Reardon 1989, 578. Contrast Indians who valued

black horses more; Philostratus, *Life of Apollonius* 2.19). With his
"bow" *(toxon,* only here in the NT), he is equipped like the light
cavalry of archers *(auxilia)* that offered flank support in the Roman
army *(Crass.* 27; *Jos. Asen.* 24.17; archers do not necessarily
come from the eastern end of the empire; see Cheesman 1975,
84, 103, 128). He receives a "crown" from one of the heavenly
beings (note 2:10-11 and 4:4; cf. Zech 6:9-14; Isa 22:21 LXX;
PGM 4.635-40, 695-705; *Ant.* 3.172; 17.197). In Revelation,
horses are consistently connected with war (9:9, 17, 19; 19:18,
19, 21; 14:20), and everything about the rider is associated with
victory in war.

The white horse and its rider is introduced in precisely the same
way as the one at 19:11: "And, look, a white horse and its rider
[AT; *kai idou hippos leukos kai ho kathēmenos ep auton*]." Those
two scenes enclose the bulk of Revelation (see the discussion of ring
composition in 1:8), which consists of visions of judgment, conflict,
and war, with intermittent visions of the heavenly throne (6:1–
19:21).

6:3-4: The second living creature calls out this time. In contrast
to the other three horses, the red horse is not emphasized. Petosiris
(a name associated with Egyptian astrology and horoscopes) says
that "red" brings war and slaughter (BAGD under *pyrros*); those
are common associations with the color red (see Becker 1994 under
"red"). The rider of the red horse takes "peace from the earth"
(contrast Matt 10:34; Zech 1:11), so that "they" (NRSV: "people")—presumably the inhabitants of the earth—"slaughter
[sphaxousin] one another" (cf. 6:9). "Earth" *(gēs)* can refer to
either the whole earth (cf. John 3:31; 12:32) or a specific "land"
(Acts 7:4, 40). The rider is given "a great sword" *(machaira
megalē),* which a warrior like Marc Antony also wore *(Anton.* 4.3;
cf. Rom 12:4; *Mar.* 25.11; *1 Enoch* 90.19).

6:5: The third living creature calls out a "black" horse, a color
associated with pestilence *(loimon;* possibly "famine," *limon)* and
death (BAGD under *pyrros;* a black horse warned Domitian of his
death, Dio Cassius 67.16). The rider comes out with a *zygon,* which

in the Greek of the Roman period refers primarily to a yoke, either one taken on as willing submission to an authority or as a symbol of oppression and forced burden. In early Christian literature, that is its only meaning, except possibly for this passage (e.g., Jesus invites the weary to take his yoke upon them, Matt 11:29; the law of Moses as a yoke, Acts 15:10; the yoke of the Lord, *Did.* 6.2; the yoke of slavery, 1 Tim 6:1). It can also refer to a balance beam or a set of scales in the shape of a yoke. For example, Ezekiel weighs the hair of his head in Ezek 5:1 and silver is weighed out at Isa 46:6. Examples of extended meanings include: "the words of the prudent are weighed in the balance" (Sir 21:25; cf. 28:25); weigh our sins (2 Esdr 3:34; *1 Enoch* 41.1; *2 Enoch* 49.2; *2 Apoc. Bar.* 41); Nebuchadnezzar is weighed on the scales and found wanting (Dan 5:27); in a papyrus from the second or third century CE "fate appears holding a balance *[katechousa zygon],* showing that justice was to be found in her" (see MM under *mēnuō*). Here in Revelation, it is not clear which meaning *zygon* has, "yoke" or "scales."

6:6: The speech of an additional voice is unique to this horse vision. The speech consists of two parts: an announcement of prices of wheat and barley and a directive not to harm the olive oil and the wine. Since the price announcement refers to volume ("quart"), the rider would not be measuring it out with a pair of scales (so the announcement offers no help in identifying the *zygon* as a yoke or as a pair of scales; cf. Ezek 45:10; *Apol. Jud.* 195.6). Regarding grain prices toward the end of the first century CE, the cost of the grain in Rev 6:6 is high, but not extreme. Compare the following prices: Here in Revelation, wheat costs the equivalent in Roman measures of thirty-two sestertii per modius, while in times of scarcity, wheat went as high as fifty sestertii per modius (for further information on prices in Asia in the first and second centuries CE, see Duncan-Jones 1982, 252; cf. *Anton.* 45.8; for price controls by Diocletian in 301 during runaway inflation—wheat is four hundred sestertii per modius and barley two hundred forty sestertii per modius—see *CIL* 3 translated in Shelton 1988, 134-36). So, grain is scarce, but famine is not extreme.

No clear connection is made between the announcement of prices and the directive not to harm olive oil and wine, or, alternatively, the directive not to dilute the olive oil or the wine. According to Philo, olive oil and wine are not food staples as are wheat and barley (*Vita Mos.* 2.223; cf. Rev 18:13; contrast Sir 39:26), but they are essential to rites in the temple (cf. *J. W.* 5.565). "Olive oil" occurs only here and 18:13 in Revelation. Elsewhere in Revelation, "wine" symbolizes divine wrath (14:10; 16:19; 19:15) or sexual passion of the whore (14:8; 17:2; 18:3). The directive to the rider in 6:6 is similar to other directives in Revelation not to harm (damage) earth, sea, trees, green growth, or grass (cf. 7:3; 9:4). Some commentators see an allusion here to Domitian's rescinded order to destroy vines and olive trees in Asia (Suetonius, *Domitian* 7.2; 14.2; Philostratus, *Sophists* 520).

The rider either judges the land or puts a yoke upon it, requiring it to submit to his authority. Whether judgment or yoke, the sense seems to be, Let things remain as they are. That directive contrasts with the prophet Elisha's announcement that famine in his time would soon end and prices would fall: "Tomorrow about this time a measure of choice meal shall be sold for a shekel, and two measures of barley for a shekel, at the gate of Samaria" (2 Kgs 7:1).

6:7-8: "Pale green *[chlōros]*" is the color of sea water, grass, and the sticks of growing trees (8:7; *Dem.* 22.6; *Herm. Sim.* 8.5), as well as the pallid color of disease, fear, and sickness (*Math.* 6.49). Petosiris associates the color with disease (BAGD under *pyrros*). The fourth living creature calls out a horse of this color, with the name (his essential quality), Death and Hades (cf. 1:18). His role is unambiguous. The fourth horseman is given authority over a fourth of the earth/land with four instruments of death: sword, famine, pestilence, and wild animals. The first three instruments are commonly grouped together, sometimes with the fourth (Jer 14:12; 21:7; Ezek 5:12, 17; 14:21; 33:27; Sir 39:29; *Pss. Sol.* 13.2; *Herm. Vis.* 73.3; *Sib. Or.* 3.335).

6:9: The fifth seal opens to a throne scene that includes an "altar" (note 8:3-4). John sees the "souls," that is, some form of continued conscious selves, of slaughtered victims (for "soul," cf. 8:8; 12:11; 16:3), but he pays most attention to their presence under the heavenly altar, not on how they were slaughtered (cf. 6:4). After being killed, they were released from death and Hades and taken into heaven, close to the Creator and the Lamb (8:3; 9:13; cf. 20:4; 12:11, 17). Because they are martyrs ("slaughtered for the word of God and for the testimony they had given"; note 1:1-2, 9b-11; cf. 12:11), they are given a special place "under the altar," where their deaths are given a sacred, sacrificial significance. (For other heavenly locations of the dead, such as "paradise" or "under the throne," see Str-B, II.264-269; also *1 Enoch* 39.7). The perfect tense of "slaughtered" *(esphagmenon)* connects them to the Lamb at 5:6 *(hōs esphagmenon)*, as does their testimony *(dia tēn martyrian hēn eichon;* cf. 1:2).

6:10-11: Although they have been raised from Hades and are present in heaven with the Creator and the Lamb, those martyred will not be satisfied until the Creator or the Lamb metes out justice "on the inhabitants of the earth" (see below). They complain in the form of a communal lament (cf. Ps 79:5-6, 10; Jer 12:4; Dan 8:13; 12:6 Theod.; Zech 1:12; 1 Macc 6:22; 2 Esdr 4:35-37; *3 Enoch* 44.7). "Sovereign Lord *[ho despotēs]*," only here in Revelation, can refer to either God (Acts 4:24; cf. *Did.* 10.3 in the eucharistic thanksgiving) or Christ (Jude 4). "Holy and true *[ho hagios kai alēthinos]*" occurs in the New Testament only here and at Rev 3:7 in connection with the Likeness of a Human (note 3:7). Given the close relation between God and the Lamb, the ambiguity is not important. The language of their lament is legal and adversarial (cf. MM under *ekdikeō*), as they appeal to the Sovereign for satisfaction and for punishment of their enemies, "the inhabitants of the earth" (non-Christians; cf. 8:13; 11:10; 13:8, 12, 14; 17:2, 8).

The verbs "to judge" *(krinein)* and "to avenge" *(ekdikein)* occur together only at one other place in Revelation, at 19:2 as part of a song of rejoicing over God's judging and avenging the blood of his servants on Babylon the whore. "To judge" is to make the appropriate descrimination or distinction among people, to punish the inhabitants of the earth, and to vindicate and deliver the saints. The verb translated "avenge" has the range of meanings found in English words derived from the Latin *vindicare:* revenge, vengeful, vengeance, vindicate. In Revelation, the meaning of the verb involves both the righting of a wrong in a judicial system (mending the moral order) and satisfying personal spite and vindictiveness (pleasure in returning harm for harm done). God, not the martyrs, takes vengeance (cf. Deut 32:35; Rom 12:19; 1 Thess 4:6; Heb 10:30; 1 Pet 2:23; 4 Macc 15:29; also "the days of vengeance" Luke 21:22; Hos 9:7. Contrast the following where humans avenge: Acts 7:24; Polyb. 3.8.10; *Anton.* 67.2; *Ant.* 9.171; 2 Kgs 9:7; Hos 1:4; 1 Macc 9:42; Plut. *Agis and Cleomenes and Gracchi* 5.5). The means by which God avenges is not stated; it could be in a quasi-automatic manner of the Erinyes, chthonic powers in Greek religion and tragedy, or by the hand of a human (2 Sam 4:8; *De garr.* 14, 509F). Here, the role of the "souls" is to be persistent in lament before God (cf. Luke 18:2-8; 2 Thess 1:8; *Prot. James* 24.2; *1 Enoch* 47). They will be vindicated, but only after their number is complete, that is, after all their brothers and sisters are martyred (2 Esdr 2:38; *1 Enoch* 47.4; *1 Clem* 2.4). Until then, they are given "a white robe *[stolē leukē],*" a festival garment of joy, freedom, and even royal status, and told "to rest a little longer" (white clothes: note 3:1-4 and 4:4; "rest": 14:13; Isa 57:21; Esth 9:17; Dan 12:13; Matt 11:28).

6:12-14: The opening of the sixth seal discloses divine judgment. Introduced by the same formula as the opening of the first seal ("And I saw when he opened *[kai eidon hote ēnoixen]*"), that formula rings the first six seals. Verses 12-14 present images of storm and sinister changes in the sky—earthquake (cf. 8:5; 11:13, 19; 16:18; Ezek 38:19; Hab 3; Matt 28:2; Luke 21:11; Acts 16:26; Diod. Sic. 16.56.8; *Sib. Or.* 12.157), darkening of the sun (note 8:12; 9:2; Isa 13:10; 50:3; Ezek 32:7; Joel 2:10), moon turning to blood (Joel 2:30; Acts 2:20), stars falling to earth (8:10; 9:1; 12:4), and the sky rolling up (Isa 34:4; Heb 1:12; *Sib. Or.* 3.80; 8.233, 413). Those theophanic signs occur in situations such as the following: Exodus from Egypt, Isa 50:3; against Pharaoh, Ezek 32:6-8; coming day of the Lord, Joel 2:30; 3:14-16; coming Son of

Man, Matt 24:29; divine judgment under Cleopatra, *Sib. Or.* 3.80; signs of the end, *Sib. Or.* 3.796-804. Mountains and islands also disappear at the pouring out of the seventh bowl (16:20).

6:15-17: All classes experience the wrath of the one seated on the throne and the Lamb, from the highest to the lowest (classes: cf. 19:18; Artem. 1.2; 3.9; *PGM* 13.251), "kings of the earth" can refer to royalty (Isa 34:12) or to magistrates (LSJ under *basileus;* Dio Cassius, 54.27); "magnates" *(megistanes),* "courtiers" or "merchants" (18:23); "generals" *(chiliarchoi),* high-ranking military officers or specifically a *tribunus militum,* commander of a cohort (six hundred men); "rich" *(plousioi),* wealthy, that is, those who do not have to work for a living; "powerful" *(ischyroi),* elite of the land (cf. 2 Kgs 24:15); "slave" *(doulos),* that is, one totally controlled by a master who may even kill him; "free" *(eleutheros),* one born free (freeman), not a slave who has been liberated (freedman).

Hiding in caves and under rocks is a commonplace in describing attempts to hide from God, especially from his wrath and judgment (Isa 2:19-21; Hos 10:8). There may also be implied here a collapse of urban living (see Jer 4:29) as well as a humbling of the rich and powerful (Isa 2:17). Being buried in an earthquake and under falling rocks is preferable to facing the divine wrath (Luke 23:30; Hos 10:7-8; Nah 1:6). Revelation 11:18 is apt commentary on "the day of wrath": "The nations raged, but your wrath has come, and the time for judging the dead, for rewarding your servants, the prophets and saints and all who fear your name" (wrath: note 11:16-18; cf. 19:15; Joel 2:11; Nah 1:6; Zeph 1:15; Mal 3:2; 2 Pet 3:10).

7:1: Instead of the opening of the seventh seal, John next sees four angels who have responsibility for the winds of the earth (not as in the LXX, winds of heaven). They keep the earth from being damaged by winds (see Jer 49:36; Dan 7:2; Zech 6:5 suggests a possible connection between these angels and the four horses in 6:1-8. On "winds," in general, see *1 Enoch* 76; on winds as vengeance, see Sir 39:28; for sacrificing to the wind gods, see Paus.

2.12.1). "Trees" ("fruit trees," *dendron*) are singled out, because strong winds could destroy them (cf. 6:13) and there were laws, at least in Jewish tradition, for protecting them (9:4; Deut 20:19; 4 Macc 2:14; *C. Apion* 2.211-12).

7:2-3: Those four angels, however, become part of the background for "another angel" who has authority over them. He comes from the east (Isa 41:25; Rev 16:12) and directs the four angels to delay their damaging winds until after he and others have placed the seal of God on the foreheads of the faithful. The seal here is a kind of brand that marks ownership (cf. *Pss. Sol.* 2.6; *Herm. Sim.* 8.2.4; note 5:1). Devotees of other deities were also branded or sealed with a mark (cf. *Syr. D.* 59; 3 Macc 2.29; see *TDNT* 7.660). The "seal" here may consist of the name of the Lamb and his Father (see 14:1), or it may be a reference to baptism (Eph 1:13; *Acts of Paul and Thecla* 25; *Acts of Paul, Martyrdom* 11.7; *Herm. Sim.* 9.17.4. A "seal" can also refer to circumcision, an apostle's converts, or death itself, Rom 4:11; 1 Cor 9:2; 2 Tim 2:19; 4 Macc 7:15; Wis 2:5). It is important to receive the seal, for in a later vision, locusts from the bottomless pit are directed "not to damage the grass of the earth or any green growth or any tree, but only those people who do not have the seal of God on their foreheads" (9:4; cf. Ezek 9:4; *Pss. Sol.* 15.6-9). The significance of the act of "sealing" is heightened by the fact that the activity of the four angels must be delayed until the sealing is completed.

7:4-8: At 14:1, John sees the 144,000 again (note 14:1), but here his attention is on their number (cf. 9:16)—12,000 from each of the twelve tribes of Israel (cf. 21:12). The names that appear in lists of the twelve tribes vary in Jewish and early Christian literature. In this list, Judah is given first position (cf. 5:5; contrast Gen 35:22; 49:1; *T. 12 Patr.*) and there is no reference to Dan (cf. *T. Dan* 5.6, "your prince is Satan"). Nor is there a reference to Ephraim. Since Ephraim has associations with accommodation to Roman life, the Essenes viewed "him" negatively; the Pharisees, positively. His absence in this list may reflect Revelation's opposition to those who are open to sharing in Roman life (see Goranson 1995, 83; note

2:20-23). "Sealed" occurs at 7:5 and 7:8, an example of ring composition (see 1:8).

7:9: A new vision *(meta tauta eidon)* focuses upon a "great multitude" *(kai idou)* that contrast with the 144,000 (cf. 2 Esdr 2:40, 42-48): The multitude is in heaven, not on earth as the 144,000; they are innumerable, not of a limited number (note repetition of *arithmon,* 7:4; *arithmēsai* 7:9; cf. 1 Kgs 3:8); and they consist of people "from every nation [*ethnous*, a social-political community], from all tribes [*phylōn*] and peoples [*laōn*, a social entity] and languages [*glōssōn*, united by a common language]" (5:9; 10:11; 14:6; 17:15; Dan 3:7; Jdt 3:8), not just from the tribes of Israel. "Before the throne and before the Lamb" is found only here (cf. 5:13; 6:16; 22:1, 3). They are "robed in white [*stolas leukas*]" (note 3:5-6; 4:4) and hold "palm branches in their hands." "Palm branches [*phoinikes*]," occurring only here and in John 12:13 within the New Testament, associate this multitude with either the Festival of Booths in Jewish tradition (Lev 23:40; Neh 8:15-16; Zech 14), rededication of the temple at Jerusalem (2 Macc 10:7), or the purifying of Jerusalem (1 Macc 13:51), or all of these. Elsewhere, Plutarch devotes a whole question as to why palm branches are awarded at all athletic festivals (*Quaest. conv.* 8.4, 724B), especially those connected with Apollo (8.4, 724C; Dio Chrys. 64.15).

7:10: The multitude stand (8:2; 20:12), rather than bow down, and acclaim ("cry out," *krazousin*, present tense; cf. 6:10; 12:10; 19:1) publicly, "Salvation [*sōtēria*] belongs to our God . . . and to the Lamb." Acclamations are made in connection with some special event, here, probably, in connection with deliverance from "the great ordeal" (7:14; see comment after 5:13-14). Elsewhere in Revelation, "salvation" is acclaimed along with "power" and "kingdom" (12:10) or "glory" and "power" (19:1). "Salvation" refers to any kind of deliverance or rescue, for example, from disease, shipwreck, possession by demons, or physical death (Matt 9:21; Luke 1:71; 8:36; Acts 7:25, 34; 27:20; 1 Clem 39.9), but especially deliverance from living a life apart from God. It contrasts with such things as "ignorance," "darkness," "afflictions," "destruction," and "death" and is virtually synonymous with "eternal life" (2 Cor 7:10; Phil 1:28; Heb 5:9; Ign. *Eph.* 18.1). So in the Hermetic writings (revelation through Hermes Trismegistus, the thrice-great), "The vice of ignorance floods the whole earth and utterly destroys the soul shut up in the body, preventing it from anchoring in the havens of deliverance" (*Hermetica* VII.1). Or, "light and other unspeakable things come from Isis [hellenistic goddess] for salvation" (Aelius Aristides, *Sacred Discourses* 3.46). In Revelation, the term occurs only in acclamations, in response to God's victory over his enemies—for example, when Satan is cast out of heaven (12:10) and when Babylon the Whore is destroyed (19:1). The day of wrath (6:16) that comes upon the people of the earth is the converse of, and simultaneously the day of salvation for the saints of God. Both occur when God judges (Rom 5:9; 1 Thess 1:9-10).

7:11-12: In response to the multitude's acclamation of "our God who is seated on the throne, and . . . the Lamb," "all the angels" (only here in Revelation; cf. Matt 25:31; Heb 1:6) bow down and worship in a lengthy doxology to God alone (note 4:9-11). This is the only passage in Revelation where "the elders" are mentioned prior to "the four living creatures" (7:11; cf. 5:11; 14:3). The "amen" rings their doxology (cf. 11:16).

7:13-14: A conversation then occurs between John (an actor in the vision) and one of the twenty-four elders regarding the identity of the great multitude that they both see. The elder asks typical questions about their identity (cf. 1 Sam 30:13; Jdt 10:12). They exchange phatic speech (which establishes sociability), in which the authority of the elder is affirmed (cf. Ezek 37:3). "The great ordeal *[hē thlipsis hē megalē]*" is a situation of much "distress" (2:22; note 1:9*a*) or "great suffering" (Matt 24:21), such as famine (Acts 7:11), slavery (Neh 9:37), political upheaval (1 Macc 9:27), or meeting a great beast, who is a "type of the great persecution which is to come" (*Herm. Vis.* 4.2.4-5; cf. 4.3.6). The Sibyl foresees a time when the Roman Empire will fall because of "unjust haughtiness," and "great affliction" will be "among men and it will throw everything into confusion" (*Sib. Or.* 3.180-90). In Daniel, the "great distress" is associated with the day of the Lord, when God comes in judgment and wrath against the peoples of the earth (Dan 12:1; cf. Jer 30:7; Zeph 1:14-16). Hermas emphasizes the importance of "enduring *[hypomenete]* the great persecution which is coming" during which the baptized should not deny *[arnēsontai]* their Christ (*Herm. Vis.* 2.2.7-8). And, later, he writes that those who suffer "stripes, imprisonments, great afflictions, crucifixions, wild beasts, for the sake of the name" sit "on the right hand" (*Herm. Vis.* 3.2.1).

The emphasis here in Rev 7:14, however, is not on details of "the great ordeal," but on the efficacy of the "blood of the Lamb" for bringing the multitude "before the throne of God" where they worship him (note 1:5; cf. Gen 49:11; Isa 1:18-20; 6:9-11). A comparable point is made later at 22:14, but there those who "wash their robes" have the "right to the tree of life" and access to the City of God (22:14). The great multitude live now around the throne, "sheltered" by God, without want (cf. Ezek 37:27; John 1:14).

7:15-17: Their idyllic conditions—stated in elemental images of food, drink, heat, water, and tears (cf. 21:3-4; Isa 4:2-6; 49:10)—are presented alternately between what they do and what the divine does: They worship; he will shelter (*skēnōsei;* cf. Exod 25:8; 29:45; 1 Kgs 8:12; Isa 4:5; Ezek 37:27; John 1:14). They will not hunger or thirst; the Lamb will shepherd, that is, rule (note that here the Lamb is the shepherd; contrast Ps 23; Isa 40:11; Ezek 34) and God will wipe away every tear. The wording of verses 17 and 18 depends upon Isa 49:10, a description of Zion's (Jerusalem's) children being brought back from exile to idyllic life in Jerusalem, though in Revelation "the Lamb" replaces the figure in Isaiah described as "he who has pity" (cf. also Job 22:7; Ps 121:6; Isa 25:6-10; Jer 31:9; Zech 14:8; Sir 43:4).

8:1: After the two visions of two groups of saints in chapter 7, the opening of the seventh seal brings silence in heaven. It serves as a marker for the reader of Revelation, as well as those who are listening, that a major segment of the writing is closed. It also indicates God's presence and presages more revelation to come (cf. 1 Kgs 19:12; Job 4:16). Zephaniah commands: "Be silent before the Lord GOD! For the day of the LORD is at hand" (1:7; Hab 2:20). Baruch wonders if at the end, "will the universe return . . . to its original silence?" (2 *Apoc. Bar.* 3; cf. 2 Esdr 6:39; 7:30). Adam, explaining the hours of the night, says to his son Seth that "the twelfth hour is the waiting for incense, and silence is imposed on all the ranks of fire and wind until all the priests burn incense to his divinity" (*T. Adam* 1.12). In the Mithras Liturgy, silence is called a symbol of the living God: "So at once put your right finger on your mouth and say: 'Silence! Silence! Silence! Symbol of the living, incorruptible God! Guard me, Silence, Nechtheir Thanmelou' " (*PGM* 4.558-60).

◊ ◊ ◊ ◊

The opening of the seven seals discloses the destiny of the world (see comment after 5:13-14). The white horse—associated with emperors and generals—conquers and brings peace, but the red horse follows, taking peace from the earth. The black horse brings pestilence and death, followed by the pale green horse bringing death by sword or famine or pestilence or wild animals. Followers of the Lamb have a special destiny: Penultimately, they are slaughtered for their witness, but ultimately, they dwell in the glory of God's presence. John's vision is probably playing on visions recorded in the book of Zechariah (1:7-17; 6:7-8). There, four colorful horses patrol the earth and report that all is still peaceful. In response to the riders' report of peace, "the angel of the Lord" asks, "O LORD of hosts, how long will you withhold mercy from Jerusalem and the cities of Judah?" (Zech 1:12; cf. Pss 74; 79:5, 10). At the opening of the fifth seal, John hears martyrs asking the question, "How long will it be before you judge and avenge our blood on the inhabitants of the earth?" (6:10). In Zechariah, the reported peace is problematic, for war must come before Jerusalem can be restored. In Revelation, those who cry out are told to wait a little longer. Then, the opening of the sixth seal moves the world's

destiny along, as the day of the wrath of the one seated on the throne
and of the Lamb comes upon all people. Chapter 7 returns to
parochial concerns about the destiny of the followers of the Lamb.
"Servants of God" are to be sealed on their foreheads (see 7:3) and
an innumerable crowd stands before the heavenly throne praising
God for his salvation (7:9-10). The opening of the seventh seal
bodes that there is more yet to take place.

Revelation 6:9-11, the opening of the fifth seal, and 7:9-17, the
multitude in heaven, are in many ways similar scenes. Those in
chapter 6 who have "been slaughtered for the word of God" cry
for vengeance before the divine throne. They are given white robes
and "told to rest a little longer." The multitude in chapter 7 have
also been killed and are before God's throne in heaven wearing
white clothes. The emotional tone of the two scenes, however, is
very different: Lamentation—linked in chapter 6 with sin, being
wronged, and vengeance—contrasts with that of joyous acclamation by those in chapter 7 who wave palm branches. That contrast
is also present in the Jewish autumn festival, from the Day of
Atonement to the Festival of Booths. G. Adolf Deissmann, in
discussing an especially poignant double inscription from Rheneia
(an island near Delos), suggests that the cry to be avenged is linked
to the Day of Atonement:

> "I call upon and pray *[axiō]* the Most High God, the Lord of the
> spirits and of all flesh, against those who with guile murdered or
> poisoned the wretched, untimely lost Heraclea, shedding her inno-
> cent blood wickedly: that it may be so with them that murdered or
> poisoned her, and with their children; O Lord that seeth all things,
> and ye angels of God, Thou before whom every soul is afflicted this
> same day with supplication: that Thou mayst avenge *[egdikēsēs]* the
> innocent blood and require it again right speedily *[tachistēn]!"*
> (Deissmann 1978, 424)

The author of the inscription calls upon the "Most High God" (cf.
"Sovereign Lord," Rev 6:10) to avenge innocent blood by making
the murderers suffer as they caused suffering (cf. Gen 9:6; Exod
21:14; Deut 19:10). Deissmann suggests that "this same day" refers
to the Day of Atonement on which there is a cry for avenging of

innocent blood. If so, the cry of "the slaughtered" that John sees in heaven may echo a liturgical cry at the Day of Atonement, just as the later scene with the palm branches echoes the later Festival of Booths (see also Ulfgard 1989).

VISIONS OF SEVEN ANGELS WITH SEVEN TRUMPETS (8:2–11:19)

Further revelation, presaged by the silence in heaven, now takes the form of seven angels blowing seven trumpets framed in with the characteristic vision marker, "I saw" *(kai eidon)*. They blow their trumpets in connection with a throne scene that centers upon a ritual of sacrifice around an altar standing before the throne (8:2-6). Six angels then blow their trumpets, one after the other (8:7–9:20). Chapter 10 describes a formal ceremony in which John's call to be a prophet is renewed (10:1–11:2). It is followed by a visionary account of the ministry of two prophets (11:3-13). Then, at the blowing of the seventh trumpet, John sees a throne scene in which God and his Messiah are once again acclaimed as cosmic kings (11:15-19). Dramatic tension is heightened in the series by the announcement that the last three trumpet blasts will bring woes to the inhabitants of the earth (8:13; 9:12; 11:14) and that the seventh blast will fulfill the mystery of God revealed to his prophets (10:7).

Blowing Six of the Seven Trumpets (8:2–9:21)

The heavenly scene initiating the blowing of the seven trumpets discloses a new feature in the throne scene—a "golden altar that is before the throne" (though compare 6:9). An angel other than the seven trumpeters offers sacrifice of "incense" and "prayers," which "rose before God from the hand of the angel." That angel concludes the sacrificial service by throwing fire from the altar to earth, which reveals God's presence in a violent storm. The angels blow their trumpets as a part of that sacrificial ritual, just as earlier, the seals were opened in connection with the enthronement ritual of the Lamb. The first four trumpet blasts form a unit, as each destroys by fire a third, respectively, of earth, sea, rivers and springs, and the heavenly lights of sun, moon, and stars (8:7-12; cf. the four horsemen at 6:1-8). With the blowing of the fifth trumpet, disaster comes to earth from below rather than above: A "star" opens "the shaft of the bottomless pit," and horrid locusts-scorpions-horses come out to torture those who "do not have the seal of God on their foreheads" (9:4; cf. 7:3). For the first time, "the bottomless pit" is opened to disclose a *cacophany,* a manifestation of evil. Then, the sixth trumpeter discloses a battle scene in which four angels, along with a large cavalry, are released from "the great river Euphrates" and kill a third of humankind (9:13-21).

◊ ◊ ◊ ◊

8:2: "And I saw *[kai eidon],*" introduces a new vision that carries through the first four trumpets. "The seven angels" are a known group of seven, probably the seven archangels (note 1:4). They may also be the seven angels of the seven churches (1:20). Trumpets are associated with divine revelation at Sinai (Exod 19:6), at a temple (Ps 47:5; Paus. 2.21.3), and in war (4:1; Exod 19:16; Josh 6:4; Ps 47:5; Zech 9:14; 1 Macc 3:54; 1QM 3; Artem. 56; also *Mart. Pol.* 22.5). They also herald the coming of the day of the Lord (Isa 27:13; Joel 2:1; Zech 9:14; 1 Cor 15:52; 2 Esdr 6:23), the Son of Man (Matt 24:31), and the return of Jesus (1 Thess 4:16; *Did.* 16.6).

8:3-6: The heavenly temple is modeled after the temple in Jerusalem: the angel first stands at the altar of burnt offerings in the courtyard of the temple and then enters the inner sanctuary, where he offers incense at the "golden altar," which stands before the invisible God enthroned upon the cherubim and the ark of the covenant (see Exod 27:1-8; 30:1; 40:5; Num 3:31; 1 Kgs 6:22; cf. Luke 1:8-10). The angel mirrors the movements of the priest on the Day of Atonement (Yom Kippur; Lev 16:12-13), though the high priest mixed incense and blood, not prayers, as he sacrificed on the golden altar (note 5:8; Isa 6:6). Incense purifies the prayers, as they are offered up (cf. Isa 6:6). In *T. Levi*, a more elaborate arrangement is described of angels relaying prayers to God (3.7; cf. *1 Enoch* 9.3). In another instance, the angel, Raphael, brings the prayers of Tobit and Sarah to God (Tob 12:12). The angel returns to the altar outside the Holy of Holies, takes fire from it, and offers it up not to God but to the earth (cf. Ezek 10:2). A theophany occurs (note 4:5-8 and 6:12-14) and the trumpeters provide the music portion of the ritual.

8:7: At the blowing of the first trumpet, a vision balloons out revealing more storm phenomena. The seventh plague on Egypt involved "thunder" and "hail": in the language of Ps 105:32, "He gave them hail for rain, and lightning that flashed through their land. He struck their vines and fig trees, and shattered the trees of their country" (cf. Exod 9:23-24; Philo, *Vita Mos.* 1.119). In other passages "hail" contributes to images indicating the presence of God (11:19; Ps 18:12; Wis 16:22), especially divine judgment (16:21; Ezek 38:22; Sir 39:29). Hail, plus "fire, mixed with blood," is "hurled to the earth." "Fire, mixed with blood" results from sacrificial burnt offerings, but the mixture can also indicate simply divine judgment (cf. *Sib. Or.* 5.377, "fire will rain on men from the floors of heaven, fire and blood, water, lightning bolt, darkness, heavenly night, and destruction in war . . ." and *Sib. Or.* 3.542-44, "and the one who created heaven and earth will set down much lamented fire on the earth. One third of all mankind will survive"). According to Sirach, fire, hail, famine, and pestilence are "created for vengeance" (39:29; cf. *Sib. Or.* 5.274). Those storm phenomena are sometimes a prelude to an imminent revelation, such as the day of the Lord (Joel 2:30-31), or in connection with the return of Nero (see comments after 17:18; *Sib. Or.* 5.375-80; cf. *Sib. Or.* 2.15-21). "One-third" occurs here for the first time in Revelation (cf. 8:9, 10, 11, 12; 9:15, 18; 12:4; Ezek 5:2; Zech 13:8; and *Sib. Or.* 3.542-44 above). The trumpeters destroy only a third of the world, not the whole of it, as will the last plagues (cf. 21:1). Damage to trees and green vegetation comes as a surprise, for they are protected by divine law, though not in the exodus from Egypt (note 7:3).

8:8-9: With the second trumpet, the sea (salt water) is burned. The spectacle of fire can only be described as a simile ("like a great mountain"; cf. 4:6; 6:6; 15:2; 19:1). This mountain of fire shares elements with the judgment of the stars in *1 Enoch* 18.13, Tyre in Zech 9:4, final judgment in *Sib. Or.* 2.195-200, and judgment at the second coming of Christ in *Apoc. Peter* 5-6. As a result of the trumpet blast, a third of the sea becomes blood, like the Nile in the first plague against Egypt (Exod 7:20; Ps 78:44). The relation between the fire and resulting blood is not clear; perhaps they are associated through color or sacrificial imagery. Some of John's hearers might think of the river in Biblos that turns blood red each year, signaling the time for lamenting Adonis (*Syr. D.* 8). "Ships" are mentioned in Revelation only here and in 18:19.

8:10-11: Though the star that falls at the third trumpet blazes "like a torch," it does not burn; it turns bitter a third of the rivers and springs (fresh water) upon which it falls. This star "fell *[epesen]*," in contrast to being thrown (*eblēthē*, 8:7, 8). The star has a name, "Wormwood *[Apsinthon]*," a poisonous, bitter shrub (Prov 5:4). The physician, Galen, refers frequently to *apsinthon*, which can heal if mixed properly with honey and wine; otherwise, it is deadly. According to Jeremiah, God judges his people and false prophets by giving them wormwood (Jer 9:15; 23:15).

8:12: At the fourth trumpet, a third of the heavenly bodies are "struck *[eplēgē]*." In Matthew, the darkening of the sun is a sign of the end (24:29); in Exodus, the ninth plague brought darkness on Egypt, except where the Israelites lived (10:21); at Rev 16:10, the fifth bowl causes darkness on the beast's kingdom; and at Rev 18:23, Babylon, when judged, is in darkness (cf. Ezek 32:7 against Egypt). According to Amos, there will be darkness at noon on the day of the Lord (Amos 8:9; cf. Isa 13:10; Joel 2:10; 3:15). "Darkness" is associated with death, the underworld, and movement down, in contrast to "light," which is associated with life, heaven, and movement up (cf. 1:16). God unleashes those "dark" powers, when he judges.

8:13: A new vision marker appears here, "Then I looked, and I heard" [*kai eidon kai ēkousa;* cf. 5:11]. "Midheaven" is directly overhead in relation to the viewer (14:6; 19:17). An eagle consistently has positive, godly associations (4:7; 12:14; Exod 19:4; Isa 40:31; though the Greek word, *aetos,* can also refer to "vulture"; cf. Job 39:27-30; Matt 24:28; BAGD under *aetos*). Baruch says about the eagle, "You have been created by the Most high that you should be higher than any other bird" (*2 Apoc. Bar.* 77.21; cf. *4 Baruch* 7.3; 2 Esdr 11). An eagle is also a sign of Zeus and sometimes other deities (Diod. Sic. 16.27.2). In contrast to the first four trumpeters that destroy the natural environment, the eagle explains that the next three trumpetings will harm people, "the inhabitants of the earth" (i.e., non-Christians, see 6:10).

9:1: Although another vision marker occurs here ("I saw"), the word order emphasizes the blowing of "the fifth trumpet." In contrast to a falling star at the third trumpet (*epesen,* 8:10), John sees a star after it has fallen (*peptōkota;* cf. 6:13; Isa 14:12). There is moral ambivalence to this star, for it comes from heaven—the place and source of divinity and goodness—but it falls downward, an image of moral and religious failing (cf. Satan at 12:9). (So, at *1 Enoch* 86.1, a falling star, referring to the Sons of God at Gen 6, mates with cows and is punished properly.) The star is a sentient being, for it takes deliberate action by opening the shaft to the abyss (cf. Judg 5:20; Job 38:7). The "shaft *[phrear]*" can be pictured as a kind of dug well with a lid on it. In fact, Pausanius refers to a "well *[phrear]*" from which one drank in order to give oracles (Paus. 9.2; cf. 10.36; also Luke 14:5; John 4:11). The "shaft," thus, may be seen as a kind of *axis mundi* connecting earth and the underworld. "Opening" is an image of transformation: To "open" is to cross a boundary not normally accessible (note 4:1; also 19:11 heaven; a sealed scroll 5:2; 20:12; heavenly temple 11:19; 15:5; earth 12:16).

The "bottomless pit" or "abyss" is rich in associations. It may indicate something general like "the unfathomable" (Dionysius of Halicarnassus 20.9.2) or a "chasm" (Strabo, *Geography* 4.6.6). Or it may be the site of chaos (*Hermetica* 3.1; Ps 33:7, 16; *Op.* 29) or the primal waters (*PGM* XIII.165-70; VI.515-20; *Sib. Or.* 1.220-225) from which the created order came—gathering "together the abyss at the invisible foundation of its position" (*PGM* IV.1145-50; cf. VII.261; *Ep. Diog.* 7.2). In the abyss dwell autochthonous powers such as Erebos, Depth, the beast, Satan, and demons (*PGM* IV.1350; Rev 11:7; 20:1-3; Luke 8:31). Through it the sun (*Hermetica* 16.5) and the moon (*PGM* IV.2835) travel. Strabo reports Herodotus saying that the sources of the Nile River are in the bottomless depth (*bathos abusson*, 17.1.52). There the dead dwell (Ps 55:23; Rom 10:7; *An. recte* 7, 1130E). According to Plutarch, the Argives call Dionysus "up out of the water by the sound of trumpets, at the same time casting into the depths a lamb as an offering to the keeper of the gate" (*De Is. et Os.* 35, 364F), a set of images used very differently in Revelation. As the Creator of all things, God has control of the abyss (*T. Levi* 3.9; *1 Clem* 20.5; 28).

9:2: "Smoke," emphasized here by repetition, is more commonly a positive, divine force, though it is also associated with destruction by fire (note 14:9-11). The smoke from the shaft is "like the smoke of a great furnace," an image of the presence of the Lord coming to bless (Sinai, Exod 19:18) or to judge (Sodom, Gen 19:28). (For the verb form, "were darkened," cf. 16:10 and note 8:12; for "air," note 16:17.)

9:3: "Locusts" (9:3, 7) appear only here in Revelation, but they are clearly demonic creatures from the abyss that God is using to ravage the earth (cf. the eighth plague on Egypt, Exod 10:12; Wis 16:9; contrast *Herm. Vis.* 4.1.6). God promises Solomon that if the people turn to the temple when locusts come in judgment, God will "heal their land" (2 Chron 7:14). More significantly for Revelation, in Joel 2 locusts are images for the coming Day of the Lord, a "day of darkness and gloom" (Joel 2:2). The locusts from the abyss have the power (NRSV: "authority") of scorpions, associated with snakes and the fangs of wild animals, all of which are deadly, desert creatures (Deut 8:15; Sir 39:30).

9:4-6: Locusts normally strip the land of vegetation; here, however, they are directed "not to damage the grass of the earth or any green growth or any tree" (note 7:1). They torture (11:10; 12:2; 14:10; 18:7, 10, 15; 20:10; Matt 8:29) only those people without the seal of God on their foreheads (note 7:2-3; cf. Ezek 9:4-6). (Throughout verses 1-4, *edothē*, "given, allowed" and *gē*, "earth" are repeated for emphasis.) "Five months" may refer to the approximate length of a locust's life cycle. Like Job, those being tortured will seek death, but will not find it (Job 3:21; cf. Jer 8:3).

9:7-10: Revelation 9:7-11 describes the locusts with an attention to detail not given since the description of the Likeness of a Human in chapter 1. Similes abound *(homoiōmata, homoia, hōs)* in language that echoes Job 39:20; Jer 51:27; and especially, Joel 2. Though they come from the abyss, they share some features of those close to God (1:13; 2:10; 4:4, 7; 14:14). In "A Babylonian Story" (second century CE), Iamblichus describes somewhat similarly horses in a procession of the Babylonian king as follows: "decked out in military fashion with frontlets, chest plates, and flank armor. . . . Tied and bound with variegated purple bands, the tails of the horses are braided like women's locks; their manes are raised in crests along both sides of their necks" (Reardon 1989, 794). "Teeth" are mentioned only here in Revelation (cf. Joel 1:6, locust; Sir 21:2, sin; *Adv. Col.* 30, 1125B, without law and culture, we return to a Hobbesian "tooth and claw"). Animals with tails tend to be associated with evil (12:4).

9:11: The ruler of these locusts is said to be "the angel of the bottomless pit," that is, the angel having responsibility for the abyss. His name is then given in Hebrew (*Abaddōn;* cf. 16:16) and Greek *(Apollyōn).* Both the Greek and the Hebrew words have the root meaning of "destroying." In the LXX and other Greek versions of the Old Testament, *apōleia,* translating MT *abaddōn,* parallels Hades (Job 26:6; Prov 15:11), the grave (Ps 88:11), and death (Job 28:22). In the *Greek Apocalypse of Ezra* (see *OTP*), Ezra is led down five hundred steps, and then down some more to the foundation of Apoleia "and there I saw the twelvefold blow of the abyss" (4.20-21). At 2 Thess 2:3, the "lawless one," who must come before the day of the Lord, is called "the son of *apōleias.*"

9:12-15: At 9:12, someone, perhaps John or the eagle, reminds the hearer that the first of the three woes (trumpet blasts) has now occurred (8:13). That reminder heightens the reader/hearer's expectations for the next two trumpet blasts. At the blowing of the sixth trumpet, a voice from the "four horns [at the four corners] of the golden altar" (note 8:3) directs the trumpeter to release four angels bound in the east at the Euphrates River, the boundary between the Roman and Parthian empires (cf. the sixth bowl at 16:12 and the four angels at 7:1; the devil at 20:2 is the only other being bound in Revelation).

9:16-19: Two hundred million cavalry soldiers (an inexhaustible supply, only here in the NT) are introduced abruptly by the phrase "I heard their number" (cf. 5:11; 7:4; 13:17; 20:8; note 7:9). Their breastplates, heads, mouths, and tails (note 9:10) are described, with emphasis on the colors of the "breastplates" of the horses and their riders—fire *(pyrinous),* sapphire *(hyakinthinous),* and sulfur *(theiōdeis)*—for those are the colors of the "three plagues" that come out of the mouths of the horses—fire, smoke, and sulfur (cf. 11:6; 16:13; Job 41:19). As we have seen, "smoke" and "fire" can be images of either a divine or demonic manifestation (note 8:8-9; 9:2); here they refer to divine judgment. Sulfur is an instrument of divine judgment (e.g., note 14:9-11; cf. 20:10; 21:8; Ps 11:6; Ezek 38:22; Luke 17:29). Philo says in connection with Sodom (Gen 19:24) that "even to this day there are seen in Syria . . . ashes, and sulfur *[theion],* and smoke *[kapnos],* and dusky flame . . . of a fire *[pyros]* smoldering beneath" (*Vita Mos.* 2.56).

The term "plagues" *(plēgōn)* occurs for the first time. This term refers to "a blow or stroke," especially blows of disaster and punishment from God (*J.W.* 1.373; Lev 26:21; Zech 14:12). It recurs fifteen times elsewhere in Revelation, in reference to the power of the two witnesses (11:6), the earth beast (13:3, 12, 14), the seven bowls of wrath (15:1, 6, 8; 16:9, 21; 21:9), the fall of Babylon (18:4, 8), and generically to all the judgments and disasters described in Revelation (22:18). In the Old Testament, plagues are associated especially with the conflict between God and Pharaoh (Exod 11:1; 12:13; 1 Sam 4:8; Jdt 5:12 [but compare Num 11:33]; 14:37; 25:8-9). Aeschylus refers to plagues from Zeus (*Agamemnon* 367). From Plutarch's point of view, John's vision is that of a superstitious man, for "in the estimation of the superstitious man every indisposition of his body, loss of property, deaths of children, or mishaps and failures in public life are classed as 'afflictions *[plēgai]* of God' or 'attacks of an evil spirit' " (*De superst.* 7, 168C).

9:20-21: The remaining two-thirds of humankind do not repent from either their idolatrous works or their immorality (cf. 16:9, 11; cf. Exod 7:13). An idol (cf. Deut 4:28; Ps 15:4; Isa 2:8; Mic 5:12; Acts 7:41; 15:20; 17:18) is a physical representation of a "demon" or deity (see Polyb. 30.25.13; Isa 2:20; Dan 5:4; 1 Cor 8:4, 7; 10:19-20; and especially, Ps 115:4-7). Sorcery and fornication are often associated as extreme forms of immorality (cf. 18:21-24).

◊ ◊ ◊ ◊

An altar in heaven provides the setting for the blowing of the trumpets, an altar on which the prayers of the saints are offered. In response to the offering of those prayers for redemption and vindication (cf. 6:10), the angels blow their trumpets. Like the plagues in Egypt, which afflict the Egyptians in order to liberate the Israelites, so the trumpet-plagues (plague occurs at 9:18 for the first time) inflict harm in order to vindicate God and his saints and to move the destiny of the world through destruction to renewal. The plagues are for the benefit of the followers of the Lamb, not "the inhabitants of the earth," who do not repent even after a third have been killed. The eagle in midheaven even announces that the last three blasts are directed against the "inhabitants of the earth."

The blowing of the fifth trumpet underscores Revelation's monism; that is, the sovereign God and his enthroned Messiah have authority and power finally over all that exists, including fallen, evil forces that oppose God and his Christ. The "star" at 9:1, like Satan at 12:9, existed in heaven and depends upon God for its being, but it has fallen. This "star" opens "the shaft of the bottomless pit [abyss]" where heinous demons and monstrosities dwell. They come up through the smoke of the abyss to earth, but they are ultimately under the control of the Lamb who holds destinies, for they harm only those who do not have the seal of God on their foreheads. Moreover, they have the form of locusts, echoing the scene in Joel where locusts/horses signal the coming Day of the Lord. Both the army of locusts and the cavalry of the sixth trumpet, described similarly to the locusts, harm and destroy those who do not follow God and the Lamb. The sixth plague ends with the observation that "the inhabitants of the earth" did not give up their idolatry or their immorality, both of which result from their misplaced commitment to "idols," "the works of their hands."

Prophecy and the Seventh Trumpet (10:1–11:19)

Before the seventh angel blows his trumpet, John sees a mighty angel holding a scroll (10:1-2). That scene has affinities with chapter 5: In both, a "mighty angel" shouts, and in both, a scroll is central. Moreover, John imitates the Lamb by taking the scroll. John's scroll, however, contains prophetic words, not tablets of destiny, and John's scene involves a renewed call to prophesy rather than a cosmic enthronement. After digesting a scroll of prophecy, John is commanded to "prophesy again" (10:11). Then he performs a prophetic sign of measuring the temple (11:1-2) and hears a narration not of his prophetic ministry, but that of two other prophetic witnesses (11:3-13). They come into conflict with "the beast that comes up from the bottomless pit," foreshadowing the conflicts between divine and demonic forces that recur in the second half of the book (chapters 12–19). The mighty angel holding a scroll had announced that "in the days when the seventh angel is to blow his trumpet, the mystery of God will be fulfilled, as he announced to his servants the prophets" (10:7). That mystery is fulfilled liturgically, in a brief service enthroning God and his Messiah (11:15-19). The sequence begun at 8:2 is concluded.

◊ ◊ ◊ ◊

10:1-2: The "mighty angel," controlling sea and land (5:2), assimilates features of several previous suprahuman beings: he is clothed in a cloud, somewhat like the "rider of the clouds" in 1:7; he has a "radiance [iris]" (NRSV: "rainbow") like that around the throne in 4:3 (cf. Ezek 1:28; Sir 50:7); his face and feet are like the Likeness of a Human in 1:15-16; and he holds a scroll in his hand like the one seated on the throne, though the angel's scroll is not sealed (5:1; note 18:21). It is clear from what follows that the scroll contains prophetic words.

10:3-7: The mighty angel roars like a lion and "seven thunders" respond antiphonally (cf. Hos 11:10; Amos 3:8; John 12:28-29). A third voice from heaven issues the first of three directives to John, "Seal up what the seven thunders have said" (a nice contrast to the Lamb's opening seals, note 5:1; Job 9:7; 2 Cor 12:4). Then, the mighty angel speaks again, swearing an oath before God that "there will be no more delay [chronos], but in the days when the seventh angel is to blow his trumpet, the mystery of God will be fulfilled [completed], as he announced to his servants the prophets" (10:6-7; cf. the speech of the man clothed in linen at Dan 12:7; the oath of Moses, Deut 32:40; vision of the end, Hab 2:3; no delay, Heb 10:37). Elsewhere in Revelation, "mystery of God" refers to an allegorical interpretation of the seven stars (1:20) and of the whore (17:5, 7). "Mystery" (also note 17:8) has many associations, for example, military secrets (2 Macc 13:21), interpretation of dreams (Dan 2:19, 27-30), or secret religious rites and teachings (Rom 16:25; 1 Cor 4:1; Eph 3:1-11; Wis 14:23). Here, however, its basic meaning is the plan of God that he makes known through his prophets (1:1-3; 22:6; Jer 7:25; Dan 9:6; Amos 3:7; Zech 1:6). In several texts, the mystery of God refers specifically to God's plan for life after death (1 Cor 2:7; 15:51; Wis 2:22; 1 Enoch 103.1-2; 1Q27). The angel's oath links integrally this scene about prophecy and prophets to the series of seven trumpets.

10:8-11: John now enters into his visionary drama more fully than anywhere else in Revelation. The heavenly voice issues a second directive to John: Take the open scroll from the mighty angel (cf. 5:7). The angel further directs John to eat the scroll, that is, to make the prophetic words his to proclaim (cf. Ps 119:103; Jer 1:10; 15:16; ; Ezek 2:8–3:3). The scroll is at first sweet, but it turns bitter (as at 8:11). After enacting this prophetic sign—ingesting as receiving prophetic words—John receives a third directive: "You must prophesy again against many peoples and nations and languages and kings" (AT; note 7:9).

11:1: There is no formal division between 10:11 and 11:1. John is given a "reed like a staff *[rabdos]*" (AT), which is an emblem of authority in both Jewish and Roman ceremony (2:27; 12:5; Ps 2:9; *Pss. Sol.* 17:23-26; *Sib. Or.* 8.248. The *fasces* is a bundle of birch wood sticks, approximately five feet long, signifying political authority in Rome. See *OCD* under *fasces; Publ.* 10.2; *Luc.* 36.2). A reed can also have a magical aspect (*Ant.* 5.284). Here it is used to execute a prophetic sign of measuring (cf. 21:15-17; Ezek 40:5; 42:16; Zech 2:1-5), that is, marking out the appropriate boundaries of a space or a sphere of activity. For example, moral judgments and punishments have their proper measure (2 Kgs 21:13; 2 Cor 10:12), and God's judgments are never disproportionate to the situation (Jer 31:37; Lam 2:8; Zech 1:16). When creating the world, God "arranged all things by measure and number and weight" (Wis 11:20), while the extended hands of Christ on the cross measured the whole world (*Sib. Or.* 1.372; 8.302). When John in his vision measures "the temple," "the altar," and "those who worship there," he marks out the boundary between the holy and the profane and limits the holy to that "inside" his measurements (cf. Thompson 1990, 86-91). This temple is patterned on the Jewish temple at Jerusalem. The altar is the one outside the sanctuary proper (note 8:3). The court or walled quadrangle that John is not to measure probably refers to the large walled yard around the temple that Herod built, called the Court of the Gentiles (cf. Matt 26:69; *J. W.* 5.190-200; a diagram at *IDB* R-Z, 556).

11:2: Since John's visions are written from an "insider's" point of view, that which is "outside" (emphasized in 11:2) is generally given a negative value (3:12; 14:20 [contrast 18:4]; 22:15). To "trample *[patēsousin]*" is to desecrate or defile (cf. Ps 79:1; Isa 1:12; 63:18; 1 Macc 3:45; 4:60). Elsewhere, Jerusalem is to be trampled in the last days (Dan 8:13; Zech 12:3; Luke 21:24). In Jewish and Christian traditions, Jerusalem is the "holy city," just as Hierapolis was in the Syrian tradition *(Syr. D.)*. Forty-two months or 1,260 days or three and a half years (all the same length of time) occur several times in Revelation; so, the time of Jerusalem's defilement (11:2) = the time of the two witnesses (11:3) = the time the woman will be nourished in the wilderness (12:6) = the time of the authority of the beast (13:5) = the time, two times, and a half time (Dan 7:25).

11:3: God's two witnesses, otherwise not identified by name (cf. John 8:17), are introduced immediately after John's prophetic act of measuring the temple. No sharp break should be made between 10:11 and 11:3:

> Then they said *[legousin]* to me *[moi]*, "You must prophesy *[prophēteusai]* again about many peoples and nations *[ethnesin]* and languages and kings." Then I was given *[edothē moi]* a reed like a measuring stick, and they said *[legōn]*, "Get up and measure the temple of God and the altar and those who worship there, but do not measure the court outside the temple; leave that out, for *[hoti]* it is given over *[edothē]* to the nations *[ethnesin]*, and they will trample over the holy city for forty-two months [1,260 days] and I will give *[dōsō]* my two witnesses authority to prophesy *[prophēteusousin]* for one thousand two hundred sixty days [forty-two months] wearing sackcloth. (AT)

In Revelation, only John (10:11) and the two witnesses (11:3) prophesy. The placement of the account of the two witnesses immediately after the directive to John to prophesy makes the story of the two witnesses to be a kind of "shadow" account that indirectly fulfills the directive to John and the destiny that he expects to carry out. Recall that throughout Revelation, John never calls himself a prophet or his activity as prophesying.

The two witnesses are identified by what they wear—as we have seen, a common way to identify a figure. "Sackcloth" is an image of mourning (2 Kgs 19:1; Esth 4:2; *T. Jos.* 15.2), submission (1 Kgs 20:32; *J.W.* 2.237), or penance (*De superst.* 7, 168D).

11:4: The two witnesses are further identified as two specific "olive trees" and "lampstands." The former allude to the two "olive trees" in Zechariah's vision (Zech 4:3, 11, 14). There, olive trees refer to Joshua the priest and Zerubbabel the king, whom Zechariah expected to complete the building of the temple after the Babylonians had destroyed it. Some of the Dead Sea Scrolls and other secondary temple literature assume a dual messiahship, priestly and royal (*T. Sim.* 7.2; 1QS 9.11). In Zechariah's vision, the two olive trees stand on either side of one lampstand, not two (Zech 4:3). The two lampstands in Revelation are different from the seven mentioned earlier (1:12, 13, 20; 2:1).

11:5-6: While prophesying, these two witnesses cannot be harmed, a point emphasized by repetition (cf. 6:6, do not harm the olive oil; for "harming," see also 2:11; 7:2, 3; 9:4, 10, 19; 22:11). In fact, if anyone tries to harm these witnesses, he or she—along with other enemies (11:12)—will be destroyed by a fiery death (9:17; Job 41:19). Fire from the mouth is an image associated with a manifestation of God (2 Sam 22:9; Ps 97:3), here, with a manifestation of the prophetic word (2 Kgs 1:10; Jer 5:14; Sir 48:3; 2 Esdr 13:10, contrast Luke 9:54-56). The two witnesses have power over rain *(brechō)* for the extent of their prophecy (1,260 days), as had the prophet Elijah (1 Kgs 17) who, according to Jas 5:17, did not allow rain for three and one-half years (1,260 days). They are also able to turn "the waters" into blood (note 8:8-9; cf. 16:4, the third bowl; Exod 7:14-24, the first plague on Egypt) and to strike the earth with plagues, as does the God of Israel (note 9:18).

11:7: Their protection lasts, however, only through the three and one-half years of their testimony/prophecy. "The beast that comes up from the abyss" is introduced abruptly. Later in chapter 13, two beasts are introduced, one coming up from the sea (13:1) and one from the earth (13:11). This beast is probably the one coming up from the sea (sea = abyss; see 9:1 and Dan 7:3; also Rev 17:8). War between the two prophets and the beast is the first of several wars that will recur in the latter half of Revelation (12:17; 13:7; 19:19; cf. Dan 7:21). The two prophets are killed, as they battle with the beast.

11:8: "The great city" by itself can refer to any major city (e.g., Jerusalem, Jer 22:8; Babylon, Rev 17:18; Nineveh, Jon 4:11; Ephron, 1 Macc 5:46; Thebes, Diod. Sic. 1.45.4). Here the great city is Jerusalem, further qualified by being "prophetically called Sodom and Egypt." Old Testament prophets also condemn Jerusalem by calling it Sodom (Isa 1:10; Ezek 16:46), but not Egypt. According to Wis 19:13-17, however, Sodom and Egypt have in common their ill treatment of the stranger. Finally, the great city is identified as "where also their Lord was crucified," which is obviously Jerusalem. Christians give a "prophetic [pneumatikōs]" interpretation to the Old Testament or to a Jewish custom in order to give it a Christian significance (cf. 1 Cor 2:14; 1 Clem. 47.3; Dial. Trypho 14).

11:9-10: For three and a half days (cf. three and a half years of prophesying; Christ, on the third day, 1 Cor 15:4), the corpses of the two prophets lie in the street, while the "inhabitants of the earth" (note 6:10-11) rejoice—an understandable response to the previously harsh judgments of the two witnesses (11:5-6). For the "inhabitants of the earth" it is a festive time, like the defeat of Satan or the fall of Babylon for the inhabitants of heaven (12:12; 18:30), the marriage of the Lamb for the multitude (19:7), or the joy at Purim for the Jews after the defeat of Haman (Esth 9:19, 22).

11:11: After three and a half days, a "breath of life [pneuma zoēs]" from God entered the two prophets and they stood "on their feet" (11:11). "Breath or spirit of life," present in all living creatures, leaves the body at death and returns to the corpse at resurrection (Gen 6:17; Ezek 1:20, comparable to the "soul of life" (psychē zoēs; NRSV: "living thing" at Rev 16:3). The language here echoes that of the resurrection of the "dry bones" in Ezek 37. In response to this marvel, the people of Jerusalem, the enemies of the two prophets (11:12), are "terrified *[phobos megas],*" that is, filled with awe and terror.

11:12-13: As the two prophets ascend to heaven, a great earthquake occurs, killing one-tenth of the city's population that totalled seventy thousand (note 6:12-14). In contrast to those remaining after the blowing of the sixth trumpet (9:20-21), the remaining citizens of Jerusalem repent (11:13, note 2:4-6). They give glory to the "God of heaven," an epithet for God occurring only here and at 16:11 in Revelation (cf. 2 Chron 36:23; Ezra 1:2; 5:11; Dan 2:18; 4:31; Jon 1:9; Rom 1:10; Tob 10:11; Jdt 5:8). If from this passage we can extrapolate an attitude toward Jews, it is ambivalent. On the one hand, they are the enemy (11:5, 12), but after the murder, resurrection, and ascension of the two prophets, they repent (11:13; cf. comment after 3:12-13).

11:14: The speaker is not indicated; perhaps it is the eagle once again: The final woe, revealing the fulfillment of God's will (10:7), will occur at the final trumpet blast (8:13). That fulfillment will occur in the form of an enthronement liturgy before the throne, which has been the primary setting for John's visions since chapter 4.

11:15: Loud voices resound in heaven (cf. 7:10; 11:12; 12:10; 19:1) acclaiming God's sovereignty and that of his anointed: "The kingdom of the world *[kosmos]* has become the kingdom of our Lord and of his Christ, and he will reign forever and ever." "Kingdom of the world" occurs only here and in Matt 4:8 in the New Testament. The verb "has become *[egeneto]*" indicates a transformation from one condition to another. Perhaps there is a notion that God has allowed Satan to rule the world (cf. Matt 4:8), even though it has always ultimately been under the control of the creator God (4:11). "Kingdom of our Lord" (and Savior Jesus Christ) occurs also at 2 Pet 1:11 (cf. Ps 10:16; 22:28; Dan 7:27; Obad 21). This is the first of three references in Revelation to "Christ" (12:10; 20:4). Though "Christ" is identified with "Jesus" in Revelation (see chapter 1), the term belongs to a broader domain of texts that refer to an agent of God who will bring eternal bliss and perfect peace to the whole world: a future Davidic king (Isa 9:2-7; 11:1-9; Jer 33:14-22; Ezek 37:24-28), a suprahuman Messiah (*Pss. Sol.* 17; *2 Apoc. Bar.* 29f; 39-42, 72-74; 2 Esdr 7; 11:37–12:34; 13:3–14:9; *1 Enoch* 37-71, especially, 48:10; 52:4; *3 Enoch* 45:5; 48.10A), Christian Messiah (*Odes Sol.* 9.3; 17.17; 24.1; 29.6; 39.11; 41.3, 15; *Apoc. Zeph.* 10.24–12.32; *Apoc. Elijah* 13.15–15.14; 25.8-19; *Apoc. Sedrach* 12; *Mart. Isa.* 9.12-13; 30-7-15; *T. Adam* 4), and the Messiahs of Aaron and Israel in the Qumran scrolls (note 11:4; 1QS 9.11; *Damascus Document* 19.10) (so Charlesworth in *OTP* 1.xxxi-xxxiii).

11:16-18: In response to the "loud voices," the twenty-four elders offer a thanksgiving to the "Lord God Almighty" (11:17-18), "for *[hoti]* you have taken your great power and begun to reign." As the Lord is enthroned, "the nations raged *[ōrgisthēsan]*," a theme in Israel's songs of enthronement; for example, Ps 99:1 "The LORD is king; let the peoples tremble! [LXX, *orgizesthōsan]*" or Exod 15, "the peoples heard, they trembled [LXX, *ōrgisthēsan*] . . . the LORD will reign forever and ever" (Exod 15:14, 18; cf. Ps 2). God responds in kind, with wrath (*orgē*, note 6:15-16; cf. 11:18; 14:10; 16:19; 19:15; Jer 30:23; Hab 3; also *thymos*, 14:8, 19; 15:1, 7; 16:1). God also judges the dead (cf. 10:7; 20:12), rewards his "servants, the prophets and saints and all who fear" him, "small and great" (11:18; see 19:5; 22:12; Ps 61:5), and destroys "those who destroy the earth" (11:18; cf. 19:2; Jer 51:25). In short, followers of God fear him, his enemies rage against him, and each receives appropriate reward (cf. Exod 15:13-18). A talion (punishment identical to the offense) recurs against the enemies: anger receives anger; destroyers receive destruction; and the desire of those "under the altar" is fulfilled (6:11).

11:19: The inner sanctuary (*naos*, note 3:12-13) opens to display the "ark of the covenant." It is an ancient palladium that preserved the people Israel, for God was present in it—especially as the divine warrior/storm God, Yahweh Sabaoth (*pantokratōr*, note 1:8; cf. 2 Sam 22:14; Ps 77:18; Isa 29:6). According to 1 Chronicles,

Solomon housed the ark in the Holy of Holies in the temple to be a "footstool of our God," covered by the cherubim (28:2; see also Exod 25:10-22; Num 7:89), and so God's kingship is closely associated with his being "enthroned upon the cherubim and the footstool-ark" (cf. 4:6*b*; 132:7; 1 Sam 4:4; 2 Sam 6:2; 2 Kgs 19:15; 1 Chr 13:6; Pss 80:1; 99:1, 5). In literature around the time of Revelation, there is speculation over the destiny of the ark: Jeremiah hid it (2 Macc 2:4-8); at the time of the resurrection, the ark will also be resurrected and placed on Mt. Sinai where all the saints gather (*The Lives of the Prophets*, 2.14-15 in *OTP*). Here in Revelation, the ark is back in the sanctuary—the one in heaven. When the sanctuary opens, God is manifested through storm images (note 4:5-8; 6:12-14; 8:7), ringing the seven trumpet sequence (8:5 and 11:19; note 1:8), and echoing the throne scene in chapter 4 (4:5).

◊ ◊ ◊ ◊

The career of the two witnesses who prophesy imitates that of Jesus: In John's vision, they appear in the city where "their Lord was crucified"; their ministry is at first successful as they do signs and wonders; then they come into conflict with evil forces—here the beast; they are martyred; and then God resurrects them—after three and a half days—and they ascend into heaven. Their biography reveals an excess of vengeance and gore. If someone harms them, "fire pours from their mouth and consumes their foes; anyone who wants to harm them must be killed in this manner." They can plague the earth "as often as they desire." Their plagues and signs mirror those of Moses, Elijah, and Jesus, but the two prophets avenge themselves against anyone who even "wishes to harm them." Then, suddenly, the beast from the abyss appears, without preparation or motivation, to conquer and kill them. The people of the earth "gaze at their dead bodies," refuse burial, "gloat over them and celebrate and exchange presents"! The whole episode seems to be archetypal, with just the quintessential elements of Christ's and a prophet's destiny: success, conflict, martyrdom, and personal afterlife.

Chapters 10 and 11 on prophecy are well integrated into the sequence of visions revolving around the blowing of the seven trumpets. In the scene of John's renewal to prophesy, the angel with the scroll announces that at the blowing of the seventh trumpet, that which God announced to his prophets will be fulfilled, and in the thanksgiving that the twenty-four elders sing, they mention specifically that "your servants, the prophets" will be rewarded. The sequence of the seven trumpets, as a whole, presents a variation on a pattern found earlier: The visions begin with the sacrificial offering of martyrs' prayers (8:3-5) and end with an enthronement scene.

Visions of Conflict, Judgment, and Deliverance (12:1–14:20)

After the blowing of the seventh trumpet (11:15-19), John sees another series of seven visions introduced by the verb "see," though they are not numbered explicitly (12:1, 3; 13:1, 11; 14:1, 6, 14). Conflict, introduced in chapter 11 between the two witnesses and the beast, also integrates these seven visions: conflict between a pregnant woman and a dragon (12:1-6, 13-17), the archangel Michael and Satan (12:7-12), a sea beast and the saints (13:1-9), an earth beast and the saints (13:11-18). Chapters 12 and 13 concentrate images of evil rarely equaled in other literatures. Virtually all references to evil in Revelation point ahead or back to those two chapters. Chapter 14 presents a divine perspective on those conflicts through a throne scene (14:1-5), announcements of judgment (14:6-13), and then two scenes of judgment (14:14-20).

Revelation 12:1 begins a new sequence of visions, but the first two sights are introduced in the same way as that in 11:19:

[19]Then God's temple in heaven was opened, and the ark of his covenant was seen [*ōphthē*] within his temple; and there were flashes of lightning, rumblings, peals of thunder, an earthquake, and heavy hail.

[1]And then a great portent was seen [*ōphthē*] in heaven. . . . [3]And there was seen [*ōphthē*] another portent in heaven. (AT)

Mother and Dragon (12:1-18)

This chapter coheres around the story of a birth. Somewhere in the heavens, a pregnant woman gives birth successfully to a royal messiah, in spite of a threatening dragon (12:1-6). Later, conflict between mother and dragon is played out again on earth (12:13-17). The transition to earth occurs by means of a war in heaven, which the archangel Michael and his angels pursues with the dragon. After losing to Michael, the dragon is thrown down to earth. In response, heaven rejoices, but woes come to earth (12:10-12). This chapter is filled with action that culminates in the dragon planning to make war on the mother's other children: "those who keep the commandments of God and hold the testimony of Jesus" (12:17).

◊ ◊ ◊ ◊

12:1-2: Word order emphasizes the portent that appears in heaven. Then the portent is described. "Portent" or "sign [*sēmeion*]" belongs to the same verbal root as "made it known [*esēmanen*]" in Rev 1:1. It indicates that more is present here than appears—the pregnant woman is more than pregnant woman, the dragon more than dragon—just as Judas's kiss signifies more than a kiss (Matt 26:48) or occurrences in temples during the second Punic war were more than occurrences (Polyb. 3.112; cf. Dan 5:9). Elsewhere in Revelation "portent" refers to the counterfeit marvels that the beast and his compatriots perform (13:13, 14; 16:14; 19:20).

The woman is located in the center of the sun, moon, and the twelve stars, and she controls them. By that location and control, she is revealed as a celestial goddess, similar to Ceres (Demeter) of Eleusis, Venus (Aphrodite) of Paphos, Diana (Artemis) of Ephesus, Proserpine (Persephone) of Hades, Mother of the Gods in Phrygia, Minerva (Athena) at Athens, Atargatis at Hieropolis, or Isis of Egypt (and in later Christianity, Mary, the mother of Jesus). The Isis inscriptions from Cyme describe her aptly: "I am she that riseth in the Dog Star . . . I divided the earth from the heaven. I showed the paths of the stars. I ordered the course of the sun and the moon. . . . I am in the rays of the sun. I inspect the courses of the sun"

(Grant 1953, 132-33; cf. Apuleius, *The Golden Ass* 11.2-4; *Syr. D.* 32). Her crown of twelve stars probably represents those stars of the zodiac (cf. Philo, *Vita Mos.* 2.124; *Ant.* 3.186), though they could be Ariadne's crown (Corona Borealis; cf. *Ap. Rhod.* 3.1002 and Tripp 1970 under "Ariadne").

Though dressed as a celestial goddess, her sole purpose in Rev 12 is to give birth. Otherwise, she acts only to flee to a divinely designated place. Birth pangs and birthing are images of transformation ("daybreak," *PGM* II.90-95; conversion, Gal 4:19; protection or restoration of Jerusalem, Isa 7:14; 26:16-21; 66:7-9; Mic 4:10; end-time events, 1 Thess 5:3; *Sib. Or.* 5.512-14).

12:3-4: The woman's antagonist is a "great fiery-red dragon," given emphasis by "behold" (RSV). He is the most powerful opponent of God in Revelation, with origins in those chaotic forces that opposed God at creation (note 9:1; Isa 27:1; *PGM* IV.994), or again in the form of Pharaoh (Ps 74:12-14; Ezek 29:3), and in the powers that try to keep Israel from returning from the Exile (Isa 51:9-10; *T. Asher* 7.3; also *ABD* under "Dragon and Sea, God's Conflict with"). Dragons usually are thought to have many heads; this one has seven (see Becker 1994 under "dragon"). Each head supports a diadem, indicating royal power (cf. *J.W.* 1.70), just as the celestial goddess's "crown of twelve stars" symbolizes royal power. He also has ten horns, as does the sea beast in chapter 13, the scarlet beast at 17:3, and the fourth beast in Daniel's vision (Dan 7:7).

His sweeping "down a third of the stars of heaven" recalls the scene at the fourth trumpet (8:12). Only here and in the trumpet visions do we encounter beings with tails (note 9:7-10). The verb "to sweep *(syrei)*" is used for "pulling" a net (John 21:8) or a person (Acts 14:19; 17:6; 4 Macc 6:1). The dragon must be located below the stars in order to pull them down with his tail (cf. Dan 8:10). This act may have occurred in connection with a battle such as that between Zeus and Typhon (Apollodorus, *The Library* 1.vi.3).

He stands before the woman, waiting for her to give birth, so that he can devour her child (compare scenes involving Python and

Leto/Apollo; see Tripp 1970 under "Leto," especially Hyginus's version; two serpents and Alcmene/Heracles; Tripp 1970 under "Heracles"; Titans and Rhea with male children, *Sib. Or.* 3.132-34; Typho and Isis/Horus, Herodotus 2.156; Pharaoh and Miriam/Moses, Exod 1; Herod and Mary/Jesus, Matt 2; *Apoc. Adam* 7; see also Yarbro Collins 1992).

12:5-6: The woman bears a male child, identified as the royal messiah by means of the image of the "iron rod" (note 2:26-29). The dragon is not able to destroy the child, for he is "snatched away" to the throne of God (cf. Acts 8:39; 2 Cor 12:2-4; 1 Thess 4:17). The woman flees into the desert or wilderness (cf. *Apoc. Adam* 7.9-16). "Wilderness" has paradoxical qualities: It is a place of drought, famine, demonic powers, dangerous animals, and akin to chaos prior to creation; on the other hand, it is a place of salvation, deliverance, and redemption (cf. CG under "desert"). Both aspects are reflected in Hosea's treatment of his unfaithful wife: "I will strip her naked and expose her as in the day she was born, and make her like a wilderness, and turn her into a parched land, and kill her with thirst. . . . Therefore, I will now allure her, and bring her into the wilderness, and speak tenderly to her" (Hos 2:3, 14). For the mother of Rev 12, the wilderness is a sanctuary, a place prepared for her by God, where she dwells for 1,260 days (note 11:2; 17:3-4; Ps 78:52; Jer 31:2).

12:7-9: This scene is introduced by a syntactical pattern similar to that of the dragon in 12:3:

Conjunction	And	And
Verb	appeared	broke out
Subject	another portent	war
	in heaven	in heaven
Explanatory clause	a great red dragon	angels . . .

Michael and the dragon engage in battle, each with a troop of angels (Michael: Dan 10:13; 12:1; Matt 25:41; Jude 9; Tob 12:15; *1 Enoch* 9.1; 20.5; 54.6; *Ascen. Is.* 3.16; *T. Levi* 5.5-6). Michael is victorious, and there is "no longer any place" in heaven for the dragon and his angels (for the idiom, "no longer any place," cf. 16:20; 18:21; 20:11).

The dragon is then identified in full (12:9). He is the ancient serpent (Gen 3:1, 14; 2 Cor 11:3; Wis 2:24; Ap. Rhod. 4.128, guardian of the golden fleece), the devil (2:10; 20:2, 10; Num 22:32; Job 1–2; Zech 3:1-2; Matt 4:1), and Satan (2:9, 13, 24; 3:9; 20:7; 1 Kgs 11:14; Luke 10:18; 2 Cor 11:14; 1 Tim 1:20). Both "devil" and "Satan" are terms for the adversary who deceives (e.g., 2:20; 20:3, 8, 10; 1 Kgs 11:14; Ps 108:6; Sir 19:15; 21:27; 2 Macc 14:27; *Ascen. Is.* 7.9-12; *Life of Adam and Eve [Vita]* 9-17). Compare this version of the "fall of Satan" to one in *2 Enoch,* where "Satan-ail" is "hurled from the height" on the second day of creation:

> But one from the order of the archangels deviated, together with the division that was under his authority. He thought up the impossible idea, that he might place his throne higher than the clouds which are above the earth, and that he might become equal to my power. And I hurled him out from the height, together with his angels. (*2 Enoch* 29; cf. Isa 14:12-15; Ezek 28:1-8)

12:10-12: A "loud voice" then acclaims God and his Messiah ("now," the time of the acclamation; "salvation," note 7:10; "power," note 4:11; "kingdom," note 1:9*a*; "authority," cf. 2:26-29; "Messiah," note 11:15). Motivation for the acclamation is threefold: First, "the accuser of our comrades has been thrown down" from heaven. The dragon-Satan is portrayed here, as elsewhere, as having been a kind of prosecuting attorney before God who brings charges against "our comrades" that is, the speaker identifies with fellow Christians (cf. 1 Kgs 22:19-23; 1 Chron 21:1; Job 1:6-12; Zech 3:1; *Apoc. Zeph.* 6.8-16). Second, the comrades conquer Satan "by the blood of the Lamb and by the word of their testimony" (note 1:5; 5:9; and 7:14). Third, the comrades "did not cling to life even in the face of death" (note 2:10 and 6:9). In the acclamation, there is no mention of the battle between Michael and the dragon or of the mother and the dragon. Moreover, salvation comes only to those in heaven. The acclamation ends, however, as does the battle between Michael and Satan, with Satan/devil being cast out of heaven to earth. The "voice" adds that Satan/devil is angry *(thymon megan)* and that he has only a short time to act on earth.

12:13-18: The dragon chase continues. This scene is not exactly a doublet of 12:1-6, for the woman has already given birth and the chase, now on earth, involves only her. She flies by the wings of an eagle (note 8:13) to "her place" in the desert, movement patterned after Israel's exodus to Mt. Sinai in the desert: "You have seen what I did to the Egyptians, and how I bore you on eagles' wings and brought you to myself" (Exod 19:4; note 12:6). Water supports the dragon, and earth is friendly to the mother (cf. "the earth laughed for joy beneath," as Leto gave birth to Apollo, *Homeric Hymn to Delian Apollo,* 118). As before, she is nourished in the desert for three and a half years (note 11:2; especially Dan 7:25; Deut 32:10-14).

The angry dragon wars not with the male child whose birth is described earlier, but with "the rest of her children" *(tōn loipōn tou spermatos autēs,* cf. Gen 3:15), "those who keep the commandments of God and hold the testimony of Jesus" (12:17; cf. 12:11). Chapter 12 concludes with the dragon standing by the seashore, where help will come from the water.

◊ ◊ ◊ ◊

The two portents—pregnant woman and great red dragon—portray the birth of a hero, who in this case is the Messiah (12:5). As typical in stories of the birth of a hero, the celestial goddess or Great Mother cries out in agony, while an antagonist seeks to destroy the child soon to be born. After the birth of the hero, one expects a reference to a battle between the Mother or Child or both, on the one hand, and the adversary, on the other, and then a sketch of the hero's life—his trials, his boon to humans, and the gathering of a community around him. Here in Revelation, however, the life of the hero/messiah is aborted: He is born and immediately ascends into heaven. (John is not writing a Gospel.) The mother also disappears, fleeing into the desert to a place prepared by God. Here, as elsewhere in John's writing, female figures are valued positively only as mother and wife; otherwise, they are portrayed as evil (2:20; 14:4; 17:3-9; 18; 19:7; 21:9). Both mother and child are relatively passive, as God acts on their behalf.

A battle with the dragon follows, but one initiated by the archangel Michael—not the hero/messiah. No motivation for the battle is given. Readers familiar with other stories about Satan being cast out of heaven might assume that Satan tried to be equal to God. Michael is victorious, and dragon/Satan is cast out of heaven to earth. A "loud voice in heaven" then acclaims, "Now have come . . . the kingdom of our God and the authority of his Messiah"; the male child reigns with God (12:10; cf. chapter 5).

Those sketches of the celestial goddess, the birth of the hero/messiah, and the fall of Satan from heaven set up the religious situation in this series of visions: conflict between those on earth who hold to "the testimony of Jesus" (children of the celestial mother, 12:17) and dragon/Satan, who was thrown to earth from heaven. Put differently, those sketches disclose suprahuman dimensions of Christian conflict with society. The conflict is moral not ontological, for evil comes into being as an act of rebellion against God, and God is the creator of all things (Rev 4), even of creatures and forces that rebel against him. The motive clauses of the acclamation allude to the religious situation set up, by referring to the brothers and sisters who have conquered "by the blood of the Lamb and by the word of their testimony" (12:11). Verse 17 makes it explicit: "Then the dragon was angry with the woman, and went off to make war on the rest of her children, those who keep the commandments of God and hold the testimony of Jesus." In short, this series of visions (12:1–14:20) describes suprahuman dimensions of the Christian situation, as John envisions it: the evil that they face, how that evil insinuates itself into society and culture, and how Christians are to conquer it.

Beasts and Saints (13:1-18)

Chapter 13 consists of two visions, one of a sea beast (13:1-10), the other of an earth beast (13:11-18). The first four verses parody the enthronement of the Lamb. The enthronement of the sea beast is, however, penultimate, for God will allow (note the passive verbs such as *edothē*) him to reign for only a short period of time. Action dominates over description, as the dragon (12:18) empowers the sea beast, and the sea beast empowers the earth beast. They are epitomes of evil: they blaspheme, entice worship, deceive with signs, and tattoo their devotees. Therefore, the saints must be watchful, faithful, and ready to endure captivity and death (13:7).

◊ ◊ ◊ ◊

13:1-2: As the dragon stands on the shore (12:18), a great beast is seen "rising up *[anabainon]*" from the sea (in contrast to the dragon who was cast down, *katebē*). The sea *(thalassa)* is an image of the abyss of chaos over which God had to be victorious in order to create an ordered world (note 9:2; 11:7; and 12:3-4; cf. Job 26:12-13; Pss 74:12-17; 89:9-10; 2 Esdr 6:52; *1 Enoch* 60.7; *Jos. Asen.* 12). Those powers of chaos continue to threaten divine creation until the monsters of chaos are overcome in the last days (Isa 27:1; Dan 7:3, 17). The sea beast has diadems (symbols of royal power) on its horns, not its head (see 12:3), and "blasphemous names" on its heads (cf. 17:3), either contemptuous names for God or names claiming divinity for the beast (note 2:8-9). "Leopard," "bear," and "lion" may allude to the beast/kingdoms of Dan 7:4-6, but they are common names for monstrous, dangerous animals (Hos 13:7-8; Wis 11:17-18; Sir 47:3-4; *Vita Mos.* 1.109; Strabo 17.3.7). According to Plutarch, Chrysippus said that the gods created "horses to accompany us to the wars . . . panthers (= leopards), bears, and lions as a school for training in bravery" (*Frag.* 193). So, for John, horses are associated with war, and the other three animals here with the dangerous and monstrous. Bears and leopards are also associated with Artemis; the lion with Cybele, Dionysus, and Aphrodite. The dragon transfers his royal power to the sea beast, so that he can make war on the rest of the woman's children. The transfer of "power," "throne," and "authority" from the dragon to the sea beast parallels and parodies the transfer of those qualities from God to Christ (cf. 12:10; note 3:21; 5:12; and 7:12).

13:3-4: Parody continues. One of the beast's heads appears "as slain" (AT; *hōs esphagmenēn;* NRSV: "seemed to have received a death-blow), like the Lamb (5:6). "Mortal wound *[hē plēgē tou thanatou]*" and "healed" form a pair analogous to "dead" and "am living" (see 1:18). The closest verbal parallel that I can find in other Greco-Roman literature is Plutarch's report of Antony's death: "Then he stabbed himself with his own sword through the belly and fell upon the bed. But the wound did not kill him quickly *[euthythanatos hē plēgē].* Presently, as he lay prostrate, the bleeding stopped and he came to himself and implored the bystanders to put him out of his pain" (*Anton.* 76.10; he eventually dies from the wound). In chapter 13 there are three versions of this wound:

Rev 13:3	Rev 13:12	Rev 13:14
And one of its heads appeared as slain unto death	the first beast whose	the beast who had
and the plague of his death	plague of his death	the plague of the sword
was healed	was healed	and he lived

The sea beast's recovery causes people to worship both the dragon and the beast, rather than God (note 3:8-9). "Who is like the beast" (cf. 18:18) mimics, for example, Ps 35:10, "O LORD, who is like you?" (cf. Exod 15:11; Ps 113:5). Finally, after the transfer of authority to the beast, the dragon recedes into the background (until his final defeat in chapter 20), as God does in the enthronement of the Lamb in chapters 4 and 5.

13:5-8: These verses recount what "was given" (*edothē,* by God) to the sea beast to do. He is allowed to blaspheme (speak contemptuously against) God, God's name, and those who live in heaven (cf. 7:15; 21:3; Dan 7:8). He is allowed authority for "forty-two months," the same length of time that the woman is nourished in the desert (12:6, 14), that the two witnesses "have authority" to perform their wonders and powers (11:6), and that "the nations" trample "the holy city" (note 11:2). The sea beast also is "allowed to make war on the saints and to conquer them" (cf. 11:7; Dan

7:21). In contrast to "the holy ones of God" on earth and in heaven, the "inhabitants of the earth" worship the dragon and the sea beast (note 6:10-11). "The book of life" has not been mentioned since 3:5 (see 3:5-6). "From the foundation of the world" goes here more naturally with "the Lamb that was slaughtered," as at 1 Pet 1:19-20, in contrast to Rev 17:8 (cf. *T. Moses* 1.14 where Moses is prepared from the foundation of the world to be the mediator of God's covenant).

13:9-10: A similar directive to "listen" ends each of the seven prophetic pronouncements in chapters 2 and 3. Revelation 13:10 takes the form of a proverbial pun: "Into captivity" has a slightly different meaning with the verb "to be" than with the verb "to go." "If anyone is destined to be a captive, he goes into captivity" (see Deissmann 1980, 120-21). The second proverb plays on "killed by a sword": "If anyone is to be killed by a sword, he is killed by a sword" (AT; cf. Jer 15:2; 43:11; Matt 26:52; Eph 4:8). The final statement calls the saints to endurance and faith (*hypomonē*; cf. 14:12; Luke 21:19, note 1:9*a*). The gist of the admonition seems to be to endure in faith rather than fight with the sword.

13:11-12: "Then I saw *[kai eidon]*" marks a new vision that calls attention to a second beast rising from the earth. In Jewish and ancient Near Eastern lore, there were two primordial beasts, one associated with the water and one with the earth:

> Then you kept in existence two living creatures; the one you called Behemoth and the name of the other Leviathan. And you separated one from the other, for the seventh part where the water had been gathered together could not hold them both. And you gave Behemoth one of the parts that had been dried up on the third day, to live in it, where there are a thousand mountains; but to Leviathan you gave the seventh part, the watery part; and you have kept them to be eaten by whom you wish, and when you wish. (2 Esdr 6:49-52; cf. Job 40–41)

According to *1 Enoch,* the earth beast "holds his chest in an invisible desert whose name is Dundayin, east of the garden of

Eden" (*1 Enoch* 60.8), and according to *2 Apoc. Bar.* "Behemoth will reveal itself from its place," and both Behemoth and Leviathan "will be nourishment" for those in the opulent days of the Messiah (*2 Apoc. Bar.* 29.4). Both primordial beasts thus have their place in the last days. The earth beast exercises the authority of both the dragon and the sea beast, and it has two horns like a Lamb (cf. 5:6; Dan 8:3). The earth beast also has authority to make the inhabitants of the earth worship the sea beast, who is here again described as "having been healed from a deadly blow" [13:3 AT]).

13:13-15: The earth beast deceives by performing great signs (*sēmeia,* note 12:1)—even making fire come down from heaven (cf. Elijah at 2 Kgs 1:10 or James and John at Luke 9:54; cf. the two witnesses, "fire pours from their mouth," Rev 11:5)—in the presence of the sea beast (on "deceiving": 2:20; 12:9; 18:23; 19:20; 20:3, 8, 10; Exod 4:8; Matt 24:24; Acts 6:8; 8:18; 2 Thess 2:9; *1 Enoch* 54.6; *Mart. Isa.* 4; Bar 2:11; *Did.* 16.4). "The beast and its image" recurs as a motif several times later (14:9, 11; 15:2; 16:2; 19:20; 20:4; Wis 14:16). The wound of the sea beast is described here as "the one who receives the blow of a sword and lived" (13:3 AT; cf. Antony at note 13:3-4). Giving breath to the image parodies the two witnesses (11:11).

13:16-17: After the living image killed those who would not worship it, the remainder—all social classes—are tattooed *(charagma)* on either their right hand or their forehead (cf. 14:9, 11; 16:2; 19:20; 20:4). A *charagma* is an imprint such as a serpent's mark, a brand on a camel, or an impress on a coin (see LSJ under *charagma;* Deissmann 1988, 240-47). It is the counterpart to the "seal *[sphragis]*" of God (7:3; 9:4; cf. 14:1; 22:4; Ezek 9:4). Both the tattoo and the seal mark the body to indicate membership in a community. For example, because of a confusion between Judaism and Dionysiac religion, Jews were branded, by decree of Ptolemy IV, "on their bodies by fire with the ivy-leaf symbol of Dionysus" (3 Macc 2:29). Initiates often have tattoos depicting dangerous or powerful animals such as serpents, scorpions, bulls, or lions (see CG under "tattooing"). Here the tattoo was of either the name of the sea beast or the number equivalent of the name. Having the tattoo had practical implications, for without it, no one could buy or sell; that is, the sea beast controlled all commerce and trade. ("Buy *[agorasai]*" is the same term translated as "ransom" in 5:9 or "redeemed" in 14:3, 4; cf. 3:18; 18:11.)

13:18: "This calls for" is the same construction as "here is a call" at 13:10 (cf. 17:9). The number of the beast, 666, is a "human number" (cf. "human measurement" at 21:17). Since each Greek letter also represents a number (John did not have available Arabic numerals), 666 was the sum of the numeric equivalents of the letters in a name. Many names have been calculated to have the sum of 666. A popular suggestion is the emperor Nero. In *Sib. Or.* 1.325-30, "Jesus" has the sum 888: "Then indeed the son of the great God will come, incarnate, likened to mortal men on earth, bearing four vowels, and the consonants in him are two. I will state explicitly the entire number for you. For eight units, and equal number of tens in addition to these, and eight hundreds will reveal the name to men who are sated with faithlessness" (cf. *Sib. Or.* 5.1-51).

◊ ◊ ◊ ◊

In this chapter, John describes, by mythic images of creation, the character and activity of evil that Christians face. Each of those beasts has its own history, but the Lord God overcame both of them in order to establish an ordered, stable world. At crucial moments in Israel's history, her opponents take on the face of one or the other of these primordial beasts, notably, at the exodus from Egypt and the Babylonian exile. They will not be overcome completely until the last days, when they will be eaten at banquet in the opulent days of the Messiah. They are dangerous to all earthlings, especially the holy ones of God, for they appear as divine powers and thereby deceive. The sea beast has divine names written on its seven heads (blasphemy from the seer's point of view). Like the Lamb, it appears "as slain." It died and came back to life—like Jesus Christ. The earth beast has two horns, perhaps in parody of the Lamb. He mimics the two witnesses of chapter 11 by making fire come down from heaven.

For the most part, parody and mythic imagery of creation are the sources for describing those two beasts, yet all of John's visions describe hidden, mythic dimensions of conflict in social life—especially, Asian life—as he envisions it. He reminds his readers of that by admonishing them at 13:9-10 and 13:18 and by the reference to buying and selling at 13:17. In a general way, the beasts disclose religious dimensions of the Roman Empire, which John sees as an evil empire (cf. Dan 7; 2 Esdr 12). Do the character and activity of the two beasts reveal anything more specific about the empire? One cannot be certain. When John describes the earth beast setting up an image of the sea beast, he may be alluding to hidden, demonic dimensions of imperial and provincial bureaucrats who erect temples, statues, and altars to the honor of emperors and Rome. So far as I know, images of the emperor at this time were never rigged up to speak. Nor were tattoos required for buying and selling. To identify them with images on coins stretches the tattoos beyond recognition. John invites his readers to calculate 666 as the number of a person, but he does not give the algorithm for calculating the number. As a visionary, John reveals the religious (mythic) rather than the social-political dimensions of the conflict between Christians and the world. He describes suprahuman forces derived from creation stories, seasonal rites, and etiologies of empires, forces that can illumine many different social, cultural situations, but especially the one John envisions for his first readers.

Judgment and Redemption (14:1-20)

This chapter consists of three visions (14:1-5; 6-13; 14-20) and seven scenes: a throne scene (14:1-5), followed by three angels, each announcing some aspect of judgment (14:6-7; 14:8; 14:9-11), a blessing (14:12-13), and two scenes describing judgment (14:14-16, 17-20). The throne scene reveals the powers that truly control the world, in contrast to the beasts who claim power in chapter 13.

◊ ◊ ◊ ◊

14:1: The Lamb was last mentioned in 7:17 (cf. 13:11) in connection with the multitude before the throne (7:17); the 144,000 were described in the scene previous to that (7:1-8). "Mount Zion" occurs only here in Revelation. It is the place to which Israel returns after the Exile and where people dwell to escape the terrible day of the Lord (Isa 24:23; 40:9-11; Joel 2:32; 2 Esdr 13:33-38). The writer of Hebrews describes Mount Zion appropriately:

> But you have come to Mount Zion and to the city of the living God, the heavenly Jerusalem, and to innumerable angels in festal gathering, and to the assembly of the firstborn who are enrolled in heaven, and to God the judge of all, and to the spirits of the righteous made perfect, and to Jesus, the mediator of a new covenant, and to the sprinkled blood that speaks a better word than the blood of Abel. (12:22-24)

Mount Zion is also the place where the king is enthroned: "I have set my king on Zion, my holy hill" (Ps 2:6). As all holy places, Mount Zion, the location of the temple in Jerusalem, opens to the heavenly throne: "The Lord is in his holy temple / The Lord's throne is in heaven" (Ps 11:4). As is clear from 14:3, "Mount Zion" here refers to a place in heaven with the 144,000 in the heavenly temple, "before the throne and before the four living creatures and before the elders."

The 144,000 have the name of the Lamb "and his Father's name written on their foreheads" (cf. 3:5, 12), in contrast to those in the previous scene who have on their foreheads the name of the beast (11:17). Throughout Revelation, the forehead is a favorite place to make a mark on the body to indicate one's identity and owner (note 7:2-3; 17:3, 5; 19:12; 22:4; possibly 3:12).

14:2-5: The voice from heaven that John hears is not identified specifically (cf. 10:4, 8; 11:12; 14:13; 18:4; Ps 103:7; Jer 51:55; Ezek 1:24; Sir 43:17). Nowhere else in Revelation is there mention of voices like harps, though the twenty-four elders have harps (note 5:8). The singers could be the harpists or heavenly angels, but from what follows, they are most likely the 144,000. They sing "a new song" (note 5:9-10) "before the throne and before the four living creatures and before the elders." Only the 144,000 who have been redeemed (*ēgorasmenoi*, cf. 5:9; 13:17) from the earth can learn the song (knowledge assumes purity, cf. 2:17; 19:12). "From the earth *[apo tēs gēs]*" occurs only here in Revelation (cf. 13:12); it may refer to being martyred (Acts 8:33; 22:22).

The 144,000 are virgins, not soiled by association with women (cf. 3:2-4, soiled/white. Examples of "soiled" or "defiled": Gen 37:31 Joseph's coat; Jer 23:10-11 prophet and priest; Cant 5:3 bathed feet; Zech 14:2 raped women; 2 Cor 7:1 Christians; Tob 3:15 Sarah). They follow the Lamb (Matt 8:19; 10:38; 19:28), having been "redeemed from humankind" (cf. 13:13, "before humankind"; NRSV: "in the sight of all") as "first fruits," a ritual, sacrificial term (cf. Exod 23:19; Jer 2:3; Rom 11:16; 1 Cor 16:15; Jas 1:18, compare Rom 16:5; Artem. 3.3). "In their mouth no lie was found" (14:5; Isa 53:9, contrast Rev 2:2; 13:5; Zeph 3:13), and "they are blameless *[amōmoi]*," only here in Revelation, but the meaning is very close to "holy *[hagios]*" (note 3:7; cf. Eph 1:4; 5:27; Phil 2:15; Col 1:22; Heb 9:14; 1 Pet 1:19; Jude 24). They are presented here as a special class of singers comparable to those of Artemis Leukophruēnē at Magnesia (*LSAM* 33.28-30; cf. 32.20).

14:6-7: Then John sees another angel (the last one was at 11:15) "flying in midheaven" (cf. the eagle at 8:13). He proclaims (*euaggelisai*, in Revelation, only here and 10:7) an "eternal gospel" (*euaggelion aiōnon*, only here in the NT) to those on earth (contrast the 144,000 who were redeemed from the earth). The content of this proclamation or gospel follows in 14:7. (Here, as in many other places, *euaggelion* refers simply to any good news; cf. Isa 60:6; Luke 1:19; *PGM* 5.142; *Tyr.* 9; *Ant.* 18.228-29). The angel urges "every nation and tribe and language and people" (note 5:9; 7:9; 13:7) to "fear God," that is, give him proper respect and awe (note 1:17-18; 15:4; 19:5), and give him "glory" (note 4:9). The hour of divine judgment provides the motive *(hoti)* for giving him glory. A final directive to worship the Creator, rather than the beast (13:12; 14:9), rounds out the proclamation (cf. 10:6). "Springs of water" are given a special category here in God's creation (contrast 10:6; "springs of water": 7:17; 21:6). The GNB translates the angel's proclamation as follows: "Honor God and praise his greatness! For the time has come for him to judge mankind. Worship him who made heaven, earth, sea, and the springs of water!"

14:8: Another angel abruptly introduces Babylon (cf. the introduction of the beast at 11:7). The collapse of her religion, government, and economy will be detailed later (18:1–19:4). "Babylon" may refer to the Mesopotamian city (Isa 21:9; Jer 51:6-10; Matt 1:12; *Sib. Or.* 5.434-46) or to Rome (1 Pet 5:13; *Sib. Or.* 5.159-60). This angel proclaims that Babylon has caused (encouraged) all nations to drink "from the wine of the passion of her lust" (AT; *ek tou oinou tou thymou tēs porneias autēs;* cf. Jer 51:7). The word translated here as "passion *[thymos]*" is the seat of emotions, including lust, anger, grief, and joy (cf. 12:12). The angel to follow will proclaim a similar phrase to refer to divine wrath: "drink the wine of God's wrath *[ek tou oinou tou thymou tou theou]*" (14:10). The two phrases should not be confused. Babylon's *porneia* echoes that of Jezebel's (note 2:20-23 and 17:1-2). As an image, "Babylon" stands for more than a reference to the city of Babylon or Rome. As a contrast to Mount Zion (14:1) and the 144,000, "Babylon" is an antonym to all that they represent, just as her *thymos* contrasts with the *thymos* of God.

14:9-11: A third angel then explains that those who worship the beast and receive its mark (13:15-16) will "drink the wine of God's wrath *[pietai ek tou oinou tou thymou tou theou]*" (cf. 16:19; 18:6, contrast the *thymou tēs porneias* above; 19:15). Moreover, this punishment will be "full strength." The image of judgment as drinking wine is a common one; for example, it is used against Jerusalem (Isa 51:17; *Pss. Sol.* 8.14), the nations (Jer 25:15), the wicked (Ps 75:8), Edom (Jer 49:12), and especially Babylon:

> "Alas for you who make your neighbors drink,
>   pouring out your wrath until they are drunk,
>   in order to gaze on their nakedness!"
> You will be sated with contempt instead of glory.
>   Drink, you yourself, and stagger!
> The cup in the LORD's right hand will come around to you,
>   and shame will come upon your glory! (Hab 2:15-16)

At Jer 51:7 Babylon is itself a "golden cup in the LORD's hand" used to punish the nations.

Further, those who bear the mark of the beast (13:16) "will be tormented with fire and sulfur" (14:10; note 9:16-19, cf. 9:5; 20:10; Matt 25:41; see also Gen 19:24, Sodom and Gomorrah; Ps 11:6, the wicked; Ezek 38:22, Gog), and their torment will be "in the presence of the holy angels and . . . the Lamb" (cf. 6:16). Seeing the blessed life with the Lamb makes the torment even greater. "Smoke" can be an image of either God's positive presence or a result of the fire of his judgment (note 9:5; 19:1-3; cf. 8:4, incense; 9:2, shaft of the abyss; 9:17, from mouths of locusts; 15:8, glory of God; 18:9, 18; 19:3, punishment of Babylon). In contrast to those who "die in the Lord" (14:13), the beast worshipers will have no rest for eternity (cf. 4:8). In brief, those who worship the beast and receive his mark will live, buy, and sell (13:15-17) in the short run, but in the long run they will meet with disaster.

14:12-13: Someone—it is not clear who—repeats part of the formula of 13:10 (see note 13:9-10), adding a further definition of "saints": "those who keep the commandments of God and hold fast to the faith of Jesus" (cf. 12:17). A voice from heaven then directs John to write (contrast 10:4): "Blessed are the dead who from now on die [united with] the Lord"; probably a martyr's death is assumed. This beatitude (note 1:3) reinforces the "call for endurance." One class of the dead, those dying steadfastly in the Lord, are blessed, for the Lord holds the keys to death and Hades (1:18). "From now on" refers to the time right around when the beatitude was announced (cf. Matt 23:39; 26:29, 64; John 14:7). In antiphonal response, the spirit elaborates their blessedness (the spirit speaks only here and at 22:17, but cf. 2:7, 11, 17, 29; 3:6, 13, 22. For "labors" see 2:2, 23; 16:11; 18:6; 20:12-13).

14:14-16: By means of cloud locomotion (1:7; 10:1; 11:12), one like a human, a divine being but not Jesus (note 1:13-16), appears in royal insignia (note 4:4), carrying a sharp sickle—an image of judgment—to reap the ripe earth (in judgment), an image that will recur six times in the rest of this chapter. An angel directs the divine being to reap the earth's grain with his sickle (cf. Hos 6:11; Joel 3:13; Matt 13:30, 39-43; Mark 4:29). Once again, it is stressed, the hour of judgment has come (14:7).

14:17-20: An angel with authority over the altar fire (note 2:1–3:22; 6:9) orders "another angel" to harvest—another image of judgment—"the clusters of [grapes]" (cf. *Cat.* 20, *tis ara tas ampelous trygēsei*). "Wine press *[lēnon]*" appears here for the first time (14:20; 19:15; Isa 63:2-3; Lam 1:15). "City" appears abruptly without identification, but its most immediate antecedent is Babylon (14:8; note 11:2). It could refer back to the heavenly Mount Zion or Jerusalem at 14:1. For the height of the wine/blood, compare *1 Enoch* 100.3, "The horse will walk through the blood of sinners up to his chest," and 2 Esdr 15:35, "And there shall be blood from the sword as high as a horse's belly. . . ." Association of "blood" and the "grape" is fairly common, because the juice of the grape resembles blood (Gen 49:11; Deut 32:14). Here "the blood of the grape" represents judgment and death, not immortality and life as in the Eucharist and Dionysiac rituals.

◊ ◊ ◊ ◊

At various points, this series of visions directs Christians on how to respond to their religious situation, that is, their situation from John's prophetic, visionary point of view that uncovers what is most fundamental for them to know. They will be victorious "by the blood of the Lamb and by the word of their testimony" (12:11). They will succeed by "not clinging to life even in the face of death" (see 12:11). They are urged to "keep the commandments of God and hold the testimony of Jesus" (12:17). They will be victorious by steadfast endurance, not by using the sword. Revelation 14:1-5 describes the destiny of one class of faithful Christians who contrast with the beasts and their followers. Although the language is different—more mythic and visionary—the motifs are the same as those in chapters 2 and 3, where the seven congregations are urged not to compromise with the forces of evil but to be steadfast and to endure patiently in tribulation so that they may reign in glory.

Messages in the second vision of chapter 14 (14:6-13) direct those who dwell on the earth—every nation and tribe and language and people—to read the religious situation correctly: God, not the beast, is to be worshiped, for God is the creator of all things; and he, not the sea beast or the earth beast, controls "earth," "sea," and "springs of water." Babylon, John's image for describing the religious dimensions of the Roman Empire, has fallen (see chapter 17). She has caused "all nations to drink of the wine of the passion of her fornication" (14:8 AT), but those who receive the mark of the beast will "drink the wine of God's wrath," tormented with fire and sulfur, without rest (14:10; cf. 20:10). The faithful dead, in contrast, will rest in blessedness from their labors.

The final vision (14:14-20) underscores the religious situation as a time of judgment. Through images of sickle and harvesting, the ripe earth is reaped and the grapes are gathered and pressed. The blood of the grape—an image of judgment and death—runs deep through a wide area "outside the city." The city is not identified. There may be a play on Babylon's causing nations to drink the wine (or blood of the grape) of the passion of her fornication (14:8) or it may refer back to Mount Zion (11:1-13; 14:1), indicating that the judgment occurs "outside" the sacred precincts.

VISIONS OF SEVEN LAST PLAGUES (15:1–16:21)

John introduces this series of visions as "another portent in heaven," just as he did the last series (12:1-3). Revelation 15:1 serves as a title for the series, which consists of a throne scene (15:1–16:1) and seven divine judgments presented under the image of "seven bowls of wrath" (see 16:2-21). Pouring out the bowls continues the wrath and judgment of God begun in chapter 14. This is the final set of numbered visions in Revelation (seven prophetic pronouncements, 2:1–3:22; seven seals, 6:1–8:1; and seven trumpets, 8:2–11:19).

Heavenly Throne Scene (15:1–16:1)

In this throne scene, John first sees "those who had conquered the beast" as they sing praises before the throne of God. They acclaim God's deeds and ways in lofty, hymnic style. A theophany then occurs, as the "temple of the tent of witness" opens to reveal the glory of God. From the open temple the seven angels with the seven plagues of God's wrath come forth to spread destruction on the earth. The scene thus involves two kinds of actions: singing and plaguing. Dramatic tension builds with this series, for these seven plagues "are the last."

◊ ◊ ◊ ◊

15:1: "Another portent," more amazing than the first two (12:1, 3), consists of the "last seven plagues" of God's "wrath" (i.e., divine desire, *thymos;* note 14:8). The finality (completion) of these plagues is emphasized through repetition ("last," "ended"; on "plague," see 9:18). In Revelation "last" *(eschatos)* refers to "last things" only in connection with these seven plagues (here and at 21:9).

15:2: John sees those who conquered the beast and its image (13:15, 17) standing upon the sea of glass before the throne (4:6), a sea "mixed with fire" (see Ezek 1:27; Dio Cassius 48.51.1). The victory of the beast (13:7) is penultimate, for the faithful conquered him "by the blood of the Lamb" (12:11; cf. 7:14). A harp (*kithara;* only here and at 5:8) is a familiar musical instrument. All young gentlemen at Teos, a town between Smyrna and Ephesus, had to play it before they could enter the city's young men's association (MM under *kitharizō*).

15:3-4: Moses sang two songs, one after victory at the Red Sea (Exod 15) and one near the end of his life (Deut 32). The two are not always kept separate (see *Ebr.* 111). The primary reference here is to the song sung at the Red Sea (though compare the opening four lines to Deut 32:4). According to Philo, the Therapeutai, a Jewish contemplative order, sang such a song at Passover (festival celebrating the exodus from Egypt), in imitation "of that one which, in old time, was established by the Red Sea, on account of the wondrous works which were displayed there" (cf. *Vita Cont.* 84-88). In the Song of Moses (Exod 15), God is praised for overcoming Pharaoh, but he is also acclaimed as victor over the waters of the chaotic deep (Exod 15:8; cf. Ps 89:8-10; Isa 51:9-10).

In Revelation, those who conquered the beast—also related to the chaotic deep (note 9:1; 13:1-2)—stand beside the sea and celebrate, praising God for their victory. They sing in a lofty, hymnic style (parallelism, rhetorical question, and "for *[hoti]*" clauses; cf. 5:9-10; also Peterson 1926, 134). As they address "Lord God the Almighty" (note 1:8) and the "King of the nations" (variant, "King of the ages"), they acclaim his marvelous deeds (Pss 111:2; 139:14) and his "just and true ways" (note 3:7; 16:4-7; Deut 32:4; Ps 145:17). Their song of praise at the same time echoes Jeremiah's taunting of other so-called divine beings: "There is none like you, O LORD; you are great, and your name is great in might. Who would not fear you, O King of the nations? For that is your due. . . . They [so-called gods] are both stupid and foolish; the instruction given by idols is no better than wood!" (Jer 10:6-8; cf. Exod 15:11). God *alone* is "holy" (*hosios*, not the more common *hagios*; see 3:7), and for that reason, those who have conquered the beast praise God. It is ludicrous to worship idols such as the beast and its image. Two more reasons for praising the Lord follow: "all nations will come and worship before you" (cf. Ps 86:8-10; Isa 2:2, at the restored Jerusalem) and "your righteous deeds *[dikaiōmata;* NRSV: "judgments"] have been revealed. "Righteous deeds" occurs only here and at Rev 19:8 where the fine linen in which the bride of the Lamb is clothed "is the righteous deeds of the saints." Note the parallel drawn between the Lord and the saints.

15:5: John's focus then shifts to the opening of the "temple [*naos;* note 3:12-13] of the tent of witness in heaven." According to Exod 40, the "tent of witness" was a portable shrine built according to a heavenly pattern (Exod 25:9). Only the priests could enter it (Lev 10:8; 1 Kgs 8:10). Elsewhere in early Christian literature, the heavenly pattern of the tent, not the earthly tent, is of interest (Acts 7:44; Heb 8:5), and it is that heavenly pattern that John sees.

15:6–16:1: The angels are dressed in linen *(linon)*, like the bride of the Lamb (19:8) and the heavenly army (19:14)—though the Greek word in the latter two instances is *byssinos*—and they have a "golden sash across their chests," similar to the Likeness of a Human at 1:13. They are given "seven golden bowls full of the wrath [thymou] of God" from which they pour their plagues (cf. 8:3, 5). "Glory [doxa]" sometimes is equivalent to light and bright splendor (18:1; 21:23), but here it creates smoke (cf. 8:4). A connection is made between the divine wrath in the golden bowls, divine glory in the temple (cf. Exod 40:34; 1 Kgs 8:10; Isa 6:4), and smoke; for the smoke of his glory fills the temple until his wrath is ended. Immediately after the statement that "no one could enter the temple," John hears a commanding voice from the temple directing the angels to pour out wrath upon the earth (cf. 16:17; Isa 66:6, "A voice from the temple! The voice of the LORD, dealing retribution to his enemies!"). The angels then begin to carry out the final plagues (cf. Ps 69:24; Jer 10:23-25; Ezek 14:19; Zeph 3:8; note 14:8, 9-11).

◊　◊　◊　◊

In this scene, victory over the beasts is set in deliberate parallel with the ancient victory of Moses and the Israelites over Pharaoh at the Red Sea. That victory is the centerpiece of the Passover celebration, which was and is probably the most important celebration in the round of festivals in Judaism. The victorious saints in Revelation are also at a sea, and there they sing the song of Moses (and the Lamb). "Lamb" resonates with Passover, for at Passover a lamb is slain (Exod 12). And the Israelites are saved by its blood (Exod 12:7), just as the saints in Revelation are victorious by the Lamb's blood (5:9-10). The destruction at the pouring out of the bowls reflects the plagues on Egypt. After deliverance from Pharaoh, the Israelites carried the "tent of witness" through the wilderness, for there Moses and others went to meet God. The victory over Pharaoh and beast also alludes to God's victory at creation, when he created order and stability by containing the primordial monsters of chaos. The seer thus draws into this scene both the cosmos-wide creation and a crucial moment in the religious history of the Israelites.

Revelation 15 draws its power from those particular understandings of creation and Exodus/Passover in Israelite/Jewish religious history. From John's Christian point of view, such usurpation of Jewish motifs was appropriate, for the Lamb and Christian congregations brought to completion that earlier history of Judaism. Jews in Asia who celebrated Passover and gathered regularly in their synagogues saw it differently: To them the Christian Lamb cannot claim rights to the Passover lamb, for the Passover lamb rightfully belongs to the Jews in their annual celebration of freedom from slavery in Egypt. If "synagogue of Satan" in the pronouncements to Smyrna and Philadelphia refer to Jews (2:9; 3:9), then one can see why the Jews of John's time were such a threat to him and his message (comment after 3:12-13).

Pouring Out the Seven Bowls (16:2-21)

In this fourth and final series of seven, as each angel pours out a bowl at command of "a loud voice from the temple," a scene of disaster balloons out. In contrast to the series of seven seals and seven trumpets, in this series, the seventh (bowl) follows immediately after the sixth. In the scenes of disaster, the pouring out of the bowls is linked to the beasts and to Babylon (especially 16:2, 10-21), looking back to chapters 13–14 and ahead to chapters 17–18.

◊ ◊ ◊ ◊

16:2: The pouring out of the first bowl brings "a foul and painful sore [*helkos,* here and 16:11] on those who had the mark of the beast and who worshiped its image" (13:14-17; cf. 14:9-10). That plague echoes the sixth plague brought upon the Egyptians through the hand of Moses (Exod 9:10; cf. also Deut 28:35; Luke 16:21).

16:3: The second bowl, like the second trumpet (8:8-9), turns the sea into blood. "Like the blood of a corpse" refers to blood that is thick and coagulated (see Galen's commentary on Hippocrates' "A Prescribed Regimen of Life" 15.782). As a result, every living thing *(pasa psychē zōēs)* in the sea dies.

16:4-7: The third bowl, like the third trumpet (note 8:10-11), destroys rivers and springs of water. Those waters turn into blood, as did the streams of Egypt: "He turned their rivers to blood, so that they could not drink of their streams" (Ps 78:44; cf. Exod 7:14-19). Angels oversee various aspects of human life and nature (note 2:1–3:22), so here the angel responsible for the waters acclaims the justness of God for turning the waters into blood (also *1 Enoch* 66.2). Addressing God, he acclaims the Holy One as just for bringing the plague (only here in Revelation; cf. 15:3; 16:7; 19:2). The talion (punishment identical to the offense) in 16:6 is given as another reason for God's being just: Those who shed blood now drink it. In an antiphonal acclamation, the "altar" —angel of the altar or those under the altar (6:9; note 8:3-4)— affirms that God's "judgments are true and just" (see 15:3; 19:2; Dan 3:27-28 LXX).

16:8-9: While the fourth trumpet (8:12) darkened the sun, the fourth bowl burns humans (contrast those before the throne whom "the sun will not strike, . . . nor any scorching heat," 7:16). In response, they blaspheme the one who brings calamities upon them (note 13:5-8). He is not one whom they care to glorify (so at the sixth trumpet, 9:20-21 and the fifth bowl, 16:11; contrast 11:13).

16:10-11: At 13:2, Satan gave his throne to the sea beast; now an angel plunges that throne-kingdom into darkness, just as the God of Moses darkened Pharaoh's kingdom (Exod 10:21; note 8:12). The allusion to the exodus from Egypt may also suggest that just as "the chaotic deep" was disclosed in the pharaoh of Egypt (note 15:3-4), so here "the chaotic deep" (the sea beast) is revealed in imperial Rome (cf. also 2:13, the throne of Satan at Pergamum). "Gnawing" can be an image of mocking the right (Philostratus, *Life of Apollonius* 7.21) as well as punishment (*Apoc. Peter* Akmim 28). As well as gnawing, people curse "the God of heaven" (note 11:13). In that sentence, *ek* forms a wordplay: They "cursed the God of heaven because of [*ek*] their pains and sores, and they did not repent of [*ek*] their deeds." Their pain and agony contrasts with those in the new Jerusalem, where there will be no pain (21:4).

16:12: The sixth angel dries up the Euphrates River (cf. the sixth trumpet, 9:13-14). Drying up a river can be good or bad depending upon whom it benefits (cf. Exod 14; Josh 3; Ps 106:9; Isa 11:15; 44:27; Jer 50:38; 2 Esdr 13:44). Some listening to Revelation may also recall how Cyrus the Persian entered Babylon by redirecting the river and walking across the riverbed (Herodotus, *History* 1.191). Drying up the river here is positive in that it allows the "kings from the east" to pass over and gather at Harmagedon and, thus, hasten the end.

16:13-14: John then sees three "unclean spirits" (AT) coming from the mouths of the dragon, the sea beast, and the false prophet (= earth beast, 19:20 and 13:14). "Unclean spirits *[pneumata akatharta]*" can refer to demons and that which is either ritually or morally unclean. For example, Xanthus says about his shrine to the god Mēn Tyrannus: "Let no uncleanness enter: Let him be clean from garlic, pigs, and woman" (MM under *akathartos*). In the Gospels, Jesus and his disciples have authority over unclean spirits (Matt 10:1; 12:43; Mark 3:11; 5:12; Luke 4:33; cf. *T. Benj.* 5.2; *PGM* IV.1227-64), and according to Zechariah, on the Day of the Lord, God will remove every unclean spirit (Zech 13:2). The "unclean spirits" are "demonic spirits" (note 9:20; cf. Ps 96:5; Acts 17:18), dwellers in desolate places (18:2). They become the agents for assembling the kings of the earth (note 1:5), including those from the east. ("To assemble *[synagagein]*" always refers in Revelation to battle preparation, 16:16; 19:17, 19; 20:8; for "war," compare the following scenes: 9:7; 11:7; 12:7, 17; 13:7; 19:19; 20:8; for "the great day," note 6:17.) In connection with the "great day," God is appropriately "the Almighty *[pantokratōr]*," the warrior god.

In Jewish law, "frogs" are unclean animals (Lev 11:9-10, 41). Artemidorus says that frogs represent "wizards, sorcerers, and cheats" (2.15). Pliny also associates them with magic and sorcery (*Natural History* 18.294.361; 32.48). In medieval Christianity, the frog is an image of the devil and heretics (see Biedermann 1992 under "frogs"). At *PGM* XXXVI.324, frogs are associated with fertility. During the second plague on Egypt, frogs swarm the land (Exod 8:1).

16:15-16: The "great day" is synchronized with the several mentions of "I" that follow. The "I" is Christ, who comes suddenly and without warning as a thief to those who are not watchful (note 3:2-4). In the beatitude, "staying awake" ("watchful") parallels "keeping one's clothes in order" (cf. "soiling," note 3:4; Jas 5:2; "pure clothes," 15:6). If not alert, one will appear naked and shamed before Christ (3:18). "Shame *[aschēmosynēn]*" refers to the exposure of the sexual organs (Lev 18:6; 1 Cor 12:23). Watchful followers of Christ cover their sexual organs, while the evil whore is naked (17:16).

The narrative in third-person plural continues (reading *synēgagon*) with the three spirits gathering the kings of the earth at "Harmagedon," more familiarly known as "Armageddon." There they will battle "on the great day of God the Almighty." In Hebrew (note 9:11), *Armagedōn* means "the hill" *(har)* of Megiddo. Explanations of the term are numerous and inconclusive (see *ABD* under "Armageddon"). For that reason, it invites speculation and has taken on much greater importance in the interpretation of Revelation than is warranted by its one-time occurrence at the pouring out of the sixth bowl. It probably should be associated in some way with Zech 12:11, "On that day the mourning in Jerusalem will be as great as the mourning for Hadad-rimmon in the plain of Megiddo." That verse in Zechariah follows the one alluded to at Rev 1:7: "when they look on me whom they have pierced, they shall mourn for him" (Zech 12:10; note 1:7).

16:17-21: The "air" between earth and sky contains demons, gods, and spirits (*PGM* XIII.825-35; VII.311-16; IV.2699; I.129). So, Plutarch writes that the priest of Jupiter does not anoint himself in "the open air and the space beneath the heavens, since it was full of gods and spirits" (*Quaest. Rom.* 40. 274B; cf. Eph 2.2; *T. Benj.* 3.4 "the airy spirit of Beliar"). After a voice from the temple declares that the final plagues are finished, the presence of God is revealed in storm imagery (note 4:5; 6:12). A voice from the temple affirms, "it is done" or "it has happened" (*gegonen;* cf. 21:6). That verbal root recurs several times in the narrative that follows:

> "It has happened." Then happened flashes of lightning, rumblings, peals of thunder, and a great earthquake happened, such as has not

happened upon earth [Dan 12:1]. And it happened that the great city [split] into three parts. (AT)

The "great city" is probably Babylon, though it could be Jerusalem (note 11:8; 14:8): "The great city was split into three parts (from the violent earthquake; cf. Zech 14:4), and the cities of the nations also fell. And so *[kai]* God remembered great Babylon. . . " (AT). The city that gave her wine-cup of sexual [idolatrous] passion to the nations now receives a wine-cup filled with the passion of God's wrath (note 14:8). The scene here described is similar to that of the Day of Wrath at the opening of the sixth seal (6:12-17; cf. 8:7 and Exod 9:23). As at the pouring out of the fourth bowl, unbelievers blaspheme (curse) God "for the plague."

◊ ◊ ◊ ◊

Those seven last plagues bring harm and destruction strikingly similar to that which came when the seven angels blew their trumpets (8:7–9:21; 11:15-19). In each series, the first four plagues bring disaster to earth, sea, rivers and springs of water, and heavenly lights, respectively. The fifth bowl that plunges the throne-kingdom of the beast into darkness parallels the darkness that came from the bottomless pit (note 16:11), and the sixth in both series involves troops coming from the river Euphrates. Finally, just as the opening of the heavenly temple brought "flashes of lightning, rumblings, peals of thunder, an earthquake, and heavy hail" (11:19), so the pouring out of the seventh bowl brought "flashes of lightning, rumblings, peals of thunder, and a violent earthquake" (16:18). The pouring out of the seven bowls is more final only because of their position in the book as a whole. The seven trumpet blasts are linked to the tablets of destiny involved in the Lamb's enthronement, whereas the seven bowls occur immediately before the final defeat of the beasts and Babylon the whore (17:1–20:10).

Those seven last plagues, along with the blowing of the seven trumpets (8:7–9:21; 11:15-19), belong to a cycle of texts in which God brings judgment against those who stand outside the circle of faithfulness: plagues in Egypt, covenantal curses to those not obedient, judgments against nations that harm Israel, events associated with Israel's exile in Babylon and return to Jerusalem, and signs accompanying the eschatological Day of the Lord (see references). The finality of the bowls points to the final day of God's judgment, but many of the images depend upon two decisive moments in Israel's religious history—the exodus from Egypt and the exile to and return from Babylon. Thus, these final plagues continue to draw heavily from Israel's religious history to portray the judgments of God, as did the prior throne scene (Rev 15). To a lesser extent, they draw from non-Jewish religious traditions (e.g., the seventh bowl).

VISIONS OF VICTORY OVER BABYLON THE WHORE AND THE BEASTS (17:1–19:10)

These visions consist of narrative, lament, and rejoicing regarding the final defeat of Babylon the whore. First, one of the seven angels from the previous series shows John "the judgment of the great whore" (17:1-6) and then explains—in a fashion—the meaning of the mystery (17:7-18). Chapter 18 recounts different responses to the fall of Babylon (alluded to in 14:8): First, an angel describes Babylon's fall (18:1-3), followed by an exhortation to the faithful to come out of her (18:4-8). Then kings and merchants lament over her (18:9-19), while heaven rejoices at her demise (18:20-24). All those around the throne rejoice at Babylon's fall, which makes way for the marriage of the Lamb (19:1-8). This sequence concludes with an exchange between John and an angel (19:9-10).

Babylon the Whore Riding the Beast (17:1-18)

This chapter coheres around a vision of a whore, which John is shown in the desert and an angelic interpretation of what that vision means. One of the angels who had the seven bowls explains the mystery along the lines of explanation given of the number of the beast (13:18). Neither unveils the mystery very much, though in chapter 17, the angel explains each item in the vision.

◊ ◊ ◊ ◊

17:1-2: One of the seven angels of chapter 16 takes the role of guide and interpreter for this vision. The angel says much the same thing to John at 21:9, where he shows John a contrasting woman, the bride of the Lamb. "Show" here suggests a disclosure that the angel will reveal (note 1:1-3). John will see a "judgment *[krima],*" a new term in Revelation (cf. 18:20; 20:4) that refers to a judicial verdict of condemnation (cf. Luke 24:20; 2 Pet 2:3; *1 Clem* 51.3). "The great whore"—we are supposed to know who she is (note 14:8)—occurs only here and at 19:2 where a multitude rejoice at her condemnation. Using the image of "whore/harlot" to describe a wicked city—"the woman you saw is the great city that rules over the kings of the earth" (17:18)—is a common motif in Old Testament prophecy. For example, Nahum calls the city of Nineveh a whore (Nah 3:4; the whole of Nah 3 is echoed in Rev 17–18), and Isaiah names Jerusalem as a whore in 1:21. Jeremiah refers to Babylon as "you who live by many waters" (Jer 51:13). "Committing fornication" usually is an image for idolatry (note 2:14-15; 14:8), but it can also refer to engaging in commerce with someone. So, Isaiah says about Tyre that she "will prostitute herself with all the kingdoms of the world on the face of the earth" (MT), which the LXX translates as, she "will be an emporium with all the kings of the earth" (Isa 23:17; cf. Rev 13:16-17; 18:3).

17:3-4: Possessed by the spirit (note 1:9*b*-10 and 4:2-3), John is taken into the desert *(erēmon),* where the mother in chapter 12 went for protection (note 12:5-6). Here, however, the desert (or wilderness)—an earthly analogue to the abyss (Ezek 26:19)—is associated, as it is later, with desolation, danger, and threatening powers such as demons, unclean birds, and unclean beasts (note 12:5-6; cf. 17:16-17; 18:2). At 17:16, the whore is "made into a wilderness" (AT; *erēmōmenēn;* cf. 18:17, 19), that is, "made desolate." The whore, "clothed in purple and scarlet," sits upon a "scarlet beast." ("Well-to-do Romans, including women, traveled on horseback [not on the back of a beast!]," *OCD* under "horses"; *Quaest. Rom.* 83, 284A; Apuleius, *The Golden Ass* 1.2). The colors of the clothing point up her wealth and high status, for "scarlet" was an honorable color worn by Roman soldiers (Matt 27:28); and in pawnshops, scarlet clothing was more valuable than white clothes (MM under *kokkinos;* cf. 2 Sam 1:24). More is involved here than high-class prostitution. Conversants in Plutarch's *Table-Talk* say: "At perfume and purple clothing, because of their excessive costliness, we quite properly look askance . . ." (*Quaest. conv.* 3.2, 646B). "Scarlet" is also an image for sin, which is intended in her description (Isa 1:18; *1 Clem* 8.4). The "scarlet beast" has "seven heads and ten horns" and "blasphemous names" like the sea beast in 13:1 (cf. Dan 7:7, 24).

The woman/city is also "adorned with gold and jewels and pearls," like the new Jerusalem (21:11, 19, 21; cf. 18:16). She holds a "golden cup"—Jeremiah calls Babylon a "golden cup in the LORD's hand" (Jer 51:7)—full of abominations *(bdelygmatōn)* and impurities (cf. 21:27; Matt 24:15 "the desolating sacrilege *[bdelygma tēs erēmōseōs]*"; and Dan 11:31. The whore is also a desolation, 17:16).

17:5-7: The placard is, of course, written from John's, not the woman's, point of view (cf. Jezebel; note 2:20-23). On her forehead—a favorite place for marking—is a mysterious statement (note 10:3-7; 17:7), "Babylon the great, mother of whores and of earth's abominations" (17:5). To complete her abominations, she is said to be "drunk with the blood of the saints and the blood of the witnesses to Jesus" (17:6). Earlier, "inhabitants of the earth" (NRSV: "all nations") were drunk on her wine (14:8); here she is drunk on blood (note 6:10-11; 16:4-7; and 19:2). John is amazed, an inappropriate response for a Christian to make; only those who do not follow the Lamb usually marvel at such things (13:3; 17:8).

17:8: The angel begins to interpret the "mystery" (note 10:3-7; cf. Dan 7; 2 Esdr 12). First, he explains the mystery of the beast that carries the woman. The beast "was, and is not, and is about to ascend from the bottomless pit," that is, the beast was alive, died, and is about to ascend from the abyss of death and Hades (cf. 11:7; note 13:3-4). The biography of the beast parodies that of Christ at 1:18. There is one major difference, however: the beast goes ultimately "to destruction *[apōleian;* see note 9:11]." Nonetheless, those "whose names have not been written in the book of life" will be amazed, for the beast "was and is not and is to come *[parestai]*," a parody of the divine epithet in 1:8 as well as of Jesus Christ (1:18; cf. the beast at 13:3, 12, 14).

17:9: As at 13:18, "wisdom" is conveyed by revelation, esoteric information from God that allows the angel to unpack the meaning of the mystery. It is a common motif in related literatures, for example, that revelation is the means for interpreting dreams (Dan 2:21-23; 2 Esdr 13.53), the stars (*1 Enoch* 82.2), or visions (*1 Enoch* 37). Wisdom here explains by allegorical interpretation.

The seven heads of the beast are seven mountains or hills. Compare *1 Enoch* 24.1-4:

> From there I went to another place of the earth, and he showed me a mountain of fire which was flaming day and night. And I went in its direction and saw seven dignified mountains—all different one from the other, of precious and beautiful stones. . . . The seven mountains . . . (in respect to) their heights all resembled the seat of a throne (which is) surrounded by fragrant trees. And among them, there was one tree such as I have never at all smelled.

Hermas, on the other hand, saw twelve mountains in a vision (*Herm. Sim.* 9.1.4). The seven mountains *(hepta orē)* may be a reference to the seven hills of Rome. When referring to Rome, however, the more common phrase is "seven-hilled *[heptalophos]*" (e.g., *Sib. Or.* 2.18; 13.45; 14.108). Plutarch discusses briefly the December festival of Septimontium (= Heptalophos), the commemoration of the addition of the seventh hill, "by which Rome was made a city of seven hills *[heptalophon]*" (*Quaest. Rom.* 69, 280D).

Almost as an afterthought, or perhaps as a further clarification, the angel explains that the seven heads are also "seven kings *[basileis hepta]*." Roman emperors are referred to as kings (*basileis, J.W.* 3.351; 4.596; *PGM* IV.2445-55), but elsewhere in the New Testament, they are referred to as Caesar (*kaisar;* e.g., Mark 12:17; Luke 2:1; John 19:12; Acts 17:7; 26:32; Phil 4:22). In the New Testament, "king," in reference to humans, is used as a term for a non-Roman ruler or as a more generic term for a ruler, which can include the Roman emperor (e.g., Acts 25:24; 2 Cor 11:32; 1 Tim 2:1-2; 1 Pet 2:13, "For the sake of the Lord, submit to every human institution, whether to a king as supreme or to governors sent by him" [AT]). The angel here is probably referring to seven Roman emperors, but his choice of words leaves it somewhat ambiguous.

17:10: Five of the seven kings have "fallen," which assumes some kind of destruction or ruin, such as falling in battle, and not simply an ordinary death (14:8; 18:2). One "is *[estin]*," that is, "is ruling," and the remaining one "has not yet come *[oupō elthen]*." "When he comes in a little while *[oligon]*, he must remain" (AT; *oligon* occurs after verbs of motion; cf. Mark 1:19; 6:31; Luke 5:3; Rev 20:3; and elsewhere in Revelation, after verbs in the subjunctive, 3:12; 6:11; 11:6; 18:21; 20:3).

17:11: The beast itself—that was and is not—is "part of the seven" (partitive genitive), for the seven heads are part of his body. Revelation 17:11 is very similar in wording to 17:8 (cf. note 13:3-4):

Rev 17:11	Rev 17:8
The beast that you saw	The beast that you saw
was and is not	was and is not
and is an eighth and part of	and is about to ascend from
the seven	the abyss
and goes to destruction.	and goes to destruction.

The parallel indicates that the "eighth" king was one of the seven kings who died and is about to ascend from the abyss as an "eighth." In other words, he will rule twice. John is probably referring here to Nero who some claimed, in the words of Suetonius, to be

> still alive and would soon return to confound his enemies. . . . In fact, twenty years later, when I was a young man, a mysterious individual came forward claiming to be Nero; and so magical was the sound of his name in the Parthians' ears [the Parthians admired Nero greatly]

that they supported him to the best of their ability, and only handed him over with great reluctance" (Suetonius, *Nero* 57; see also Tacitus, *Histories* 2.8-9; Dio Cassius 64.9; *Sib. Or.* 3.63-70; 4.119-20, 130-39).

17:12-14: The angel continues to explain: The "ten horns . . . are ten kings," who have not yet taken/received (the verb can mean either) their kingdom, but they take/receive authority as kings for one hour, along with the beast (cf. Dan 7:24). They offer *(didoasin)* their power *(dynamin;* note 4:9-11) and authority *(exousian;* note 12:10-12) to the beast—a statement that can be read either strictly politically or liturgically (cf. especially 4:9). These kings—the ten along with the "eighth"—will fight a losing battle with the Lamb and his chosen cohort. (Only here in Revelation does the Lamb "make war" *[polemēsousin];* cf. 2:16 and 19:11.) The Lamb conquers, for "he is Lord of lords and King of kings" (cf. 19:16; 1:6, as a divine epithet; Ezra 7:12; 1 Tim 6:15; 2 Macc 13:4; *1 Enoch* 9.4). Elsewhere the Lamb and his followers conquer through his blood (e.g., 12:11). Only here in Revelation are the Lamb's followers given the epithets of "called *[klētoi]*" and "chosen *[eklektoi]*"; elsewhere, those terms characterize angels (1 Tim 5:21; *1 Enoch* 39.1), the Israelites (Ps 88:4; Isa 65:9), and Christians (Rom 1:6; 8:33; 1 Cor 1:24; Titus 1:1).

17:15-18: The angel makes three more identifications in the vision. The "waters" are various groups of people (note 7:9; cf. Jer 51:13). The "ten horns" are further qualified as ten kings who with the beast will, at divine instigation, turn against the woman who rides the beast. The conflict, which is both political and sexual, is horridly brutal: They will make her desolate, that is, a desert *(erēmōmenēn,* note 12:5-6; 18:1-2), like a primordial abyss. In connection with Tyre, Ezekiel writes in the name of God:

> When I make you a city laid waste [LXX, *erēmōmenēn*], like cities that are not inhabited, when I bring up the deep *[abysson]* over you, and the great waters cover you, then I will thrust you down with those who descend into the Pit, to the people of long ago, and I will make you live in the world below, among primeval ruins, with those

who go down to the Pit, so that you will not be inhabited or have a place in the land of the living. I will bring you to a dreadful end, and you shall be no more; though sought for, you will never be found again, says the Lord GOD. (Ezek 26:19-21)

They will strip her naked (note 16:15-16; Ezek 16:39 Jerusalem; Ezek 23:29 Oholibah; Hos 2:5-6 Gomer), "devour her flesh" (cf. 19:18, 21; 1 Kgs 21:23; Ps 27:2; Mic 3:2-3), and "burn her up with fire" (18:8; Lev 21:9; Jer 34:22; *Sib. Or.* 5.367-69). This divinely initiated liaison between the ten kings and the beast against the woman will last "until the words of God will be fulfilled" (note 10:3-7; 19:9). It is not clear when this brutality occurs in relation to the war against the Lamb at 17:14. The angel interpreter then gives his final allegorical interpretation: "The woman . . . is the great city" (note 11:8 and 14:8; also, Isa 24:21; 2 Esdr 10:25-28). Her rule "over the kings of the earth" is not ultimate, however, for Jesus Christ rules over them (note 1:5-6).

◊ ◊ ◊ ◊

Only in this chapter and at 1:20 does a suprahuman give to the seer an interpretation of a vision. The interpretation gives a parallel, subtle meaning to what John sees. That meaning relates to the Roman Empire, but it is not simply an encoding of people and events, as is, for example, *Sib. Or.* 5.1-51. For that reason, the reader cannot identify unambiguously images in the interpretation with specific emperors or particular events in Roman history. For example, by using the Greek phrase *hepta orē* rather than *heptalophos* for the seven hills or mountains on which the woman is seated (17:9), the angelic interpretation joins chapter 17 with texts such as *1 Enoch* 24, where seven mountains surround the throne of God (note 17:9), as well as with references to the seven hills of the city of Rome. Or, by using the phrase *basileis hepta* rather than *kaisares hepta*, the angel does not refer simply to imperial heads of Rome. The angel's interpretation is a meditation on social, political life in the empire, not a representation of it. He sees the religious depths of the empire, not its surface manifestations. When an emperor dies, more occurs than a succession of emperors or a change in political dynasties. Suprahuman forces are in action: Rome is more than

Rome, and the emperor (whoever he is) is more than emperor. Religious forces are at war, and human allegiance is at stake. The mind that has wisdom knows the victor and to whom allegiance should be given.

In describing the beast/king who is one of the seven, but will reign as the eighth, John is probably alluding to rumors that circulated about the emperor Nero. Besides the reference by Suetonius quoted above, numerous other texts describe Nero's return from the dead or from hiding. Since he was especially popular with the Parthians to the east of the Roman Empire, stories circulated that Nero had secretly escaped to them (*Sib. Or.* 4.119-24; 5.137-54) and would come from the Euphrates (cf. Rev 16:12, roughly the boundary between the Parthian and the Roman empires) with armies of Medes and Persians (ancestors of the Parthians) to destroy, among other places, Rome itself (cf. *Sib. Or.* 5.137-54, 361-72; 8.151-58):

> He himself will destroy . . . the Romans. For the empire of Rome, which then flourished, has perished, the ancient queen over the surrounding cities. No longer will the plain of luxuriant Rome be victorious when he comes from Asia, conquering with Ares [the God of war]. (*Sib. Or.* 8.142-46)

Several impostors traveling in the eastern end of the Roman Empire claimed to be Nero revived (Tacitus, *Histories* 2.8-9). Moreover, in books 3, 4, and 5 of the *Sibylline Oracles,* the appearance of Nero is connected to the end time. He appears in opposition to the messiah or to godly forces, and sometimes he is specifically named the "Evil One," Beliar, or the anti-Christ (*Sib. Or.* 3.63-70; 4.130-46; 5.93-110, 214-37). A writer, writing near the time of Revelation, describes the return of Nero as follows:

> Beliar will descend, the great angel, the king of this world, which he has ruled ever since it existed. He will descend from his firmament in the form of a man, a king of iniquity, a murderer of his mother— this is the king of this world—and will persecute the plant which the twelve apostles of the Beloved will have planted; some of the twelve will be given into his hand. This angel, Beliar, will come in the form of that king, and with him will come all the powers of this world,

and they will obey him in every wish. . . . And he will do everything he wishes in the world; he will act and speak like the Beloved, and will say, "I am the Lord, and before me there was no one." And all men in the world will believe in him. They will sacrifice to him and will serve him, saying, "This is the Lord, and besides him there is no other." . . . And the power of his miracles will be in every city and district, and he will set up his image before him in every city. And he will rule for three years and seven months and twenty-seven days. (*Mart. Isa.* 4; cf. the language to Rev 13)

In Rev 17 and in describing the battle of Harmagedon at 16:12-16, the seer likely draws upon this lore about Nero. That connection makes sense not only of a king who comes to reign again, but also of a king gathering ten other kings to war against the whore/city, Rome. From John's point of view, however, it is not so important that readers identify the seven heads and ten horns with specific political leaders of the time as it is to understand that there are dark, powerful forces of evil at work in the Roman Empire, forces that will amaze the "inhabitants of the earth," but will ultimately be destroyed by the Christian God and the Lamb. In short, the seer is putting these stories about Nero at the service of strengthening religious commitment and not simply of historical prediction.

The Fall of Babylon (18:1–19:10)

With these visions, speech dominates over sight, the ear over the eye. John sees "another angel coming down from heaven" (18:1), but then speech takes over (18:2-20). First, the voice of an angel proclaims the fall of Babylon (18:2-3), then "another voice from heaven" makes a lengthy speech, either speaking in his own voice of Babylon's fall (18:4-8, 14, 20), or as he expects that kings (18:9-10), merchants (18:11-17), and shipmasters (18:18-19) will lament over the fall. After these laments and hymns of rejoicing, a "mighty angel" performs a prophetic sign of casting a millstone into the sea, the meaning of which he then explains (18:21-24). After that, John hears a ritual of praise within a throne scene: A multitude praises God for judging the whore (19:1-3); the twenty-four elders and the four living creatures respond antiphonally

(19:4); a voice from the throne then exhorts all to praise God (19:5). After that a "great multitude" acclaims God's kingship: "Hallelujah! For the Lord our God the Almighty reigns" (19:6). The ritual of praise concludes with a directive in first-person plural—"Let us rejoice"—to celebrate "the marriage of the Lamb" (19:7). The scene ends with the angel reminding John that only God is to be worshiped and that "the testimony of Jesus is the spirit of prophecy" (19:9-10).

◊ ◊ ◊ ◊

18:1-2: The glory *(doxēs)* of "another angel," that is, a different one from the "interpreting angel" of chapter 17 (cf. 10:1-6), "lights up the earth" (AT)—"glory" either lights up its surroundings or fills them with smoke (note 4:9-11; 15:6–16:1). Only he and the sea beast have "great authority." His proclamation emphasizes the transformation of Babylon into a "dwelling place" (cf. Eph 2:22) or "haunt" *(phylakē,* translated as "prison" at 2:10 and 20:7) of uncleanness (NRSV: "foul"). (If "foul and hateful beast" is the correct reading, compare to 17:16 "the beast will hate the whore.") In short, the city is transformed into a "desert" or "wilderness" (note 17:15-18), a common image for divine judgment on a city (cf. Isa 13:19-22; also Isa 34:9-15 Edom; Jer 9:10 Jerusalem; Jer 50:39; 51:37 Babylon; Baruch 4:35 Babylon; Zeph 2:14 Nineveh).

18:3: There are three interrelated causes of Babylon's fall: nations have drunk of her passionate fornication (note 14:8; 19:2), kings have fornicated with her (note 17:1-2), and merchants have grown rich from the power of her *strēnous*—"arrogance or luxury or sensuality" (only here in the NT; cf. 2 Kgs 19:28, Assyrian king). "Merchants" occurs for the first time (note 17:2), but the "voice from heaven" later speaks for them (18:11-17; cf. Ezek 27:12 and Isa 23:8 Tyre). Thus, images of fornication, luxury, commerce, and wealth indicate the causes of her fall (cf. 3:17).

18:4-5: The opening directive of the "voice from heaven" addresses "my people," that is, the "saints" (cf. 21:3). The directive opens with synonymous, parallel lines:

> Come out from her, my people
> So that you do not take part in her sins
> And from her plagues,
> So that you do not partake. (AT)

Both Isaiah and Jeremiah speak in similar language about Babylon: "Go out from Babylon, flee from Chaldea, declare this with a shout of joy, proclaim it, send it forth to the end of the earth; say, 'The LORD has redeemed his servant Jacob!' " (Isa 48:20). All of Jer 51 is echoed in this passage in Revelation:

> Flee from the midst of Babylon, save your lives, each of you! Do not perish because of her guilt, for this is the time of the LORD's vengeance; he is repaying her what is due. Babylon was a golden cup in the LORD's hand, making all the earth drunken. . . . Suddenly Babylon has fallen and is shattered. . . . Come out of her, my people! Save your lives, each of you, from the fierce anger of the LORD!" (Jer 51:6-8, 45; cf. 2 Esdr 16:40-48)

The punishment of the city is imminent, and so God's people must have nothing more to do with the whore/Rome.

Her sins are many—they pile up to heaven—and God remembers them (cf. Jer 51:9). "To remember" is often an image for describing a situation soon to be transformed. When one—including God—remembers, conditions change, toward deliverance or judgment (e.g., 2:5; 3:3; Acts 10:4; 1 Macc 7:38). The term, "iniquities [adikēmata]," occurs only here in Revelation, but it contrasts with "righteous" or "just" (dikaios), which occurs several times (15:3; 16:5, 7; 19:2; 22:11).

18:6-7: According to the syntax of the passage, "my people" (18:4) continue to be directed; they are to "render" and "repay." Nonetheless, some commentators assume that another group is now being addressed: angels of judgment or even the ten kings (17:16-17; see S. Elliott 1995). Babylon's "deeds" are the standard of measurement for the doubling (cf. 22:12). Measure for measure is insufficient: give her back *double* for what she has done and "mix a double draught for her" (so also Ps 137:8; Jer 50:29, Babylon;

Isa 51:17; Jer 16:18; *Pss. Sol.* 8.14, Israel; see notes 14:8, 9-11). Reciprocity is repeated: "As she glorified herself and lived luxuriously, so give her a like measure of torment and grief" (18:7). Elsewhere in Revelation, "glory" and "glorify" are used only in relation to the divine (note 4:9-11; 11:12-13). The merchants and kings who once shared in her "luxury" (18:3, 9) now "grieve" (18:11; NRSV: "weep and mourn for her"; contrast 21:4). Babylon's arrogance motivates the divine response: "in her heart she says, 'I rule as a queen; I am no widow, and I will never see grief,'" as a widow grieves (Isa 47:8, Babylon; all of Isa 47 is instructive). "She says," but her claim is not true (cf. 2:2).

18:8: "Therefore" (i.e., on account of the previous clause, "because in her heart she says . . ."), her plagues will come upon her shortly (cf. 18:10)—death [pestilence], grief, and famine (note 6:7-8; contrast 21:4). Similarly, Isaiah condemns Babylon: "both these things shall come [future] upon you in a moment, in one day: the loss of children and widowhood shall come upon you in full measure, in spite of your many sorceries and the great power of your enchantments" (Isa 47:9; more remotely, Jer 50:31). "Burning with fire" repeats the actions of the ten kings (see 17:16). A final cause for all this is then given: "for *[hoti]* mighty is the Lord God who judges her" (cf. 6:10).

18:9-10: The "voice from heaven," who is speaking (18:4), expects that "the kings of the earth" will "weep and wail *[kopsontai ep;* only here and 1:7]" over Babylon, their former ally in luxury. (The two verbs occur also in Luke at the lamentation over a dead girl, Luke 8:52.) "Torment" also comes upon those who do not have the seal upon their forehead (18:7, 10, 15) and who worship the beast (14:11). In their woe, the kings repeat language used previously (16:19; 17:18; 18:8).

18:11-14: Now the "voice from heaven" (18:4) anticipates the lament of merchants. Their motive for lamentation is economic loss: "Because *[hoti]* no one buys their wares [NRSV: "cargo"] anymore" (AT). The "voice from heaven" lists many of their wares in 18:12-13 (cf. lists in Ezek 16:9-13, Jerusalem; Ezek 27:5-24 against Tyre)—J. Nelson Kraybill calls the list a "bill of lading" (1996, 103). They include items precious to elites: ornaments, fine clothing, natural resources, perfumes, edibles, animals, and slaves. The objects are imported from many different countries, so they involve shipping on the sea (see Bauckham 1991, 58-75 for an excellent discussion of this list). The merchants lament the loss of the "good things" ("the fruit for which your soul longed"), "the glitter and the glamour" (NEB), that once was in Babylon (cf. Wis 4:12; Sir 23:5; *PGM* XVIIa.9).

18:15-17a: The merchants behave as do the kings (cf. 18:9-10). They describe her enormous wealth ("clothed in fine linen, in purple and scarlet, adorned with gold, with jewels, and with pearls," note 17:4), but the cause of their lament is different: "For in one hour all this wealth has been laid waste," that is, has become a wasteland, a desert (*erēmōthē;* cf. 12:5-6; 17:16; Jer 51:29 against Babylon; Ezek 26:19 against Tyre). Earlier, it was mentioned that they lament "since no one buys their cargo anymore" (18:11).

18:17b-19: Reference to shipmasters and sailors occurs only here in Revelation (cf. Wis 14:1-7). They are a class of merchants, but they make a separate response to the loss of Babylon. As Babylon burns (18:9; Isa 35:10 Edom), they ask a rhetorical question, "What city was like the great city?" (note 11:8), which parodies God (note 13:3-4). In Ezek 27, mariners lament over Tyre, the seafaring emporium of old:

> The mariners and all the pilots of the sea . . . wail aloud over you, and cry bitterly. They throw dust on their heads and wallow in ashes. . . . In their wailing they raise a lamentation over you, and lament over you: "Who was ever destroyed like Tyre in the midst of the sea? When your wares came from the seas, you satisfied many peoples; with your abundant wealth and merchandise you enriched the kings of the earth." (Ezek 27:29-33)

Throwing dust over one's head is a sign of grief (cf. Josh 7:6; Lam 2:10). They lament because they "grew rich by her wealth" (18:19), but now that wealth is gone as well as their own prosperity.

18:20: The "voice from heaven" completes a long speech with a hymn of gladness over the fall of Babylon: "Rejoice" (see 12:12; Jer 51:45 MT, Babylon). The directive is to "heaven, saints, apostles, and prophets," all of which are on "God's side," whether in heaven or on earth (cf. 2:2; 12:12; 16:6; 18:24). The rejoicing is motivated by God's retaliation for her judgment on the saints and apostles and prophets: "For God has imposed on her the sentence she passed on you" (Bratcher and Hatton 1993, 268). That which the angel promised to show John (17:1) occurs here in the narrative.

18:21-24: After the long speeches of the "angel" (18:1) and the "voice" (18:4), the narrative from 18:1 continues. A mighty angel performs a prophetic sign by casting "a great millstone" into the sea. (The "mighty angel" holding a little scroll in Rev 10:5 also "raises" something here: *aggelos ischyros ēren,* there an arm, here a millstone. Both passages have probably been influenced by Jer 51:63-64: "When you finish reading this scroll [which had on it all the disasters that would come on Babylon], tie a stone to it, and throw it into the middle of the Euphrates, and say, 'Thus shall Babylon sink, to rise no more, because of the disasters that I am bringing on her.' ") Both millstone and Babylon will disappear, never to be found (cf. Ezek 26:21 Tyre).

The "mighty angel" then shifts to a second-person address, speaking to Babylon directly: "and the sound of harpists . . . will be heard in you no more." So, according to Ezekiel, music will be silenced in Tyre (Ezek 26:13; cf. Isa 24:8, throughout the earth; Jer 25:10, Jerusalem). Without the light of a lamp, Babylon will be in darkness, in contrast to the new Jerusalem, which will be lit without a lamp (22:5). Normal human activities such as working at crafts (note repetition of "millstone") and marrying will cease (cf. Jer 7:34; 25:10).

Three causes are given for Babylon's destruction. "Your merchants" were magnates (here again Revelation's bias against wealth and prestige). "All nations were deceived (note 2:20-23, "beguiled") by your sorcery." For the third cause, the "mighty angel" shifts to third person: "In *her* was found [cf. 18:21] the blood of prophets . . ." (cf. Ezek 24:7, Jerusalem; Matt 23:35-37, Jerusalem). The "slaughtered *[esphagmenōn]*" refers only to Christians (cf. 6:9, though also cf. 6:4).

"Sorcery," *pharmakeia,* refers to magical drugs or potions, often associated with love-spells that cause fornication or adultery (9:21; 21:8; 22:15; Jezebel, 2 Kgs 9:22; Babylon, Isa 47:9; Nineveh, Nah 3:4: "gracefully alluring, mistress of sorcery, who enslaves nations through her debaucheries, and peoples through her sorcery"; Cleopatra, *Ant.* 15.93, cf. 19.193; Potifer's wife, *T. Jos.* 2.7). There is also a reference in *T. Reuben* 4.9 that refers to the "Egyptian woman" who brought potions to Joseph and tried to cause him to stumble with the aid of Beliar, prince of demons. But Joseph withstood the temptation on both the human and the demonic level: "For if promiscuity does not triumph over your reason, then neither can Beliar conquer you" (4.11). In Revelation, the great whore, Babylon [Rome], who is in league with the demonic beasts, deluded people by "the wine of her fornication" (see 14:8; 17:2; 18:3; cf. 17:6 where she is drunk with the blood of the saints). "Potions" may also have medicinal properties of healing (Sir 6:16). When Ignatius boldly names the Eucharist "medicine of immortality" *(pharmakon athanasias),* he has in mind its healing, salvific qualities, but opponents of Christianity could easily view the Eucharist as a magical potion. In Revelation, as in all of the above examples, by indicting the "other" as one who beguiles by magical potions, a sharp differentiation is made between "them" and "us," between Babylon/Rome and the saints of God. Insofar as the "wine of her fornication" may also involve "the blood of the saints" (17:6), the third cause, "in you was found the blood of prophets and of saints" (18:24) is closely related to her magical potion. Both the "sorcery" and the "blood" thus serve John in "marshalling the battle lines and demarcating 'insiders' from 'outsiders' " (Elliott, J. H. 1993, 271).

19:1-3: A "loud voice" sings in acclamation before the throne (7:9; 11:15; 12:10; Dan 10:6, note 7:10). Within the New Testament, "Hallelujah" appears only in Rev 19; it is a liturgical formula in Jewish and, later, in Christian worship that means "Praise the

Lord" (in Pss 104-150; Tob 13:17; 3 Macc 7:13; *PGM* 7.271; *Odes Sol.*). Common attributes are given to God ("salvation," note 7:10; "glory" and "power," note 4:9-11). The motive for the acclamation is two-fold: "His judgments are true and just" (note 15:3-4; 16:5-7), and he "judged the great whore," avenging "the blood of his servants" (note 6:10-11; 17:1; 18:20; Deut 32:43). The whore is said to "corrupt the earth with her fornication," only here in Revelation (note 14:8; cf. 11:18; Jer 51:25). The multitude speaks a second time (*eirēkan,* only here and at 7:14). "Smoke" here reflects destruction (note 14:9-11; Isa 34:9-10, Edom).

19:4-5: Verse four makes clear that the scene (19:1-10) is set before the throne, as the twenty-four elders and the four "living creatures" worship the one sitting upon the throne by affirming what the "loud voice" said. A "voice" then "came" "from the throne" (see 16:17; 21:3), directing the servants of God to praise him. "Praise" *(aineite)* occurs only here in Revelation (other terms for praise in Revelation: "Hallelujah," 19:1-3; Pss 22:23; 135:20; *eulogia,* 5:12, 13; 7:12; *doxazō,* 15:4; 18:7).

19:6-8: The voice—apparently that of an angel see 19:10—is described the same as those of the 144,000 at 14:2 (note 14:2-5). The voice repeats, "Hallelujah," with the motive (*hoti,* "because"), "The Lord our God the Almighty reigns" (cf. the blowing of the seventh trumpet, note 4:8 and 11:15). Then the speaker directs both himself and his hearers to "rejoice" (cf. 11:10, "celebrate"), "exult" (i.e., "be glad," only here in Revelation), and "give glory" (note 4:9-11; 11:13; 14:7; 16:9), paralleling "hallelujah" (cf. Matt 5:12; 1 Pet 4:13). They rejoice because of the marriage of the Lamb, an image that suggests that the Lamb is not celibate. (The 144,000 at 14:4 are a special class of followers of the Lamb, but not "holier" because of their celibacy.) The bride is allowed to wear "linen, bright and pure," which is identified as "the righteous deeds of the saints" ("linen": 18:12, 16; 15:6; 19:14; "bright": 15:6; 18:14; 22:1, 16; "clean": 15:6; 19:14; 21:18, 21; "righteous deeds": 15:4). "Marriage" is a common image for expressing the relation between God and his people (Isa 54:5; Hos 2:19-20; 2 Cor 11:2).

19:9-10: A directive is then given to John, to write down a beatitude (note 1:3; 14:12-13; 21:5): "Blessed are those who are invited to the marriage supper of the Lamb" (19:17; Luke 14:15). Angels are not to be worshiped ("Worship God"), for they are fellow servants (6:11) of those "who hold the testimony of Jesus"— either "Jesus' testimony" or "testimony to Jesus" (also 22:9). I incline to translate it, "the testimony given by Jesus" (note 1:1-3), and the following explanation (*gar;* "for") as "the testimony given by Jesus is what inspires a prophet."

◊ ◊ ◊ ◊

In these scenes (18:1–19:10), people engaged in Roman society— kings, merchants, and shipmasters—become more visible. The religious situation is also depicted more along apocalyptic times as popularly understood today—war, judgment, destruction, and disaster. The destruction of Babylon/Rome is imminent, and John hears various responses to her fall. The laments of the kings and merchants appear in a complex linguistic situation, for they speak words put in their mouths by an angel, which gives their lamentations an ironic twist, and the angel appears in a vision that is filtered through John's understanding. Nonetheless, by drawing upon Isaiah's judgment of the nations in Isa 34, Ezekiel's lamentations over Tyre in Ezek 26:1–28:19 (also Isa 23), and Jeremiah's prophecy of the doom of Babylon (Jer 51), the speakers portray the responses of classes of humans who experience the loss of their political and economic supports.

John warns Christians, "Come out of her, my people" (18:4), for otherwise they will be destroyed with Rome. There is little doubt that some Christians in the cities of Asia shared in the prosperity of Rome. The peace of the empire brought opportunities for provincials to benefit from Rome's thriving economy, especially during the reigns of the Flavians (69–96 CE). J. Nelson Kraybill has shown that those provincials engaging in commerce included Christians: Lydia of Thyatira, dealer in purple cloth (Acts 16:14); Paul of Tarsus, tentmaker and leather worker; Phoebe, a deacon of the church at Cenchreae (Rom 16:1); Hermas, a freedman possibly of some wealth (*Herm. Sim.* 1.1); and Marcion, a wealthy shipmaster

(Kraybill 1996, 94-101). Jews were involved in both overland and maritime trade, dealing in "incense, perfumes, spices, silk, precious stones, gold, expensive textiles, animal skins, and rare woods" (cf. Rev 18:11-13; S. Applebaum 1976, 667-68, quoted in Kraybill 1996, 185). Those Jews who converted to Christianity, like Paul, most likely continued in their trade. From John's point of view, those Christians are in great danger if they do not "come out," that is, detach themselves from Rome and her economic institutions.

The voices that John hears reflect his attitude toward the Roman Empire, which, as we have seen before, he regards as an evil, satanic, impermanent empire. The voice from heaven delights in Rome's fall and the loss of her "dainties." Her reversal of fortune begins to reveal the true nature of things: Those apparently poor and powerless, suffering martyrdom, are the truly rich who will reign. Conversely, the apparently powerful and rich will be destroyed. The call from heaven to "come out of her, my people, so that you do not take part in her sins" expresses the same point of view stated in the Likeness to a Human's objection to Jezebel and her followers in his pronouncement to those at Thyatira (2:18-29) and his support of poverty over riches in the other pronouncements: Christians must not collaborate with Rome, for it is impossible to serve both Rome and the Lamb.

VISIONS OF A GRAND FINALE (19:11–22:5)

Revelation 19:11 uses a major vision-marker that occurred previously only when the heavens first opened to John in 4:1 ("I saw . . . and there"). He now sees visions of truly eschatological (end-time) events: the beasts and their armies are defeated decisively (19:11-21), the devil (Satan) is imprisoned (20:1-3), Christians reign for one thousand years (20:4-6), Satan is defeated decisively and joins the two beasts in the lake of fire (20:7-10), the dead are judged (20:11-15), and John sees a new heaven, a new earth, and a new Jerusalem (21:1–22:5).

End-time Events Prior to the New Earth (19:11–20:15)

A messianic epiphany (19:11-16) introduces end-time events in Revelation. The Messiah battles and is victorious over the two beasts (19:17-21). That scene is followed by the temporary binding of Satan in the bottomless pit (20:1-3), a millennial reign with Christ (20:4-10), and the final judgment (20:11-15). In all of the scenes, judgment recurs as a key theme.

◊ ◊ ◊ ◊

19:11-16: John describes the royal messiah by images used previously: an "open heaven" (4:1), a rider on a white horse (note 6:2; contrast *Pss. Sol* 17:33 where the non-military messiah "will not rely on horse and rider and bow"), called "Faithful and True" (3:14), who judges and wars in righteousness (16:5; 17:14; Ps 72; Isa 11:4). His eyes are like "a flame of fire" (1:14), upon his head are "*many* diadems" (contrast 12:3; 13:1), and he has a name that only he knows (2:17). His robe has been dipped in the blood of war and sacrifice (cf. Isa 1:9; 5:9; 63:1-3). Like the "all-powerful word" of God that came upon the Egyptians, the rider comes as "a stern warrior carrying the sharp sword" (Wis 18:15-16; cf. Isa 11:4; John 1:1; Rev 1:16; *Pss. Sol.* 17.35).

He is accompanied by a heavenly army (9:16) dressed very much like the bride of the Lamb (19:8; Suetonius, *Augustus* 98). He will shepherd the nations with "a rod of iron"—the hero/messiah of chapter 12 now fulfills his mission (note 2:26-27; 12:5; Ps 2; *Pss. Sol.* 17.23-24; *Sib. Or.* 8.245)—and "will tread the wine press of the fury of the wrath of God the Almighty" (note 14:6-20; Isa 63:2-3). Written along the leg of his garment is an epithet given to the Lamb at 17:14. By means of those images, the rider of the white horse is identified clearly as the royal messiah, the "King of kings and Lord of lords."

19:17-21: The angel calling the birds and foreshadowing the results of the battle is "standing in the sun" (cf. 12:1; Ps 19:4-5 LXX; Phaethon, *VH1* 12; Heracles, *De Is. et Os.* 41, 367E). In a similarly worded passage in Ezekiel, birds and wild beasts are gathered to a sacrificial feast *(thysia)* associated with the burial of

Gog (Ezek 39:17-20; cf. also Rev 17:16; *T. Judah* 21.7-9). The narrative moves quickly through the battle to the capture of the sea beast and the false prophet (earth beast). "Signs," "deception," "tattoo," and "worshiping the image" all refer back to chapter 13. "Fire" is, of course, an image of judgment. "River of fire" or "stream of fire" is more common than "lake of fire" (cf. Dan 7:10; *1 Enoch* 14.19; *2 Enoch* 10.2; *Sib. Or.* 2.196-200, 252, 286; 3.84; 8.411; *Apoc. Peter* 8). Isaiah's description of the Lord's judgment on Assyria includes a "burning place":

> And the LORD will cause his majestic voice to be heard and the descending blow of his arm to be seen, in furious anger and a flame of devouring fire, with a cloudburst and tempest and hailstones. The Assyrian will be terror-stricken. . . . For his burning place has long been prepared; truly it is made ready for the king [Molech], its pyre made deep and wide, with fire and wood in abundance; the breath of the LORD, like a stream of sulfur, kindles it. (Isa 30:30-33)

Later in Revelation, the devil, Death, Hades, anyone whose name is not written in the book of life, and various types of sinners will be cast into that same "lake of fire" (cf. 20:10, 14, 15; 21:8). In the cosmic geography of Revelation, the "lake of fire" (the place of punishment; cf. 19:20) is located at a different place from "the bottomless pit" (where all go at death).

20:1-3: An angel (cf. 10:1; 18:1), the main actor, moves down the *axis mundi,* to reverse the action of the fallen star at 9:1-3 (note 9:1). He throws the dragon (note 12:7-9) into the pit of the dead (cf. the plight of the astral deities and kings of the earth at Isa 24:21-22 and fallen angels at Jude 6). In *1 Enoch*, the archangel, Raphael, binds the desert demon Azazel:

> And secondly the Lord said to Raphael, "Bind Azazel hand and foot and throw him into the darkness!" And he made a hole in the desert which was in Dudael and cast him there; he threw on top of him rugged and sharp rocks. And he covered his face in order that he may not see light; and in order that he may be sent into the fire on the great day of judgment. (10.3-6)

One manuscript of *1 Enoch* states that fallen stars are imprisoned for ten thousand or ten million years (18.6; 21.6; cf. *Barn.* 15.4-9).

20:4-6: While the dragon is imprisoned, the authority to judge (note 17:1-2) is given to "those seated on [thrones]." Probably "those seated" are "those who had been beheaded," (epexegetical *kai*), though they may be a second group. "Beheading," seldom referred to in the literature, is a more humane form of executing criminals than crucifixion, burning, being thrown to beasts, tearing by scourging, or drowning in a sack (cf. *Mart. Pol.* 2-4; Ste. Croix 1981, 458. On Antony's decapitation of the Maccabean king, Antigonus, see *Anton.* 36.4; Strabo, quoted by *Ant.* 15.8-9. Other examples: *Ant.* 14.39.3; 20.117; Diod. Sic. 32.26.2; 36.2.4. Strabo 16.2.18). Their beheading results from their testimony and their rejection of the beast (cf. 1:2, 9; 6:9; 12:17; 19:10; all of chapter 13). If "those beheaded" are the ones who reign and judge, then the millennium reign is limited to an elite group of martyrs who are resurrected first ("resurrection," *anastasis,* occurs here for the first time in Revelation). According to P. Billerbeck, Rabbi Eliezer, in about 90 CE, also refers to a one thousand-year messianic reign (Str-B III.824-27. See also Excursus 29, Str-B IV.799-976; 2 Esdr 7:26-30; also possibly 2 *Apoc. Bar.* 30, 39). Paul speaks of an interim messianic reign in 1 Corinthians:

> for as all die in Adam, so all will be made alive in Christ [= Messiah]. But each in his own order: Christ the first fruits, then at his coming those who belong to Christ. Then comes the end, when he hands over the kingdom to God the Father, after he has destroyed every ruler and every authority and power. For he must reign until he has put all his enemies under his feet. . . . When all things are subjected to him, then the Son himself will also be subjected to the one who put all things in subjection under him, so that God may be all in all. (1 Cor 15:22-28)

20:7-10: The saints' camp (cf. Heb 11:34) lies in or around Jerusalem, "the beloved city." Satan is eventually released from "his prison" (20:2-3; *phylakēs,* note 2:10-11; 18:1-2) and gathers an army from the four corners of the earth. Much of this scene is drawn from Ezekiel's description of Gog, prince of the land of Magog (Ezek 38–39; after the battle, it takes the Israelites seven months to bury all the bones of this army, even after the birds and wild animals feast on them). In later Jewish visionary literature, however, both Gog and Magog become lands or kingdoms that oppose God and his people at the time of the end, for example: "And I saw all the battles and wars which Gog and Magog will fight with Israel in the days of the Messiah, and all that the Holy One, blessed be he, will do to them in the time to come" (*3 Enoch* 45.5; cf. *Sib. Or.* 3.319-22, 512; *Eldad and Modad* in *OTP*). Fire from heaven immediately destroys the enemy, as it does Magog in Ezekiel: "I will send fire on Magog and on those who live securely in the coastlands; and they shall know that I am the LORD" (Ezek 39:6; cf. 2 Kgs 1:10-12).

20:11-15: The last judgment occurs before "a great white throne" (cf. Dan 7:9, 27; *1 Enoch* 90.20). Earth and heaven disappear, in preparation for the "new heaven and new earth" (21:1; *1 Enoch* 91.16). All humans stand before the throne to be judged (cf. Dan 7:10; 2 Esdr 6:20; *2 Apoc. Bar.* 24). The judge opens two sets of books: one contains a record of people's deeds (*erga;* note 2:1-3, 19; *Apoc. Peter* 6), and the other is the "book of life" (note 3:5-6; 13:5-8; cf. Isa 4:3; Dan 12:1). Those of the sea, Death, and Hades are associated by water (note 9:1). The "lake of fire" is "the second death" (2:7, 11; 19:20; 20:6, 10).

◊ ◊ ◊ ◊

In these scenes, all previous horrors and judgments are brought to completion. The royal messiah whose birth is mentioned in chapter 12 now battles victoriously against his evil opponents, the beasts, who act on behalf of dragon/Satan. Then those two beasts who oppressed and persecuted the saints are cast into the lake of fire and sulfur. That completion carries the religious situation into a new stage, an end time when God and his righteous ones bring final judgment against all evil, cosmic forces. Never again will they deceive and lead people astray. Before Satan is judged and cast finally into the lake of fire, the Messiah and at least some of his followers reign for a thousand years. Then the last judgment follows.

Heaven and earth, as known up to that point, pass away. All social and cosmic structures are destroyed. Judgment and punishment reduce virtually everything to nothing, for transformation and renewal can occur only then. One of the differences between ancient and modern apocalyptic images lies in the significance of destruction: in the modern, destruction is usually seen as final; in the ancient, destruction is but a necessary stage in renewal, like winter followed by spring. John has not fallen out of the natural cycle of birth, death, and rebirth or creation, dissolution, and re-creation. From death and destruction, God creates (transforms) the new heavens and new earth. In Christian myth and rite, that pattern can be seen in baptism, where the person "dies," is buried in the waters of chaos, in order to "rise," "be born anew" in Christ. Mystics experience that cycle in the dark night of the soul, the "night of the spirit" in which nothing remains but emptiness. Drawing primarily upon Jewish visionary tradition, John presents his point of view about the cosmic dimensions of this death, prior to the rebirth of heaven and earth.

New Heaven, New Earth, and New Jerusalem (21:1–22:5)

These scenes consist of a brief narrative describing the new heaven, the new earth, and the new Jerusalem (21:1-2), followed by two proclamations: the first one spoken by "a loud voice" (21:3-4) and the second by God himself (21:5-8). The proclamations explain and elaborate the meaning of the narrative. God's proclamation brings the visions to their final climax: "All is accomplished" (21:6; NRSV: "It is done!"). Revelation 21:9–22:5 then describes in detail the new Jerusalem mentioned at 21:2: The splendor of its wall, gates, and foundation (21:11-14, 18-21); its huge dimensions (21:15-17); and its sacredness, purity, and glory. Nothing profane and impure can enter, though its gates are open (21:22-27). Simple, primal needs of water, food, and light are met by "the river of the water of life," "the tree of life," and "the Lord God" (22:1-5). The final sentence in the visions confirms the enthronement of the saints: "they will reign forever and ever."

◊ ◊ ◊ ◊

21:1-2: Immediately after the judgment of those cast into the "lake of fire," John sees "a new heaven and a new earth" to replace the old ones (20:11; cf. Isa 65:17; 66:22; 2 Pet 3:13; *Sib. Or.* 5.512, 530; *Greek Apocalypse of Ezra* in OTP 4.38; *Jub.* 1.29; 4.26; *1 Enoch* 45.4-5; 72.1; 91.16; *2 Apoc. Bar.* 32.6; 57.2). The sea disappears, for it is associated with the chaotic waters of the abyss (note 13:1-2; cf. *Sib. Or.* 5.155-61). Then the heavenly Jerusalem comes down from God adorned as a bride (21:10; 22:19. Cf. "Beautiful garments" and "wedding garments" of Jerusalem, Isa 52:1-2; 61:10; 62:5; Jerusalem as woman, Gal 4:26; Jerusalem comes down from heaven, Rev 3:12; new Jerusalem, *T. Dan* 5.12; *1 Enoch* 90.29). The image of marriage also occurs in seasonal rites of renewal involving Attis and Cybele, which makes it apt for John's description of a new universe (see Gaster 1966, 68-69). Paul describes this novelty in terms of Christian existence: "So if anyone is in Christ, there is a new creation: everything old has passed away; see, everything has become new!" (2 Cor 5:17).

21:3-4: Speech dominates the rest of this scene. First, a "loud voice from the throne" speaks (16:17; 19:5). The voice describes this new situation, first positively: God and his people now dwell together (7:15; 13:6; 15:5; cf. Ezekiel's restored kingdom, Ezek 37:27; many nations will dwell with the Lord, Zech 2:10-11; Jeremiah's new covenant, Jer 31:1; those obedient to the divine law, Lev 26:12; Solomon's dedication of the temple, 1 Kgs 8:27). Death, pain, and lamentation will be no more, for they belong to the "first things" that "have passed away" (cf. 7:17; Isa 25:8; note also the return from exile at Isa 35:10; 43:18 and the new Jerusalem at Isa 65:19).

21:5-8: God himself then makes a rare speech, repeating in first person much of what has already been said. The one on the throne for the first time orders John to write (cf. 3:14; 19:9). Once again, readers hear, "All is accomplished" (*gegonan*; cf. 16:17). God speaks in a theophanic "I am" style (note 1:8). Like the Lamb at 7:17, God gives water from the springs of life to those who are thirsty (cf. 22:1, 17; Isa 55:1; Zech 14:8; John 7:37). The expression, "those who conquer," echoes the end of each of the pronouncements in chapters 2 and 3. The God/child image associates the saints with those in Israel's covenantal relation to the Lord, especially the king (Lev 26:12; 2 Sam 7:14; Pss 2:7; 89:26-27; Jer 3:19; Ezek 11:20; Zech 8:8; *Jub.* 1.24). God then completes his speech by contrasting those who conquer with various kinds of sinners (cf. 22:15; Rom 1:29; 1 Cor 5:9-11; 6:9; Gal 5:19-20; 1 Tim 1:10; Titus 1:16). The portion *(meros)* of those sinners will be the "lake that burns with fire and sulfur," in contrast to those who will rule with Christ (20:6).

21:9-14: John introduces the "wife of the Lamb" in exactly the same way as he did the whore/city at 17:2: "Then one of the seven angels who had the seven bowls full of the seven last plagues came and said to me, 'Come, I will show you. . . .' " He is deliberately contrasting the two female figures (note 17:1-2, 3-4; cf. Ezek 40:2). This scene also adds detail to 21:2 ("And I saw the holy city . . . coming down out of heaven." Cf. Isa 62; 2 Esdr 10:25-28). The "heavenly Jerusalem" existed from the beginning, long before David founded the "historical" Jerusalem. So God explains to Baruch:

> "And I showed it to Adam before he sinned. But when he transgressed the commandment, it was taken away from him—as also Paradise. . . . I showed it to my servant Abraham . . . again I showed it also to Moses on Mount Sinai." (2 *Apoc. Bar.* 4; cf. 2 Esdr 7.26; 13.36)

It shines with "the glory of God" (note 4:9-11; 21:23; Isa 60:1; Ezek 43:2-5) and has a "radiance like a very rare jewel," specifically, "like jasper," as has the one seated on the throne (note also 4:3, for "rare jewel"; 17:4, the whore; 18:12, cargo; 18:16, Babylon; Isa 54:12, restored Jerusalem; Tob 13:16, new Jerusalem). It is a walled city with twelve gates, each guarded by an angel (cf. Isa 62:6; Ezek 40:5; 48:30-35; and the breastplate of the priest, Exod 28:21). John seems to refer to the twelve "apostles of the Lamb" as people different from him, that is, the writer of Revelation is not one of the twelve apostles.

21:15-17: For the significance of "measuring," see 11:1 (cf. Ezek 40:3 where a "man" does the measuring, as also Zech 2:1-2). The city forms a square (NRSV: "foursquare"), as do many other cities, temples, and altars (Ezek 43:16, an altar; 48:16, Jerusalem; Strabo 12.4.7, Nicaea in Bithynia; Diod. Sic. 13.82.2, a temple of Zeus at Acragas). The height of the heavenly Jerusalem equals its length and width; thus, it forms either a cube or a pyramid, either shape appropriate for a sacred place (for example, the Kaaba in Mecca derives from the Arabic, "cube"). All the measurements are in multiples of twelve (the number of the tribes of Israel, the disciples, and the signs of the zodiac; note 12:1-2).

21:18-21: Typical of "utopian buildings and cities, as well as fairy tale castles and castles in the sky," the walls, foundation stones, and gates of the new Jerusalem are built of precious stones (Becker 1994 under "jewels"). They are also the materials for crowns of kings and the breastplate of Israelite priests. Precious stones and jewels are images of perfection, holiness, and permanence (cf. Exod 28:15-23; Isa 54:11-14; Tob 13:15-17). Identification of the specific stones cannot always be made with certainty: "Every jewel," Tob 13:17. "Jasper," 4:3; Exod 28:15; Isa 54:11; Ezek 28:13. "Sapphire," Exod 28:15; Isa 54:11; Ezek 28:13; Tob 13:17. "Agate" *(chalkēdōn),* rare, uncertain meaning. "Emerald," Exod 28:15; Ezek 28:13; Tob 13:17. "Onyx," buttons on priestly garb, *J.W.* 233. "Carnelian," Exod 28:15; Ezek 28:13. "Chrysolite," Exod 28:15; Ezek 18:13. "Beryl," Exod 28:15; Ezek 28:13; Tob 13:17. "Topaz," Exod 28:15; Ezek 28:13. "Chrysoprase," a rare word, an apple-green variety of quartz. "Jacinth," a priestly garment, *Ant.* 3.164. "Amethyst," Exod 28:15; Ezek 28:13. "Pearls," 17:4; 18:12, 16; Matt 13:45-46. "Pure gold," 11:8; 22:2; Exod 28:15; Ezek 28:13; Tob 13:17.

21:22-27: The order of the Greek words is "A temple I did not see in the city, for the Lord God Almighty is its temple, and the

Lamb." "The Lamb" could be seen as an afterthought, an addition to an earlier text, or in an emphatic position. In any case, both Lamb and the Lord are identified as the temple *(naos)* of the city (note 3:12-13), and their "glory" provides constant light to the city (cf. Isa 24:23; 60:1, 19; Zech 14:7). As with Isaiah's expectations of the restored Jerusalem, nations and kings will come to the light of God's glory (Isa 60:3), bringing their glory with them (i.e., fame, honor, riches; cf. Ps 72:10; Isa 60:11, 13). "Nothing profane" will be able to enter, for something "profane" *(koinon;* NRSV: "unclean") opposes the holiness of divine glory. ("Profane" here is virtually synonymous with *akatharta;* note 16:13-14; Isa 35:8; 52:1). Only the saints, "those who are written in the Lamb's book of life," whose robes have been made "white in the blood of the Lamb" (7:14), may enter. Note, however, that the gate stands open between the saints inside and the sinners outside.

22:1-5: The angel now reveals to John the final scene in his visions. Utopian settings in the Bible often contain rivers (cf. 4:6; 21:6; Ps 46:4; Ezek 47:1-6; Joel 3:18; Zech 13:1; 14:8). The river in John's vision flows "from the throne of God and of the Lamb," reminding the listener that the Jerusalem coming down from heaven is another version of the throne scenes that began in chapters 4 and 5.

One tree seems to grow on both sides of the river. In similar scenes, especially those of Ezekiel that have influenced John's vision, there is more than one tree (cf. Ezek 47:12; *Pss. Sol.* 14.3). At one point in *1 Enoch,* the whole renewed earth will bear trees with plenteous fruit (10.19), and, at another point, the "throne" is "surrounded by fragrant trees," among which one is very special. The archangel Michael explains:

> And as for this fragrant tree, not a single human being has the authority to touch it until the great judgment, when he shall take vengeance on all and conclude (everything) forever. This is for the righteous and the pious. And the elect will be presented with its fruit for life. He will plant it in the direction of the northeast, upon the holy place—in the direction of the house of the Lord, the Eternal King. (25.4-5)

This circle of texts, of course, draws upon the story of the "tree of life" in Gen 2:9 and 3:22. In the last days, the righteous will be allowed to eat of that which was forbidden to Adam and Eve (note 2:7). This tree bears fresh fruit twelve times a year, once each month (cf. *1 Enoch* 25.4; 2 Esdr 8:52). In Revelation, the "leaves of the tree" are also valuable "for the healing of the nations" (22:2). Ezekiel had similarly stated,

> On the banks, on both sides of the river, there will grow all kinds of trees for food. Their leaves will not wither nor their fruit fail, but they will bear fresh fruit every month, because the water for them flows from the sanctuary. Their fruit will be for food, and their leaves for healing. (Ezek 47:12; cf. *1 Enoch* 24.4)

Probably, the healing power of the tree and the reference in 22:3 to "accursed" also allude to the cross of Jesus (Acts 5:30; 10:39; Pol. *Phil.* 8). "Accursed" *(katathema)* occurs only here in the New Testament, though in Galatians, Paul writes, "Christ redeemed us from the curse *[kataras]* of the law by becoming a curse for us—for it is written, 'Cursed *[epikataratos]* is everyone who hangs on a tree' " (3:13). The term for "accursed" in Revelation occurs also in a fairly obscure passage in the *Didache* in a description of the end times: "they who endure in their faith will be saved by the curse *[katathematos]* itself," probably a reference to the cross (16.5).

In the final sentence of the visions (22:5), the enthronement of the saints is celebrated: "and they will reign forever and ever" (cf. Dan 7:18, 27). This declaration echoes the thought of the initial doxology of the book, "To him who loves us and freed us from our sins by his blood, and made us to be a kingdom, priests serving his God and Father" (1:5-6). There is, however, an important difference. Those qualities of "affliction" and "patient endurance" along with "royal power," so essential to Christian existence in John's time (note 1:9*a*), will not be required in the heavenly Jerusalem. For all evil is overcome, and those around the throne—with their name in the book of life and God's name on their forehead (7:3; 9:4; 14:1)—will worship the Lord God and the Lamb "face to face," in the light of their glory (1 John 3:2; Pss 17:15; 42:2; *T. Zebulon* 9.8; 2 Esdr 7.97-99).

◊ ◊ ◊ ◊

In the new Jerusalem, set amidst a new heaven and new earth, boundaries are relocated from where they were in the days of the old Jerusalem. Heaven collapses into earth, for the heavenly throne of God comes down to the new earth in the form of the new Jerusalem: "See, the home of God is among mortals. He will dwell with them as their God" (21:3). The glory of the Lord God and the Lamb light up the new Jerusalem, so "they need no light of lamp or sun," a radical change from the old heavens. Temples—earthly places where people approach the heavenly deity—are no longer needed, for in the new Jerusalem, heaven and earth merge, and God and the Lamb dwell in the city. In contrast to earthly life since the expulsion of Adam and Eve from the Garden, those dwelling in the new Jerusalem drink from the "river of the water of life" and eat from the "tree of life." Finally, in contrast to the high, impervious boundary between good and evil, which John labors to create throughout the earlier sections of the book, the gates of the city are open. Clean and unclean cannot mingle, but the open gates suggest that in the time of the new Jerusalem, boundaries are more porous, and there is the possibility of the "unclean" to repent and to enter the city.

CONCLUSION TO THE VISIONS (22:6-21)

The conclusion to Revelation takes the form of a dialogue:

Angel: "These words are trustworthy and true . . ." (22:6).
   Jesus: "See, I am coming soon!" (22:7).
   John: "I, John, am the one who heard and saw . . ." (22:8).
   Angel: "You must not do that . . ." (22:9-11).
   Jesus: "See, I am coming soon . . ." (22:12-16).
   Spirit and Bride: "Come . . ." (22:17).
   Jesus: "I warn. . . . I am coming soon" (22:18-20a).

Congregants: "Amen. Come, Lord Jesus!" (22:20*b*).
John: "The grace of the Lord Jesus . . ." (22:21).

◊ ◊ ◊ ◊

22:6-11: The trustworthiness of the words in Revelation has been a theme throughout the book (cf. 3:14; 19:9-10, 11; 21:5). "Spirits of the prophets" occurs only here in Revelation (cf. 19:10 and 1 Cor 14:32, "And the spirits of prophets are subject to the prophets . . ."). "Servants" can refer to either prophets (10:7; 11:18) or all believers (2:20; 7:3; 19:5; 22:3). The beatitude at 22:7 and the virtually identical one at 1:3 ring the entire book. At 22:8, John, like Jesus, speaks in first person, blurring the distinction between seer and Jesus (cf. comments at Rev 1:13-20). The angel's response to John (cf. 19:10) may suggest that the worship of angels was an issue in the churches of Asia (cf. Col 2:18, and Stuckenbruck 1995). In contrast to some visionaries who write at a time distant from the end, John writes near the end and should not seal up his prophecy (cf. 10:4; Dan 12:4, 9; *2 Enoch* 33-35). Compare the sequence in 22:10-11 to this one in Daniel: "Go your way, Daniel, for the words are to remain secret and sealed until the time of the end. Many shall be purified, cleansed, and refined, but the wicked shall continue to act wickedly" (12:9-10). "Filthy" can refer to immorality or ritual uncleanness, and in connection with the heavenly Jerusalem both are applicable. "Holy" also has a double significance: both free from sin and dedicated to God.

22:12-16: At 22:12, Jesus makes three assertions: He is coming soon (1:7; 3:11; 16:15; 22:7, 20), he is coming to judge according to everyone's work (cf. 11:18; also 2:23; Pss 28:4; 20:12, 13; 61:12; Prov 24:12; Jer 17:10; Rom 2:6; *1 Clem* 34:3), and he encompasses all things (note 1:8, 17; 2:8; 21:6; Isa 44:6). The words echo those of Isa 40:10, "See, the Lord GOD comes with might, and his arm rules for him; his reward is with him, and his recompense before him." Jesus then confers a final blessing on those "who wash their robes," rather than wear "filthy" garments (Zech 3:3-4; Jas 2:2; and see the discussion of "filthy" above), so that they have access to the "tree of life" (2:2; 22:2) and the city (Ps 118:19-20). Except for "dogs," this list of vices repeats that at 21:8. (In Revelation, as in much of Jewish and Christian literature, dogs are not "man's best friend," but rather are unclean animals; cf. Ps 22:16, 20; Matt 15:26, 27; Phil 3:2; Ign. *Eph.* 7.1). For "sorcerers," note 18:21-24, cf. 9:21; 21:8; "fornicators," note 17:1-2, cf. 2:14, 20, 21; 9:21; 14:8; 17:4, 5, 15, 16; 18:3, 9; 19:2; 21:8; Eph 5:5; "murderers," 9:21; 21:8; "idolaters," 2:14, 20; 9:20; Eph 5:5; "falsehood," 2:2; 3:9; 14:5; 16:13; 19:20; 20:10; 21:8, 27.

At 22:16, "you" is plural, referring to Christians, "I, Jesus, have sent my angel to announce these things to you in the churches" (GNB), rather than singular, referring to John (Rev 1:1). Jesus concludes by claiming two messianic epithets for himself: "the root [shoot] and the descendant of David" (5:5; Isa 11:10; Rom 1:3; 15:12) and "the bright morning star" (2:28; Num 24:17).

22:17-19: "Spirit" and "bride" respond (note 2:7; 19:6-8). They are either invoking Jesus to come or inviting others to come to Jesus. Given the way the verse ends, they are probably inviting others (cf. Isa 55:1; John 7:17, 37; 21:6). At 22:18, the speaker is not identified clearly; probably it is Jesus (22:18, *martyrō*, "I warn . . ."; 22:20, *ho martyrōn*, "the one who testifies"). The conditionals in verses 18 and 19 ("If anyone . . .") remind one of the blessings and curses in Deuteronomy (chap. 28), which also contains a warning not to add to or delete from what is written (Deut 4:2; 12:32). Such curses also are found at the end of other writings (*Ep. Arist.* 311; *Greek Apocalypse of Ezra* 7.5-13; *1 Enoch* 104.10-11; *2 Enoch* 48.7). As at the beginning of the book, Revelation is called "prophecy" (1:3; 22:7, 10, 18). The plagues probably refer especially to the seven bowls (Rev 16).

22:20-21: This concluding exchange has the quality of a liturgical benediction. In the *Didache*, "Our Lord come" concludes the eucharistic liturgy (*Did.* 10.6; cf. 1 Cor 11:26). It, along with verse 21 also, however, closes letters (cf. Rom 16:20; 1 Cor 16:22-23; 2 Cor 13:14; Gal 6:18; Rev 1:4), which were of course read in services of worship.

◊ ◊ ◊ ◊

The conclusion to the visions (22:6-21) returns to much the same language as that in the introduction (1:1-8, 9): John repeats to those listening that his testimony is true, the prophecy that he writes comes to him from an angel of Christ or God, the time is near, and blessed therefore is the one who keeps the words of this book. The epithet, "Alpha and Omega," is repeated at 22:13 from 1:8.

Through that language, John ends his visions by turning from the future new Jerusalem to his readers living in the province of Asia. By returning to those listening to his writing, John reminds them indirectly that his visions reveal and clarify religious dimensions of their situation in Asia, their home. Their present life is not totally isolated from life envisioned in the new Jerusalem. Put differently, the new Jerusalem is not a purely future event tacked on "at the end," for the vision of the new Jerusalem also gives added meaning to that term, *hypomonē,* so central to John's understanding of Christian existence (note 1:9*a*). That is John's only term for "hope" in Revelation. The hope implied in "enduring steadfastly" has nothing essentially to do with predicting the future. *Hypomonē* (hope) is an orientation toward the present. As Vaclav Havel said at Hiroshima in 1995,

> hope is humanity's profound and essential archetypal certainty—though denied or unrecognized a hundred times over—that our life on this earth is not just a random event among billions of other random cosmic events that will pass away without a trace, but that it is an integral component or link, however minuscule, in the great and mysterious order of Being, an order in which everything has a place of its own, in which nothing that has once been done can be undone, in which everything is recorded in some unfathomable way and given its proper and permanent value. (Havel 1997, 2)

John writes in a different idiom from Havel, yet their point is strikingly similar with respect to hope. For both, humans endure steadfastly because their life "is an integral component . . . in the great and mysterious order of Being." John describes that "order of Being" in a certain way, within a certain religious tradition, one that he shares with his readers in Asia (even if they do not all share his view of Rome as the evil empire). His visions of hope ground everyday life in Asia in those larger, religious realities.

There is a "not yet" to life in Asia that is asserted in Jesus' repeated statements that he is coming soon. For those who share in the hope of his coming, however, the present becomes fuller rather than emptier, for the present Lord of the church is the coming Lord of the universe. As in holographic photography, every part of the whole is present in every other part. Those who gather in the congregations of Asia walk in the streets of the new Jerusalem, partaking of the living water and the tree of life, reigning forevermore. In short, John's visions of the end disclose that which is most fundamental, most comprehensive, the hub of the web of all that exists. John gives it a dual name: God and the Lamb.

SELECT BIBLIOGRAPHY

WORKS CITED IN THE TEXT
(EXCLUDING COMMENTARIES)

(Reference works especially helpful for this commentary are marked *)

Achtemeier, Paul J. 1990. "*Omne Verbum Sonat:* The New Testament and the Oral Environment of Late Western Antiquity." *JBL* 109:3-27.

Artemidorus. 1975. *The Interpretation of Dreams.* Translated by Robert J. White. 2nd ed. Reprint, Torrance, CA: Original Books, 1990.

Augustine. 1991. *Confessions.* Translated by Henry Chadwick. Oxford: Oxford University Press.

Bauckham, Richard. 1991. "The Economic Critique of Rome in Revelation 18." In *Images of Empire,* 47-90. Sheffield: JSOT.

*Becker, Udo. 1994. *The Continuum Encyclopedia of Symbols.* Translated by Lance W. Garmer. New York: Continuum.

Berger, Peter. 1970. *A Rumor of Angels.* Garden City, NY: Anchor.

Berry, Wendell. 1990. *What Are People For?* New York: North Point Press.

*Betz, Hans Dieter, ed. 1986. *Magical Papyri in Translation.* Chicago: University of Chicago Press.

Bickerman, E. J. 1980. *Chronology of the Ancient World.* Ithaca, NY: Cornell University Press.

Biedermann, Hans. 1992. *Dictionary of Symbolism.* Translated by James Hulbert. New York: Meridian.

Brandi, John. 1991. *In the Desert We Do Not Count the Days.* Duluth, MN: Holy Cow! Press.

*Brenton, Lancelot C. L. 1851. *The Septuagint with Apocrypha: Greek and English.* Reprint, Peabody, MA: Hendrickson, 1990.

Broughton, T. R. S. 1938. "Roman Asia Minor." In *An Economic Survey of Ancient Rome,* edited by Tenney Frank, 499-918.

Cheesman, G. L. 1914. *The Auxilia of the Roman Imperial Army.* Reprint, Chicago: Ares Publishers, 1975.

*Collins, John J., ed. 1979. *Apocalypse: The Morphology of a Genre; Semeia 14.* Missoula, MT: Scholars Press.

Colwell, Ernest Cadman. 1939. "Popular Reactions Against Christianity in the Roman Empire." In *Environmental Factors in Christian History*, edited by John Thomas McNeill, Matthew Spinka, and Harold R. Willoughby, 53-71. Reprint 1970, Port Washington, NY: Kennikat.

Couliano, I. P. 1991. *Out of This World: Otherworldly Journeys from Gilgamesh to Albert Einstein*. Boston: Shambhala.

*Deissmann, G. Adolf. 1901. *Bible Studies*. Translated by Alexander Grieve. Reprint, Peabody, MA: Hendrickson, 1988.

*———. 1922. *Light from the Ancient East*. Translated by Lionel R. M. Strachan. Reprint: Grand Rapids, MI: Baker Book House, 1978.

Duncan-Jones, Richard. 1982. *The Economy of the Roman Empire: Quantitative Studies*. 2nd ed. Cambridge: Cambridge University Press.

*Elliott, J. K. 1993. *The Apocryphal New Testament*. Oxford: Clarendon.

Elliott, John H. 1993. "Sorcery and Magic in the Revelation of John." *Listening: Journal of Religion and Culture* 28, 3: 261-76.

Elliott, Susan M. 1995. "Who Is Addressed in Revelation 18:6-7?" *BR* XL:98-113.

Frye, Northrop. 1990. *Words with Power*. San Diego: Harcourt Brace Jovanovich.

Gager, John G. 1992. *Curse Tablets and Binding Spells from the Ancient World*. New York: Oxford University Press.

Gamble, Harry Y. 1995. *Books and Readers in the Early Church*. New Haven, CT: Yale University Press.

*García Martínez, Florentio. 1994. *The Dead Sea Scrolls Translated*. Translated from Spanish by Wilfred G. E. Watson. Leiden: E. J. Brill.

Gaster, Theodor H. 1966. *Thespis*. New York: Harper & Row.

Gilliard, Frank D. 1993. "More Silent Reading in Antiquity: *Non Omne Verbum Sonabat*." *JBL* 112:689-94.

Goodman, Felicitas D. 1990. *Where the Spirits Ride the Wind*. Bloomington: Indiana University Press.

Goranson, Stephen. 1995. "The Exclusion of Ephraim in Rev. 7:4-8 and Essene Polemic Against Pharisees." *Dead Sea Discoveries* 2.1:80-85.

*Grant, F. C. 1953. *Hellenistic Religions: The Age of Syncretism*. Indianapolis: Bobbs-Merrill.

Hall, Donald. 1995. *Principal Products of Portugal*. Boston: Beacon.

Hall, Stuart George, ed. 1979. *Melito of Sardis, On Pascha and Fragments*. Oxford: Clarendon.

Hammond, Nicholas G. L. 1981. *Atlas of the Greek and Roman World in Antiquity*. Park Ridge, NJ: Noyes.

Havel, Vaclav. 1997. "The Future of Hope." *Religion and Values in Public Life* (The Center for the Study of Values in Public Life at Harvard Divinity School), 5.2/3:1-3.

Hillman, James, and Michael Ventura. 1992. *We've Had a Hundred Years of Psychotherapy—and the World's Getting Worse.* New York: Harper-Collins.

*Himmelfarb, Martha. 1993. *Ascent to Heaven in Jewish and Christian Apocalypses.* New York: Oxford.

Hvidberg, Flemming Friis. 1962. *Weeping and Laughter in the Old Testament.* Leiden: E. J. Brill.

Jones, A. H. M. 1971. *The Cities of the Eastern Roman Provinces.* 2nd ed. Reprint, Amsterdam: Adolf M. Hakkert, 1983.

Kittel, R., et al., ed. 1990. *Biblia Hebraica Stuttgartensia.* Stuttgart: Deutsche Bibelgesellschaft.

Kraabel, Alf Thomas. 1968. "Judaism in Western Asia Minor under the Roman Empire." Doctoral thesis, Harvard University.

*Kraybill, J. Nelson. 1996. *Imperial Cult and Commerce in John's Apocalypse.* JSNTSup 132. Sheffield: JSOT. Quoting S. Applebaum, 1976. *The Jewish People in the First Century,* II. Philadelphia: Fortress.

Kumar, Krishan. 1995. "Apocalypse, Millennium and Utopia Today." In *Apocalypse Theory and the Ends of the World,* edited by Malcolm Bull, 200-224. Oxford: Blackwell.

Le Guin, Ursula K. 1991. "The Writer on, and at Her Work," in *The Writer on Her Work,* vol. 2. Edited by Janet Sternburg. New York: Norton.

Lewis, Naphtali. 1974. *Greek Historical Documents, The Roman Principate: 27 B.C.–285 A.D.* Toronto: Hakkert.

McGinn, Bernard. 1984. "Early Apocalypticism: The Ongoing Debate." In *The Apocalypse in English Renaissance Thought and Literature.* Edited by C. A. Patrides and Joseph Wittreich, 2-39. Ithaca, NY: Cornell University Press.

*MacMullen, Ramsay. 1966. *Enemies of the Roman Empire.* Cambridge, MA: Harvard University Press.

Meeks, Wayne A. 1983. *The First Urban Christians.* New Haven, CT: Yale University Press.

———, ed. 1993. *The HarperCollins Study Bible.* New York: HarperCollins.

Melton, J. Gordon. 1992. *Encyclopedic Handbook of Cults in America.* New York: Garland.

Meyer, Marvin W. 1976. *The "Mithras Liturgy."* Missoula, MT: The Society of Biblical Literature.

Mitchell, W. J. T. 1993. "Image." In *The New Princeton Encyclopedia of Poetry and Poetics*. Princeton, NJ: Princeton University Press.

Nock, Arthur Darby. 1944. "The Cult of Heroes." *HTR* 37:141-70.

Peterson, Erik. 1926. *HEIS THEOS: Epigraphische, formgeschichtliche und religionsgeschichtliche Untersuchungen*. Göttingen: Vandenhoeck & Ruprecht.

————. 1964. *The Angels and the Liturgy*. Translated by Ronald Walls. New York: Herder & Herder.

Philo. 1993. *The Works of Philo Complete and Unabridged*. New updated edition. Translated by C. D. Yonge. Peabody, MA: Hendrickson.

Pilch, John J. 1993. "Visions in Revelation and Alternate Consciousness: A Perspective from Cultural Anthropology." *Listening* 28.3:231-43.

Pinker, Steven. 1995. *The Language Instinct*. New York: HarperPerennial.

*Potter, David. 1994. *Prophets and Emperors: Human and Divine Authority from Augustus to Theodosius*. Cambridge, MA: Harvard University Press.

Reardon, B. P. 1989. *Collected Ancient Greek Novels*. Berkeley: University of California Press.

Rice, David G., and John E. Stambaugh. 1979. *Sources for the Study of Greek Religion*. Missoula, MT: Scholars Press.

Ricoeur, Paul. 1981. *Hermeneutics and the Human Sciences*. Edited and translated by John B. Thompson. Cambridge: Cambridge University Press.

Schmidt, Roger. 1988. *Exploring Religion*. Belmont, CA: Wadsworth. Quoting Mokichi Okada. 1984. *Johrei: Divine Light of Salvation*. Kyoto, Japan: Society of Johrei.

*Schürer, Emil. 1986. *The History of the Jewish People in the Age of Christ*. III.1. Revised and edited by Geza Vermes, Fergus Millar, and Martin Goodman. Edinburgh: T&T Clark.

Seeley, David. 1992. "Blessings and Boundaries: Interpretations of Jesus' Death in Q." *Semeia* 55:131-46.

Shaw, Brent D. 1996. "Body/Power/Identity: Passions of the Martyrs." *Journal of Early Christian Studies* 4:269-312.

*Shelton, Jo-Ann. 1988. *As the Romans Did: A Source Book in Roman Social History*. New York: Oxford University Press.

Sherk, Robert K. 1988. *The Roman Empire: Augustus to Hadrian*. Cambridge: Cambridge University Press.

Ste. Croix, G. E. M. de. 1981. *The Class Struggle in the Ancient Greek World*. Ithaca, NY: Cornell University Press.

Stuckenbruck, Loren T. 1995. *Angel Veneration and Christology. Wissenschaftliche Untersuchungen zum Neuen Testament, 2. Reihe 70.* Tübingen: Mohr-Siebeck.

*Thompson, Leonard L. 1990. *The Book of Revelation.* New York: Oxford University Press.

———. 1996. "Social Location of Early Christian Apocalyptic." *Aufstieg und Niedergang der Romischen Welt* II.26.3: 2615-56.

Torrance, Robert M. 1994. *The Spiritual Quest: Transcendence in Myth, Religion, and Science.* Berkeley: University of California Press.

*Tripp, Edward. 1970. *The Meridian Handbook of Classical Mythology.* Originally published as *Crowell's Handbook of Classical Mythology.* New York: New American Library.

Turner, Victor. 1974. *Dramas, Fields, and Metaphors.* Ithaca, NY: Cornell University Press.

Ulfgard, Hakan. 1989. *Feast and Future: Revelation 7:9-17 and the Feast of Tabernacles.* ConBNT 22. Lund, Sweden: Almqvist & Wiksell International.

*Whiston, William. 1995. *The Works of Josephus: Complete and Unabridged.* New updated edition. Peabody, MA: Hendrickson.

Wilder, Amos N. 1971. *Early Christian Rhetoric.* Cambridge, MA: Harvard University Press.

Wilken, Robert L. 1984. *The Christians As the Romans Saw Them.* New Haven, CT: Yale University Press.

Yamauchi, Edwin M. 1980. *The Archaeology of New Testament Cities in Western Asia Minor.* Grand Rapids, MI: Baker Book House.

Yarbro Collins, Adela. 1992. "Revelation, Book of" in *ABD.*

COMMENTARIES (BOTH CITED AND NOT CITED)

Aune, David E. *Revelation.* WBC. 3 vols. Word: Waco, TX. — Forthcoming commentary that treats extensively the text, language, and historical setting of Revelation. Extensive discussion of Greek grammar and syntax. Argues that there was an earlier and a later edition of Revelation.

Boll, Franz. 1914. *Aus der Offenbarung Johannis: Hellenistische Studien zum Weltbild der Apokalypse.* Stoicheia: Studien zur Geschichte des Antiken Weltbildes und der Griechischen Wissenschaft. Leipzig: B. G. Teubner. — Influenced by the history of religions school at the beginning of the twentieth century. Especially interested in the influence of astrology on Revelation. Bruce J. Malina has adapted and translated much of this material in *On the Genre and Message of Revelation: Star Visions and Sky Journeys* (Peabody, MA: Hendrickson, 1995).

Boring, M. Eugene. 1989. *Revelation*. IBC. Louisville: John Knox Press. — Views Revelation as a pastoral letter written to churches in crisis. Punctuated throughout the commentary are separate, extended reflections that consider more difficult themes in the Revelation such as violent imagery and universal salvation.

Bousset, Wilhelm. 1906. *Die Offenbarung Johannis*. Göttingen: Vandenhoeck & Ruprecht. — Another (along with Charles) classic commentary on the Revelation. A shaping member of the history of religions school.

Bratcher, Robert G., and Howard A. Hatton. 1993. *A Handbook on the Revelation to John*. New York: United Bible Societies. — An invaluable commentary intended for those translating Revelation into different languages. Both RSV and GNB are included, often along with other translations.

Caird, G. B. 1966. *A Commentary on the Revelation of St. John the Divine*. HNTC. New York: Harper & Row. — A careful historical and literary study in the finest British tradition of biblical scholarship.

Charles, R. H. 1920. *A Critical and Exegetical Commentary on the Revelation of St. John*. Edinburgh: T&T Clark. — Originally published in 1920, it continues to be one of the finest, most thorough commentaries on Revelation. Draws extensively on Charles's commentaries on Jewish apocalyptic and pseudepigraphic works.

Farrer, Austin. 1949. *A Rebirth of Images*. Reprint, Boston: Beacon, 1963. — An eccentric commentary written by a philosopher/literary critic. Some jewels amidst the elaborate development of various patterns in Revelation.

Ford, J. Massyngberde. 1975. AB. Garden City, NY: Doubleday. — Soon to be revised. Valuable references to parallels in the *Dead Sea Scrolls* and to patristic writings. Also some use of contemporary art. The revision will take out the argument that a stratum of the book belongs to John the Baptist.

Lohmeyer, Ernst. 1953. *Die Offenbarung des Johannes*. Handbuch zum Neuen Testament. Zweite, Erganzte Auflage. Tübingen: Mohr-Siebeck. — Interested in applying form criticism to Revelation, with special attention to metrics.

Richard, Pablo. 1995. *Apocalypse: A People's Commentary on the Book of Revelation*. Maryknoll, NY: Orbis. — Reads Revelation through the eyes of the oppressed who can identify with Revelation's ultimate message of hope.

Schüssler Fiorenza, Elisabeth. 1991. *Revelation: Vision of a Just World.* Proclamation Commentaries. Minneapolis: Fortress. — Presents Revelation as a genuine prophetic document in the history of liberation from unjust political regimes. Combines rhetorical analysis and feminist political interpretation to show how the social location of the reader influences interpretation.

Yarbro Collins, Adela. 1990. *The Apocalypse (Revelation).* NJBC. Englewood Cliffs, NJ: Prentice Hall. — A succinct commentary by one who has contributed significantly to the interpretation of Revelation.

INDEX